BAD IDEA
The Anthology

First published in the United Kingdom in 2008 by
Portico Books
10 Southcombe Street
London
W14 0RA

An imprint of Anova Books Company Ltd

ISBN 9781906032302

A CIP catalogue record for this book is available from the British Library.

10 9 8 7 6 5 4 3 2 1

Printed and bound by WS Bookwell, Finland.

This book can be ordered direct from the publisher.
Contact the marketing department, but try your bookshop first.

Cover and illustrations by Bill Bragg.
Additional art direction by Steve Sawyer.

www.anovabooks.com
www.badidea.co.uk

BAD IDEA
The Anthology

PORTICO

Contents

Cultural Revelations

Introduction
Daniel Stacey & Jack Roberts

Our journey in magazine publishing began in a class led by an energetic septuagenarian who, in decades previous, had spun the world of magazines around at his fingertips like a light wooden top. Clay Felker – *New York* magazine's founder, former editor of *Esquire* and owner of *The Village Voice* – stood before our class at Berkeley's Graduate Journalism School one day and asked us a question.

"Do you think the Internet has changed the way you think about magazine journalism?"

Over the previous five years he had noticed an increasing interest in the obscure, in the trivial and private, as young people launched personal websites and made efforts to 'broadcast themselves'. The Internet age had at once been an information revolution and a false education for many in our class.

"I don't think many people your age really understand what a magazine is anymore," he said. "It's something that captures a single, large scale idea. A magazine has to stand for values that a lot of people care about, and take an interest in. It has to be about a BIG IDEA."

We nodded our heads while secretly wishing away his advice. The force of our youth meant we were right. We would make magazines about the intersection of Gadamer's hermeneutics and reappraisals of 19th Century Californian pottery, about the underground, the fabulous and the intellectual. Millions of people would want to read these publications because they were unique, clever, and – most importantly – extensions of *us*.

Eventually though, over the course of many weeks of patient counseling and behavioral osmosis, Mr Felker's vision began to win us over. Journalism was a wild, dirty business, and we'd better ditch the obscurantist personal obsessions and get ready for it.

Good long-form journalism – from Felker and his gang of *New York* writers like Jimmy Breslin and Tom Wolfe, from Hazlitt to Orwell, from *Nova* magazine to the *NME* in its late 70s heyday, and *The Face* in the 80s and 90s – required that you make your ideas big and learn to communicate with a large audience in a language that was bold and meaningful. Broadcasting yourself wasn't so important as outgrowing yourself.

Truly great magazine journalism captures the flavour of people and their lives: the inflections of modern speech, the style and texture of generational change; it chisels a chip from our contemporary experience, polishes it up and fashions it into the shape of something universal; but it's a form of writing that requires patience, an eye and an ear for detail, 15 plus edits. It's a form of writing young journalists have to fight for, as the media rapidly fragments: the blogosphere generating an omniverse of underfunded news outlets where editors are called 'moderators', and 'churnalism' becomes a necessity with so little time to research. In this frenzy of ceaselessly updated content it's rare to find a business model that allows for considered, long-form journalism online: more often the Internet age forces the written word to become a cheap, trite mimicry of the manic news cycles of television.

Young writers can't rest their hopes in established media either. After we left Berkeley, many of the writers from our class discovered that the editors of the commercial publications employing us weren't particularly interested in our generational perspective, unless it came with the currency of 'cool' or a command knowledge of the private lives of the famous and mediocre. If we had stories to tell, if we had big ideas, that would just have to wait till later, after we'd clawed our way over the seething heap of editors, elder journalists, careerists and ink-tanned hacks that had stacked up in front of us, like a grand pile of dead wood barring the path to the means of production. If you couldn't get these big stories, or if people wouldn't let you write them, then your only other function as a journalist was to provide readers with raw information or dull punditry. The reality facing the young journalist was therefore stark: you were to become an administrator, a writer cum data entry assistant, force feeding a thousand plus words a day to the hungry, pragmatic masses; a food writer, the office hand collating lists of the best websites about celebrity dog breakdowns; or, worse, a sports journalist, pouring the fruits of a long, heady education into circles of desperate prose, gasping attempts to enliven the usual platitudinous clichés about ball-chasing wife-beaters with clumsy allusions to Camus and Van Gogh.

As our class's graduates became aware of this horror, they quickly started looking for their 'big story' elsewhere, most opting for an escape into book writing. Sarah M. Broom left her position as an associate editor at *Oprah* magazine to work for and write about Burundi's only independent radio station. Lauren Gard, writing for the *East Bay Express* about private detectives, saw a story bigger than anything else on her daily beat, and quit her staff job to start working for and piecing together a book about the firm she was investigating.

After forays into broadsheet journalism in the UK and Australia, we could also smell the rot, but for some reason decided to do something much more frivolous and foolish. We decided, just as print journalism seemed to be entering a phase of slow, terminal decline, to create a magazine where young and ambitious writers could take a run up and charge at their subject matter, where they could write their big stories: a broad features magazine about the lives of those in our generation, based on something magnanimous, a magazine that would attempt to wed intelligent young writers with intelligent young readers.

Launching a magazine on the basis of ideals, instead of the lip-licking, cash-hungry intentions that drive any sane publishing venture, is an experience of false steps, and of greying, unabating worry.

Early in the process we met with Nick Logan, founder of *The Face*, *Smash Hits*, *Arena* and *Frank*, who kindly brunched with us at the Zephyr Hotel in Farringdon. After telling us to include more photography, and suggesting we revise our choice of fonts, he stared ruefully over both our heads and said:

"Whatever you do, don't go into publishing. That is my ultimate advice. It is not what you think it is."

Jaded by years of plucky, derisory editors heckling him about independence in an industry so crucially linked to its advertisers, and of decades of ad sales recessions and booms, readership dips, weariness, and the final humiliation of watching *The Face* self-destruct following its sale to EMAP in 1999, Logan warned that in all earnestness publishing would prove, in the final summation, to be a disappointment to both of us, an unrewarding and relentless slog resulting in the exhaustion of all our dreams and the sacrifice of our supple, joyous youth. Suffice to say he was also unwilling to give us any money.

Andrew Neil was our next port of call – former editor of *The Sunday Times* but perhaps most famous for his weekly appearance in *Private Eye*'s letters column, in an oft requested photograph that captures him coddling a woman half his age. His response to our request for a meeting, channelled through a PA, was short and succinct:

It's not something we would wish to invest in and he feels it will be quite difficult to raise funds for this project, he is concerned of his blunt response [sic] but wishes you to know it is also honest.

Other consultations followed, including some sagacious business advice from Roger Law, founder of the comedy puppet show *Spitting Image*, and a meeting with the publisher of *Prospect* magazine, a short barking pugilist who wanted to be our publisher, and hurled abuse at us when we wouldn't let him.

Most of our meetings were generously arranged by our constant supporter and mentor Lou McLeod, who was then a publisher at

News International; among the more memorable was a morning spent discussing brand strategy with Stef Calcraft, CEO of Mother, the multinational creative agency. His offices in the Tea Building in Shoreditch, a salubrious 5000 square ft. open plan hall where his team of well-heeled young creatives networked on leather ottomans and rubberised concrete tables, were a palace to his perseverance – having built his company from scratch over 11 years.

The two of us sat with Mr. Calcraft at one of the informal lounge and table clusters in the far corner, sipping the rich coffee handed to us by secretarial gazelles. This particular day we were especially down, after the promises of yet another advertiser had evaporated, and the boulder we'd been edging up the incline to publishing Valhalla slipped back to base camp for the umpteenth time, our personal fortunes with it.

"Keep going boys," said Calcraft, his perfect, feathered haircut and levitating cashmere sweater a beacon of success. "It will work out for you. I mean, I can see it's tough for you right now… you, well, you look *poor*."

As he purveyed our choppy, home-cut hairstyles and tatty cardigans, it became clear that Calcraft's gaze was not one of condescension, but of recognition. Inside every successful institution there is hidden a history of the ragged, desperate lives of its founders – months and years of coffee soaked terror, broken social lives and minor pulmonary episodes, as the weighty Zeppelin is stitched by hand and puffed with a miasma of hope, fear, cunning and the cold, venal impulse to succeed. If that Zeppelin finally manages to fly, the grim history of its manufacture is erased as quickly as the lickspittle polish of cash can wipe its unappealing smear away. Calcraft recognised us for what we were, a pair of bright-eyed hobos, linked like everyone else to the sad dimmer switch of time and struggle.

"It's like this for everyone at the start," he said. "But you've got a good idea, keep going."

That was a rare moment on our journey; Calcraft offered us an honest, firm variety of sympathy, when many other veterans were more intent on ignoring us, and by extension, feigning non-recognition of their grim, human origins.

Prior to this meeting, David Hepworth, publisher of *Word* magazine and founder of the publishing house Development Hell, had delivered a withering rejection of young publishing ventures, although not spoken to us in private but as a publicly addressed litany of jeremiads in the media section of *The Guardian* newspaper.

The kindest thing you can say [to someone trying to launch a new magazine] is 'no, no, a thousand times no'… [D]on't delude yourself that you're pitching your idea to somebody who hasn't already considered it. Most publishers can scribble down on a piece of paper all the ideas that are currently being entertained by their competitors. *

His crowing echoed a spirit typical among many of the veterans we spoke to, who collectively had chosen to forget they and their publications had ever been anything less than they were now. Of course, Hepworth has business savvy, and a back catalogue of publishing successes, but the message was more a broad indictment of one generation by another: 'Do not bother to do anything new, you will fail!'

Hepworth's message was primarily one of cynicism and fear dressed up to look like pride, or rather a snarling sub-*Goodfellas* personae adopted by all those whose young ambitions have been ground into the dust by the compromises they've made. And here is where it is perhaps appropriate to bring out the long knives. He and the many other creative industry gatekeepers, sitting aloft and aloof, conducting public, simmering topographies of landscapes they consider their personal fiefdoms, remember that the mistakes of the young often overcome the successes of the old, that the flawed but colourful performance, the enthusiastic outward looking and imaginative act triumphs over the chiselled professional delivery of the inveterate, dispassionate hack.

* 'Got a new magazine idea? I don't want to hear it', *The Guardian*, April 10, 2006.

When Hepworth refers to the primary function of a magazine cover as attracting a "moron in a hurry", or that "all magazines are picture magazines," he lapses into that bottomless cynicism that becomes the attribute of publishers who long ago realised the only thing they were good at was making money. People like this exist in the film industry as well – they make Tim Allen flicks at Christmas time, or have Richard Curtis on speed dial. In the music industry they're putting the finishing touches on the launch single for this year's *X-Factor* winner. They are the people who will tell you that magazines and art can never meet, that the reading public is irredeemably stupid and worthless and, like battery hens, should be fed the cheapest and least nutritious content. They are the LAST people on earth any young publisher should listen to – let bitterness accumulate in your life of its own accord, rather than take on the burden of someone else's.

While we've made a litany of mistakes launching our magazine, and have had any number of citable lectures delivered to us – about letter-setting our title, changing the title itself, developing Cartesian layouts for our covers, adding and deleting sections – the one thing we've never shied away from was creating a magazine of intelligent journalism by and for young people, open to and actively sourcing new talent. Following the insights of Mr. Felker we've tried to create something capturing a broad yearning, which we see as a yearning of the young and literate for a magazine that engages them with rich and well written stories about their lives today. Ours is a magazine for the curious and the optimistic – for thinkers. From launch we've searched for outward looking writers who can entertain and capture something of the whole: writers that satisfy a desire in younger readers for signs of intelligent life beyond their own.

So this is our first anthology, and perhaps the beginning of many. The quality and variety of new writers will be the supporting latticework that builds this institution, as the tide of British youth culture flows back towards a desire for intellectualism, substance, and ideas that are undeniably of a new, unique generation. We believe this tide is gaining in momentum, hurdling pitfalls and false paths with the frothy surge of its unquestionable inertia, a wave of fresh, sanguine blood washing away the choleric, yellow bile of the past... or some other apt and forceful metaphor for collective rabble rousing.

And if it all ends in flames so be it.

OUT OF THE ORDINARY

Short Struggles With A
Malevolent Universe

Pub Quiz Hotshots • Hindu Life Advice
When Dad Dies • Sexual Hairdressing
Batman & Robin • Bye Bye Baby • Brian Wilson

Death, Respawn
Nikhil Gomes

We sat hunched on the sofas, transfixed on the TV. Laser, Winker-with-an-A and me. It was gone one in the morning and we'd been out for a quiet drink in The Champ, which had dice-rolled into a few cocktails in the Maypole.

We were drunk. Silent, teeth gritted, eyes focused on the screen, our thumbs rapidly hammered away at the undersized *GameCube* pads in our hands. We'd only got a *GameCube* because Laser loved *Zelda*, but ever since we discovered *Smash Bros.* we'd all become addicted.

An ultra-fast platform fighter in which classic characters from Nintendo's past beat each other across and off the screen, it was a game constructed around a gluttony of death, and beat drinking six *Red Bulls* mixed with a crushed packet's worth of *Pro Plus*, chased down with an espresso.

"Do you ever wonder whether all this death devalues the real thing?"

Winker-with-an-A was losing. He only chatted when he was losing, an attempt to distract us. I didn't reply – Laser was winning and I always had to be better than him.

"No really, it's just death, respawn, death, respawn, a pointless, endless loop."

Laser laughed. "That's only because you're playing so badly that you're not getting any kills."

That shut Winker-with-an-A up, and he unleashed his strongest attack upon Laser's screen persona, allowing me to nip in and kill them both. My character was alone on screen and so taunted his dead opponents. And in those short seconds where my character belittled death, it struck me that maybe Winkerwith-an-A was right. We're the generation that has grown up with death as an inconvenience, an automatic kickback to the last save point from where you could run headlong into death again, the generation for whom ideas of everlasting life through computer coded selves inhabits the gap between science and fiction, the generation whose parents will live long and fairly healthily while we choke our arteries with fat, the generation that killed Captain America but brought back Bucky, the generation who believe Kurt, Tupac, Richie Manic and Biggie are all still alive, the generation for whom suicide bombings are no longer worth putting on the evening news. Death means nothing to us.

I opened my mouth but Laser smashed my pixelated body far off the screen and only obscenities coloured the air. As I waited to respawn I remembered that the US army uses first person shooters to entice new recruits.

Pub Quiz Hotshot
Leesha McKenny

His name was Alan. He was an electrician with a passion for restored cars and mini golf. He was trying to give up smoking. I was pretending to start. I don't think we would have stopped to speak to each other otherwise. Alan and I only ever met at the pub down the road, and only ever on Wednesdays. He told me how his team, The Dirty Half Dozen Or So, hadn't gotten anywhere near the top teams in weeks and there was talk of quitting. I told him about They Might Be Onto Something's embarrassing tendency to get completely drunk by the end of the eigth round and then fall asleep. I soon found myself looking forward to the weekly trivia, but especially toward our hurried meetings out the back by the cigarette machine.

Before long we were meeting up between rounds to compare answers. We would discuss the periodic tables in passionate, husky tones one minute, only to return breathless and guilty to our teams shortly after. If They Might Be Onto Something noticed anything they said nothing. When I told them I was up to a pack a day they only gave me money for more. But before long, Alan began to resent our success.

"Do you know who won the 1976 Ashes series or not?" I asked.

"What does it matter? We're too far behind to catch up now," he replied.

"We don't have time for this," I snapped.

I was impatient. He looked hurt. He accused me of only wanting him for his answers. He had "made me" he said, and he demanded to know why I still refused to break away and start our own team. He was right, but it was more complicated than that. Things had started to go well with They Might Be Onto Something. We had stopped drinking so much. We were winning rounds. And besides, I needed them for a lift home. But Alan looked past me and into the glow of the Winny Blue cigarette machine.

"We can't do this anymore," he said.

"The other teams are beginning to suspect anyway."

He left before I could respond. More than ever, my walk back to They Might Be Onto Something felt cheap and lonely. I was over trivia. Nothing could be worth the emotional turmoil and eventual remorse and shame.

But then, we did win the meat tray.

Attack Me, Big Boy
James Daly

Richard and I must have been eight years old. He had a beautiful big house in Wimbledon: much bigger than mine, because his father was the regional manager of a popular chain of restaurants. We were upstairs playing in his room when we both started to feel peckish, and decided to go downstairs and ask his mother (an extraordinary, glamorous woman with long dark hair and a striking figure whom I would later develop a painful crush on) if she would make us some sandwiches. At the top of the large staircase, which square-spiralled around all four walls down two storeys to the main hallway, I held a piece of silly putty over the edge of the banister and, giggling like a girl, let it go. After a few seconds listening for a thud, I looked over the banister and saw Richard's sister Hannah lying on the floor laughing, having been struck by the putty.

Richard and I ran downstairs: from staircase to landing to staircase to landing, all around the centre of his huge house. Hannah, who was a year younger than us, still lay on the floor laughing. She had pulled her knickers around her ankles and lifted her skirt around her chest.

I stopped at the second or third step up from the hall and stared. Richard was behind me. She looked at me.

"Attack me!" she shouted.

"What?" I asked, confused and not a little scared.

She spread her legs apart and repeated what she had said.

Richard ran on into the kitchen, laughing, completely unsurprised, while I stood on the stairs, shocked. I had no sisters, you see.

Hannah laid her head back, not looking at me anymore, and slid her bare feet along the wood floor, bending her knees.

"Attack me," she said, not shouting this time.

After a moment I joined Richard in the kitchen with his

mother, who wore a black and white check skirt and smelled of what I now know to be *Chanel No. 5*. She made me a sandwich – lettuce, tomato, cucumber and wholegrain mustard: diagonal cut – and poured me a glass of pineapple juice, with ice cubes that came out the front of their enormous refrigerator with a wonderful rattling noise.

My Left Breast
Jean Hannah Edelstein

All of my friends are doing it.

"Life-changing," Leah declares. "Turns out I'm a 34C. C!"

"30F," Melissa says. "I'm a 30F. Now I have to get mine from a speciality shop. You have to go."

I gaze down at my own pair, remembering the birthday party a few weeks ago at which, after a few cocktails, it occurred to me that my cleavage was a handy spot to stash a small bottle of *Bombay Sapphire*. Maybe I have outgrown my 36B.

Indeed, it's high time that I, too, pay a visit to the Selfridges free bra-fitting service. When I get there, the man (man?!) behind the desk checks a chart and hands me a number.

"Wait in a cubicle," he says, "and take your top off."

The dressing room is pink and black and satin and velvet; it's a little brothel-y. I strip off my shirt and too-small bra and stand, half-naked, shivering in the chill of the air-con. Then my personal bra-fitter arrives.

"I'm coming in," she cries, in strong Essex tones, and then sweeps back the curtain before I have a chance to cover my cold-hardened nipples. She leans in, stares, and without warning takes one breast in each hand for a thorough grope, manipulating them with the delicacy of a randy 16 year-old.

"This is so weird!" she exclaims, mouth slightly agape.

"This boob is so much bigger than the other one. It's freaky!"

I try to keep smiling as she hands me something in an E-cup.

"I mean, usually you try to fit the larger one," she says, forehead creased with consternation. Are my breasts her greatest professional challenge?

"But in this case..."

My smile is tighter than a 30A bra on a 42FF chest.

"Imagine," I think to myself, "If I were a man, and these kinds of comments were being made about my penis: 'Dude, your cock totally bends to the left!' Inconceivable!"

But just as I am getting a little worked up, a little inclined to storm out of there, Miss Personal Bra-Fitter presents me with a black lace 32DD number. I slip it on, and there it is, magic: my brand new, perfectly supported, perky silhouette.

"I guess that will have to do," she says, shaking her head.

No matter: demeaned, mortified, officially a freak, I walk out of that cubicle a new woman, able to smile smugly with the knowledge of my impressive dimensions. On the left side, at least.

No Future for You
Nikesh Shukla

While the women toil in the kitchen, the men toil in front of the television, wincing as another wicket falls and as their beers edge to the bottom of their cans. I've asked the women if I can help. They've all laughed and told me to sit with the men.

They appreciate the offer but kitchen-work is their Hindu boon in life and they can handle it. It doesn't stop them having a dig at me for being a man though.

"Go and sit with all the men. Go on."

I sit with the men. My dad and uncles are engaged in serious cricket watching. It's an India–Pakistan grudge match, so their eyes are glued. India aren't doing very well.

My grandfather recognises my ambivalence towards cricket and asks, "So, what is your job at the moment?"

"I'm a writer, grandfather. I write. I've just written a novel."

"What about money? You can't work for no money."

"I get paid, grandfather. Making loads of money doesn't bother me."

"That's nice. You could be a well-paid lawyer right now. Instead of being unemployed."

"Money isn't everything."

"Money is God. Are you a communist?"

"No, I just want to make enough money to be happy."

"You sound like a communist."

"Why?"

"Just making sure you're not living like a vagrant. I worry about your money. Would you like to borrow some? I haven't got much, but I would gladly give you money."

"I'm fine."

"No you're not. This is not a good career for you. No future. Not like a lawyer. You could make much money, you could buy a huge house for everybody."

"I'm fine, grandfather. I get by and I'm doing well. I am happy."

"So, all these concerts you do, how do you come home?"

"By taxi or bus or whatever."

"What precautions do you take from being attacked?"

"I'm careful."

"No you're not. You don't know what people are like these days. They're just after your money."

"Granddad, we live in leafy Middlesex."

"Just make sure you keep your money in your sock or make a

special secret pocket in your jacket. And always offer them your watch first. That way, you don't lose any money. If they say no, then offer them your jewellery or phone. If they say no, they can check your wallet and it will be empty."

"Why carry a wallet then grandfather?"

My grandfather laughs at my stupidity and hits me on the knee.

China Spy Showdown
Sorrel Neuss

Working as a journalist for the *China Daily*, I have all my needs attended to but have forfeited the right to choose my own home. In my decrepit Beijing apartment building, all the *lo wei* (foreigners) have been placed on the 13th floor. Wei Wei also lives on our floor, in a 1.5 metre squared window box, furnished with a ripped leather couch.

Unsubtly disguised as a lift attendant, Wei Wei's main job is to spy on us.

After a hard night's drinking, I come home at 5.30 am with a big bag of booze, my well-fed breasts bursting out of a nipple-stiffening top. I look up to find Wei Wei staring at them.

"Is so cold," she growls.

Without taking her eyes off my jugs, she swivels on her high chair and presses number 13. The lift doors close in, the lights spark, and we ascend at depressingly slow speed. First floor. Her eyes now roam over to my arse.

"You late today," she says, pirate-like.

'Was that a question, statement or accusation?' I think.

Looking down, I can see she has her usual scrap of the *China*

Daily clutched between podgy thumb and forefinger. She's always reading the paper and tearing out little bits of 'evidence': the floor of her window box is littered with them.

Fifth floor.

"Cutting articles out means you can't read what's on the other side of the paper," I squeak feebly.

Wei Wei's English is basic – there's no response. My Chinese can barely get me a packet of fags.

10th floor.

Raising a duster to the broken phone she barks, "You drink alone?"

I stall, imagine she doesn't exist, and look up at the numbers, desperately waiting for

13. When the doors slide apart, the rush of relief prompts my hangover to kick in. But even when safely locked in my flat I can hear her vicious cough. Feel her staring at me from her window box. I can't sleep. Got to stop her.

I throw my door open to find Wei Wei perched on the shitty sofa looking straight ahead.

"Look. I fucking hate you. Give me a break. I'm not boning the ugly toff next door. I'm not making bombs in my kitchen. I'm not plotting to overthrow the Party. So get out of my face… and stop gawping at my tits."

Wei Wei doesn't even flinch, and continues to sift through old scraps of the *China Daily*.

Get a Grip
Matt Prins

It's dizzying to be standing on these steps halfway around the world, where I stood two months ago on trial for the job I start today. This was my choice: copywriting over a longstanding love. Now the Italian girl I developed a crush on those two months ago is in front of me and she's giving me air kisses on both cheeks.

The guy I'm working next to, Ali, creates hip-hop lyrics on the spot; I pretend to listen and then compliment him on his "mad rhyme skillz".

Ali says nice things to all the office women, about their shirts or hairdos. When my crush walks past, Ali states as a fact that, "She's a cute-toot-tootie," and that, "She was really excited to know you were coming." So when she passes by I tell her, "That's a really nice shirt. And you have nice hair today."

I'm invited to breakfast at her place with a bunch of other people. I help her wash up and we laugh and smile, and when I wink at her she looks down into the sink.

Another time we're at a bar together with a few other people. It's loud there, because of a fußball match and music by the band Wings. We stare at each other and grin beside the fußball table. I grab her face and kiss her forehead and then say something about work.

When I get back home, I open Internet Explorer. I've got a few messages to read in my Yahoo! account. One message is from Zoe:

Matt. I love you. Somehow I get the feeling that you don't want to talk. Maybe I'm reading too far into your words (or lack of). I miss you so much.

I turn hot and bothered. So hot and bothered that sweat trickles into my eyes.

"Zoe. You can't expect me to call or write so often. We are

broken up."

That was her choice: breakup over long-distance. Suddenly I've got some very urgent things to say to my crush. Not urgent enough to be said at work though, so I try to talk to her in a bar, surrounded by our co-workers. But she's listening to someone else's conversation – for the whole night. Then she leaves without talking to me.

Back at my new apartment, I try to cover my walls with pictures from back home. Zoe at the beach. Puckering her lips. Waving at me.

I sit on my bed and masturbate.

Beach Boy or Beached Whale?
Alyssa McDonald

Our band arrives at UCLA's Royce Hall in the twinkling Californian sunshine. As the support band for Brian Wilson, we've been told we aren't allowed alcohol, food, or guests backstage. So we sit and wait in our band room, Beach Boys songs wafting through the air conditioning ducts from the rehearsal upstairs.

Eventually someone takes pity on us, letting us loose on the remains of Brian Wilson's band's buffet. We're used to having a rider backstage – bottles of beer and water, some sandwiches and fruit – but this is a *buffet*, like at a wedding or business convention.

Nervously nibbling at plates of pasta and pieces of cake, we try not to stare as a familiar figure walks past. He moves his large body like a toddler, concentrating on every step. His royal purple cowboy shirt has white piping around the seams.

"Hi Brian," says Green, our bandleader, saucer-eyed. Brian

says nothing, and plunges both hands into a big packet of crisps, then shovels them into his mouth. It's like we've bumped into the Queen at a supermarket.

Bob, bassist for Brian, session player for Madonna and others, appears next to me and enthusiastically palms me his card.

"So, what other musical projects are you involved in at the moment?" he says.

"Uh, well, I don't… I'm just doing this at the moment."

"Oh."

He looks at me hard. I begin to wonder how many people have twigged that I don't really belong here, that this is my first proper band, that I'm not really a professional musician. It's not until I'm introduced to Brian Wilson, and shake his limp hand, that I start to think I might not be the only one.

Our gig goes well, and we come off stage elated, until we realise the bar has shut and there's no booze backstage. Admitting defeat, we take our seats in the back row of the hall for Brian's set.

Two hours of Beach Boys classics follow, beautifully played. But Brian isn't there. The same fat body we'd seen in the green room sits behind the keys, surrounded by 11 stunningly talented support musicians. Brian's voice is shot though. In fact, I'm fairly sure that for long parts of the gig his keyboard isn't even switched on.

Copy Shop Hag
Louis T. Fowler

It's a small, generic copy shop on Lexington Ave, and it has a generic name – 'Copies.' I'm stood at the shop's only black and white copier, working through my artwork originals, which are stacked on a nearby mounting table.

I often copy my work to create poster montages. It usually takes a bit of time, so I load the copier with a whack of change.

An old lady walks into the shop, papers in her hand. She looks towards me for a moment, but then walks over to the counter. I continue my work, sifting distractedly through my originals at the mounting table. When I turn around, the old lady – who wears big, dark lunette glasses and a beige *Barbour* jacket – is standing at MY black and white photocopier, using MY money to photocopy her papers.

Okay, no problem. I give her some time to finish up, walk over, and then reach across the copier to retrieve my original.

She slams the copier lid down on my hand.

"MINE!" she rasps.

It hurts. A lot. Everyone else in the room is staring at me now.

"Look lady, I just want my original."

Be mature now. Act the bigger man. She raises a spindly finger and points to the overflowing bin next to the counter. My artwork lies on its cusp… crumpled.

"IT'S MY TURN."

I swear she's grinning now. Everybody is still staring – the happy couple copying wedding invitations, the slightly overweight counter clerk. They think it's her turn – just because she's a little old lady. But it's NOT her turn. I want to shout it out loud, but know how childish it would sound.

"You know what? You're very rude you know – a very rude lady."

I pack my art originals and photocopies up into my bag, and saunter towards the door, head held high. But as soon as I turn my back on her –

"YEAH? WELL YOU'RE A WEEEIRD MAN."

She looks at me and raises a single, quivering finger to the door in some kind of pseudo-Biblical gesture.

Outside the shop, I'm stewing. It was my turn, my money… How can she get away with this? How many more must suffer? I bolt back in.

"YOU STUPID CUNT!"

Then I bolt right back out again. After that, I feel horrible for the rest of the day.

Birthday Blog Victim
Anneka Hartley

My 25th birthday is going well, until I check my MySpace messages. It's Paranoia69:

The following is a special note just for you/
I wish you perfect sunny days with a gentle breeze to ease your cares away.
I also hope you are able to find laughter and love in everything you do/
I guess what I'm trying to say is HAPPY BIRTHDAY to you sweetheart!

I can taste bile rising in the back of my throat. This attempt to find a birthday date through MySpace – and in the process get some new material for my dating blog – has transmogrified into a tiresome, depressing chore. Whence came this endless stream of socially inept, lumbering wife-hunters?

I read the poem to my housemate Katherine, accompanying it with cries of horror, but strangely she doesn't react, just sits there placidly. Eventually her sweet, puzzled face guilt-trips me out of standing him up, and, disturbed, I head out into the night.

Paranoia69 is late when he stumbles through the barriers at Notting Hill tube station. He looks like a prematurely aged teenager: ripped designer jeans and a bleached mini-Mohican that might have been fashionable five years ago.

"Hi," I mutter icily and peck him on the cheek.

"Are you okay?"

"No, I'm stressed. And I can only stay for one drink."

"What happened?"

"Look, I was an idiot to think I wanted to spend my birthday with someone I barely know."

"You're not looking for a relationship then?"

"Er, no…"

Rather than taking the sensible option of abandoning me there and then, he ploughs on with his plan – a gastropub recommended by a friend. Guilt propels me. He loses his way in the residential streets of Ladbroke Grove though, and at this point I become panicky.

"Please, I just want one drink," I whimper, and by the time we arrive at his swanky gastropub I reach a hysterical pitch.

"I'm not eating! I can't stay!"

A confused waiter directs us towards a table as I drag my feet, muttering frantically. Unfortunately, Paranoia69 is well versed in crisis training: he used to be in the Navy. He employs a soothing tone, persuading me to sit down and stay for food.

Eventually I insist on leaving – by now I'm itching to relate the horror to my MySpace faithful. As I look for the exit, Paranoia69 assumes the hopeful, pleading look of a starving child.

"Look, sorry for being a prima donna," I say.

"If anything, it's made you even more sexually appealing," he replies.

In your cyberdreams, blog victim.

Bye Bye Baby
Amelia Coulam

The doctor told me I had to be 100% certain that I actually wanted an abortion. She even had it written down on a *Post-It* note to remind her, underlined, "100% CERTAIN". Lest she forget I suppose. I made a mental calculation of how certain I was, but somehow the numbers didn't add up to a perfect 100. So I smiled and left, making sure to organise a follow up appointment so that she could refer me for a vacuuming of my womb. Like a spring clean, I thought.

Tom and I spent a lot of time together, lying on his bed, watching DVDs, eating whatever food I could stomach. We had decided straight away what we needed to do, as though it was assumed, as though my maternal default setting was switched to "Off". Or perhaps "Automatic Denial".

Together we would nod our heads and say, "It's the right thing to do," telling ourselves that we believed it, all the way, 100%. So the appointments were made – doctors, consultations, D-day – and I peed in pots, gave up my arm for blood tests, smiled bravely and told them I was sure.

My mum had told me, "Watch out, soon the hormones will kick in." Right on cue, thoughts of no money, no job, no home were replaced with babies in hand knitted cardigans, a baby next to me in bed, a small body full of everything good, nothing bad. And it wasn't just me: one day I caught Tom looking at pictures of the two of us, comparing features.

"I was wondering what he would look like." He was apologetic as though what he was doing might frighten me.

Secretly I was just thinking, "Well actually, it's a girl". My stomach was already sticking out ever so slightly, my boobs growing.

I kept thinking, "Right now, I'm a mother". The thought would make me cry randomly, tears dropping into the soup I was heating up for lunch, onto the platform at the tube station. When I was with Tom, my face would scrunch up like a little girl's; one minute smiling, the next minute sobbing. I'm still a little girl, I thought.

My mum confirmed this: "You always did things too soon," she said.

I trudged on, believing less and less in 100%, less and less in right and wrong. Amidst my mixed feelings I counted the weeks. Nine weeks pregnant. One week and it will all be over. One week till I take it all back.   –

What I Wouldn't Do for a Head Massage
Jake Barnes

Emma introduces herself and then beckons me to the far side of the room.

"Just go over there, Tina will deal with you."

I walk across the floor, sit down on the reclining seat and slowly dip the nape of my neck into the groove of the porcelain basin. In the hairdresser's mirror I see myself trussed up in a black cotton bib.

Tina is also in the reflection; a pretty teenager with honey skin, flickering enhanced lashes, and eyes of purest boredom. She has jet hair, cut up in an ethereal pixie stylllywwwooooooooah!

A warm sensation is flowing down the right side of my head.

"Temperature okay, yeah?"

A pang of cold hits me as she turns off the water stream. My front teeth rattle together.

"Rrrrrrggh."

There's a wet slapping noise as she greases her palms with gunk. Her insect fingers crawl along the tight skin on the back of my head and sharply scrunch in and out.

"OoooooohAAAAAAAhoooooh."

I look through the top of my eyelids and technicolour orange cascades into a lush ocean green. She rips her hands free and it's cold again.

"Hwoooooooooh."

I hear more slapping, then feel a deliberate pulling motion through the hair-ends behind my earlobes. This is followed by a spray of warm wetness and more colours.

"You okay, yeah?"

"UrrrHrrrr."

"Lift your head up."

She pulls out a yellow towel and vigorously goes to work on my skull. Then her grip loosens. Dark waves of self-loathing crash against my pale sense of self-worth.

"Er... Thanks."

She nods, and then stands there, looking through me with a blank expression.

"I'll sit myself down," I say.

I sit on the revolving chair in front of Emma's mirror and stare at my bedraggled form. Emma turns up with a mug of hot tea.

I feel strangely dirty.

"Tina's pretty good at that, eh? So, what do you want it to look like this time?"

Cheap even.

"Come again?"

Superzeros
Nick Gillott

Batman and Robin arrive at the fancy dress party. Robin is young and fresh faced; Batman looks stalwart and dynamic. Capes, masks and artificial physiques are all in place. They're very late and need to do some catching up; they scan the room for drink. Robin looks at his token contribution, a two litre bottle of Asda best bitter, which he abandons in favour of the host's supply of *Stella*. Batman is already downing a bottle of *WKD*.

Rapidly advancing towards extreme intoxication, the duo move to finger food, pushing their Lycra outfits to the limit. A loosening of the utility belt is required before the obligatory dance. A girl dressed as Noddy is spun dramatically around and a male Mother Theresa also gets some action. It's not long before time is called and the pair decide to walk home.

Quiet streets allow the dynamic duo to enact their fantasy, leaping in and out of the shadows, chasing an imaginary Joker, BANG, THWACK, KABOOM.

Soon competition between the two superheroes overheats; Robin challenges Batman to a feat of strength in a narrow, dark alley. Who can climb the highest by bracing themselves between the two walls? Pressing his back to one wall and both feet on the other side, Robin climbs, tensioning his body between the two buildings.

Not to be outdone, the Dark Knight follows, catching his partner some six feet above the ground. Robin accepts defeat and scrambles down, his limbs aching. He calls Batman down, but is ignored. He decides to leave for home.

Above, the Caped Crusader is still climbing. He is 15 feet up when he realises his colleague has disappeared. Not sure how to get down, he sits, poised between the two walls. Below him, a couple enters the alleyway for some clandestine time together. They embrace, the young man's hands all over her body as he pushes her against the wall to kiss. Then Batman feels a sharp, intense pain in his left leg… cramp. His grip on the wall falters, his knees weaken, and he plummets.

The preoccupied couple only notice his black form when it drops next to them – feet first, cape flapping. Regaining composure as he falls, the Dark Knight lands with a classic knee bend finish, his hands on his hips – ready for action. Facing the shocked couple, he leans in menacingly, and whispers "Good evening citizens," then runs from the alleyway.

Confessions of a Serial Coat Snatcher

Nicholas Royle

Recently my publisher, Pete Ayrton, came to spend a night at our house.

"Nice coat, Pete," I said.

It was a black raincoat with a rubbery texture. In the morning, Pete forgot his coat. I saw it hanging on a hook next to one of my jackets.

I was reminded of a book launch at which I spotted Geoff Dyer across the room. He was wearing a yellow zip-up jacket with a double black band. Discreet logo: 'ONEWORLD'.

"Lovely jacket, Geoff."

"Thanks."

It really was a lovely jacket. It looked good. Geoff looked good in it. I told him so again.

At that time I worked on a London listings magazine. A colleague, Chris Hemblade, had a red satin bomber jacket. Every time he wore it I complimented him on it. He told me the brand. I tried every shop in London that stocked Chevignon clothing. I called Chevignon in Paris. I tried stores in New York. I hoped Chris would tire of his jacket sooner or later. As a fashion journalist, he wouldn't want to be seen around town in something outdated, so all I had to do was wait for it to go out of fashion. Finally, Chris said I could borrow it for a few days. A few days became a couple of weeks. I wore the jacket every day, so that he'd see it would break my heart to give it back. Eventually, I realised this couldn't go on and handed it back. It hung on the back of his chair for three days before he came and placed it on the back of my own chair.

"It's yours," he said.

It wasn't long after this that a parcel turned up in the post. I opened it. It was Geoff Dyer's jacket. In a note, he explained that he'd washed it and it had shrunk and no longer fitted him so well.

Perhaps it would fit me? It did, kind of. So what if it hung off my shoulders slightly? I could get away with it. In that jacket I could get away with anything.

I've been wearing it for years now, alternating it with Chris's. There's an inside pocket an inch and half wide and five inches deep. The only thing it's good for is a pen. When I inspected this pocket closely for the first time I saw it was from a different material to the jacket lining. I wonder if he does this to all his jackets that don't have inside pockets? Adds his own little pen pocket…

I take down Pete's coat from the hook. I read the label. *Adolfo Dominguez*. There's some stuff in the pockets, but there are limits. I try the coat on, nevertheless, and look in the mirror. It's a little bit big for me, but that hasn't stopped me before.

When Dad Dies
Amanda Caverzasi

Approximately 20 years before I learned dad had an estimated eight years to live, I told him, "When you die, you will look like this." Mouth and eyes wide open, I wagged my head until he scooped me up and said, "Bedtime, you."

How do people actually look when they die? Bill, an octogenarian I befriended in my sophomore year at university, appeared badly bruised. Hands on his, I tried not to stare at the purple mass that spanned his shoulder and chest. He sobbed quietly, tearlessly. He had dried up. Karen Kristin, my dance teacher, dragged her oxygen tank up East 64th Street. I admired her pixie do and she patted where she once styled her bun. In her eyes, I read peace: the glimmer that yogis (suspect ones) and mothers-to-be radiate. She said, "Live for the moment." I nodded when I should have asked how.

Once dad told us he had Chronic Lymphocytic Leukemia – cancer of the lymphocytes, treatable, not curable – mom sometimes cried suddenly. But she echoed Karen Kristin.

"In some ways this is a blessing, Mandy. We live for today."

How? What I noticed was that if dad snapped or bullied, or, as he once joked "had a beer in the AM," she remained composed, gentle and patient.

"You love well," I told mom.

"I hope to love Marko so well."

"So you asked Marko to propose? And he did, and you accepted?" she asked.

"I live for the moment."

Before the ceremony, I asked dad, "You ready? For our entrance? Our big moment?"

I expected dad to say, "love you, kid" or quote Shakespeare or Einstein, "Gravitation is not responsible for people falling in love," or something funny or wise.

But he murmured, "Did you tell anyone? About my illness?"

"No."

But probably people had guessed. He had postponed chemotherapy for Marko and me, and the abnormal lymphocytes in his glands had caused his neck to swell nearly past his ears. Plus he tended to "rest his eyes" every time he sat.

"Because your grandparents said I looked strange."

"I heard Grammie tell Gramps you only looked strange because you didn't shave."

Dad smiled up to his nostrils. His eyes seemed distant, dead. Today dad is slender, pale and minus muscle mass. Shirtless, his spine and shoulder blades protrude dreadfully. So I focus on his eyes. I see weariness, scepticism, humour, a great dad, and more life than I can currently comprehend.

But what about when the chemo eventually kills him? How will he look then?

Highway Robbery
Ailsa Caine

"Got just the thing girls. Gimme a minute, I'll call Mickey; he's got the keys but he's at the footy."

We sat on our hands like nervous children, looking up at him and nodding slowly.

"Mickey! All right geeza, it's Spence. You at the game? Good, I've got a couple of ladies here wanting to look at Moham Walk and I've no sodding key. 'Av a look on your keychain… yeah, the gold one."

He looked at us and rolled his eyes.

"Ok, later mate."

He snapped his phone back together and picked up his jacket.

"Come with me, I can show you what you're getting but we can't go inside."

Ignoring the oxymoron, we followed dumbly. His beige, lowered sports car was parked on a double yellow line. Spence opened the door, pulling back the passenger seat whilst simultaneously whipping a disabled sticker off the dashboard, all with the smooth confidence of a repeat offender.

Stuffing it into his pocket, he glossed over the offence with a smile and gestured towards the back seat. Ignoring every single "stranger danger" campaign I had ever witnessed, I climbed in. Ele was given the front. Sticking to the leather seat whilst my knees hovered inches from my chin, we weaved through the East London traffic, pulling up at the property in a cloud of Guns 'N' Roses and unnecessary revs.

"It's a nice East End estate, not like that shit you get Stratford way," Spence said.

I waited until Ele clocked the large, fluorescent pink 'SEX' graffito scrawled on the wall.

"Come 'av a look," he said, and pressed his nose up against the murky glass. We schlepped to the window with the enthusiasm of teens at a family wedding, as Spence, like a drunken uncle, waxed lyrical.

"Five bedrooms," "one en suite," and "a fully fitted kitchen" later, we'd heard it all; it jarred somewhat with reality. Leaning in conspiratorially, Spence dealt his final blow.

"Like I said, this is a great estate, proper East End residents, 'cause I ain't being racist, but…"

We were ready to leave. Ele displayed admirable tenacity, brushing off Spence's invitation to the pub with an ideal mixture of humour and force. We made our excuses and left. Out of earshot, I revealed my accomplishment.

"Found 50p."

"Nice, where?"

"On the floor of the car."

Ele spat out laughter.

"You're so frugal. That's theft!"

I stood in shock; I hadn't thought, but she was right, this was theft, and there were no intoxicators for an excuse.

"Can of *Coke*?"

We looked at each other.

Taking the moral high ground is never easy.

Mr Garden Variety
Federay Holmes

I'm walking back from dropping my kids at school. I haven't had a shower and I'm wondering if I can smell myself. This is when a dad I often nod to at this time of day jogs up beside me. He's a heavy chap, and folds his arms valiantly as he walks, hugging himself. It looks tiring. He's trying to tell me about old-fashioned mums he knows who don't work, but starts the conversation as if it began 10 minutes ago, leaving me a bit wrong-footed.

One mum he particularly dislikes has a nanny, a cleaner, and an "ironer" (shouldn't that be ironing lady?). Apparently, she spends all day complaining about the taxman trying to take all her money and talking about how busy her life is. He is her gardener.

As we stop outside my house, he starts giving me tidbits of info about plants I've just put in my garden. He gets some of them wrong.

'You know something, mate, it's not a cherry, it's a crab apple,' I think to myself.

Many of the other things he points at don't go by the names he's using either. He rocks about a bit on his heels, leaning backwards and tucking his chin in. It occurs to me he is waving his dick about at my garden.

I am getting one of those headaches that start in your jaw.

The conversation returns to his client, this mum who has lots of money and her only child in full-time childcare, yet still wants a low-maintenance garden.

"You know... something with grasses... slate chips... I don't know."

I want to say: "Leave the poor woman alone, she's telling you about her money worries and how busy she is, probably because you make her feel worthless. She's clearly depressed, and doesn't need staff fiddling outside her curtains all day, shaking their heads and tutting. I imagine she probably has nothing to do but weep into her waffle cotton duvet cover – and you're the problem. Piss off."

Instead, I snort, and say:

"Goodness! An ironer! Ha!" shaking my head in disbelief. Pleased with himself, he says,

"Ha!" too, and smiles a very wide smile. I watch him roll away while I feel for my keys. I relate this to two separate people. And do you know what they both say?

They say: "He fancies you."

Boiling Natasha
Tat Usher

Although it's not easy to tell whether a tortoise is dead or just hibernating, Lloyd is convinced that Natasha is dead and that we should boil her. At our allotment by White Hart Lane, in North London, I watch Lloyd building the funeral pyre. Natasha is in a shoebox in the back of the van.

Lloyd got the tortoise-boiling idea from *The Swiss Family Robinson*. In Chapter 47, the Family boil some unfortunate tortoise they'd slaughtered. The shell emerges, shiny and beautiful, and they use it as an unusual bowl. They also enjoy the nutritious tortoise soup that ensues. Lloyd thinks that *The Swiss Family Robinson* is the greatest book of all time, and he's read to me from it throughout my entire life.

I'm bored senseless by *The Swiss Family Robinson*, and I don't want to boil Natasha. I want to bury her, give her a proper funeral and sing hymns.

Lloyd has unearthed a rusty iron pot from somewhere. He whistles as blue smoke drifts across the allotments towards the football stadium. I glare at him from under the hood of my red anorak and consider informing him that normal dads don't boil their kids' pets. I know this would be a mistake, however, as he despises "normal" people and doesn't like hearing about what they get up to, or don't get up to.

Lloyd fetches the shoebox from the van, and I shut my eyes and block my ears so I can't see or hear him plonking Natasha in the pot. Then I stand around not knowing what to do with myself.

I've let Natasha down. I should've stood up for her and refused to let this happen. I should've given her a decent burial with flowers and blessings. I fiddle with my anorak zip and kick at the dirt with my welly boots. Lloyd puts more wood on the fire and tells me how he once ate roasted guinea pig in Mexico. Apparently it was delicious. I make a mental note to take Gerald back to the pet shop.

Eventually Lloyd decides it's time to check on Natasha. He beckons me over and I take a deep breath. I peer into the iron pot.

Instead of the beautiful, shiny shell there's just some sticky, mushy stuff. I can hardly believe that this brownish mess is all that's left of Natasha.

"Well," says Lloyd cheerfully, "it looks like the tortoise in *The Swiss Family Robinson* was a different kind of tortoise."

My Cinephiliac Shame
Niven Govinden

I'd become unsociable in stages. Bars, parties, dinners: scrapped. My writing was to blame. I was in the thick of my new novel, and its mechanisms were all I could think about. I'd grown used to the home lockdown, started to like it. Anything that took me out of my cocoon-state was too energetic and to be avoided.

When I wasn't at my desk, I liked to sit in the dark, especially the cinema. It was the one extension of my personal space I allowed myself. There was nothing deeper than the matinee experience, immersing myself in Story. Somehow, it helped keep me focused on my novel.

For a month, the only words out of my mouth were the film's name, ticket quantity and screening time, spoken abruptly to whoever was manning the kiosk. To make life easier, I booked online where possible for those cinemas I knew had ticket-collection machines.

I spent weeks in the city this way, snaking my way through swathes of people without speaking to a soul. Only at night did I worry, singing in my flat to exercise my voice box. I was terrified that if I didn't I'd lose it for good.

One day I went to see a double of Charles Vidor films. It started with a turkey, but ended with *Gilda*, which made it all worthwhile. I'd set up camp in my usual seat – aisle stage right, two rows from the back – throwing my coat across two further seats to deter anyone who might consider getting friendly. There had been a situation earlier, and I wanted to avoid any unnecessary contact.

The guys who ran the cinema had a certain form that kept me coming back. They denied all recognition of their patrons, knowing that the regulars preferred blank, anonymous exchanges, but on the day of the Vidor double I was served by the newbie: a guy normally consigned to the confectionary concession. He was young, and unaware of the protocol.

"Wow. You must really like movies."

"I guess."

"I see you here a lot. Third time this week, right?"

"Possibly."

Wait. Was he lumping me in with the cinephiles? With their packed lunches and preferred seating? Couldn't he see the difference between them and me? When people talked of being mortified I'd always taken the piss, unaware, but this is what it felt like. To be thoughtlessly sized up by a kid in week-old *Converse* killed.

I resumed my socialising after that.

Tory Prankster
David Gaffney

Danny and Gill asked us to stay at their house whilst they went to Budapest. They needed some time alone, to sort a few things out, get some perspective. We were about to settle down to a DVD on Danny's giant plasma TV when the new Tory leader, David Cameron, appeared on the news. And we noticed that he was the spitting image of Danny: the same moonish face, the same springy, puppy-dog gait. Pundits wagered Cameron would run to fat, and we'd said the same about Danny.

So when Danny rang from Budapest to remind us to switch off his lawn sprinkler, Adelle asked him straight away if he knew that he looked exactly, precisely, UNCANNILY, like David Cameron. Danny protested violently, and Adelle couldn't understand why. After all, Cameron was fairly handsome, in his Converse all-stars and faded jeans – even a bit fancyable, if you allowed Tories a sexual dimension.

But I understood.

Danny was unutterably pompous about his Trotskyite past. The fact that a famous Tory looked like him reminded him of how far he had betrayed his socialist roots. It was hilarious. So the night before he was due back I printed out dozens of smarmy publicity shots of Cameron.

We sought out unusual and surprising sites for our poster campaign: under the toilet seat, inside cupboard doors, the bottom of the bread bin, beneath the dried food in the cat's bowl, the bottom of Gill's underwear drawer.

The pictures were everywhere and the next day we left the house exhilarated by our grand joke, looking forward to the amused phone call from Danny. But the call we got the following evening was from Gill, and it wasn't like that at all. She'd returned alone. Danny had left her. He'd been seeing someone else. It had gone on for quite some time. Now, she couldn't get his face out of her mind. His lying, cheating, shit-eating smile. In fact, she'd got a bit angry, smashed a few things up. But we shouldn't worry. She'd been about to redecorate, anyway. Starting with the hall. The hall is most important place, didn't I agree?

Gill was right: a hall is where the private and public world meet. If the hall isn't right, nothing's going to work.

TELL IT LIKE A STORY

Dispatches From The Frontiers
Of A Savage Age

New Rave MySexuals • The Honeytrapper
The Death Files • Iraqi Road Trip
Hurricane Katrina • Bobbies in Jamaica

New Rave and the MySexual Revolution

Daniel Stacey

Groups of early and pre-teens flow down the Gower Street pavement, jagged little bunches of gold and silver and neon, shiny sparks of light. For the boys, the idea is to look like the elf James Righton from Klaxons: drainpipe jeans in red and yellow and white. Bright high-tops: silver or gold. Hoodies with cartoon references, or a colourful pattern. A little eye makeup, big hair. The girls wear the ugliest tights they can find, puffer jackets, shiny high-tops, bumbags. Oversize neck chains.

Computer Game F A N T A S Y!!

Day-glo O P T I M I S M!!

*The Carto o o o n Came Jumping, Breathing From My TV set, effulgent GREEN flames B U R S T i n g through the phosphorescent coating, And>>and>>>>*and near the venue two young boys walk back in the wrong direction, flashing spiky, conspiratorial eyes, wrestling with tryptamines, paranoia, an absolute loss of inhibition: verging on an impulse to violence. They stare at me, look down at the ground, stare again, smile, frown, introspect, walk on.

"They're shit, don't bother! Shit!" Snarls a girl in a group exiting down the stairs, leering at the crowd gathered outside. She and her friends disappear quickly along the pavement towards Euston station, a giggling, bitchy breeze of tights and bangles and ski-jackets.

Upstairs, past the bewildered African security, in the University of London Union's concert hall, *Super Super* magazine's first all ages rave is at full capacity.

L e i g h B o w e r y for NEOphytes. Multicoloured spinning F R A C T ALS eating suburban style tribes, N E O P H I L I C P R E P O S T E R I T Y !!!

The black, undecorated hall is awash with neon, silver and gold. A girl, maybe 12, in tights, puffer jacket, with a black star painted on her cheek, dances to Michael Jackson's *Black or White*, then falls over. Brightly coloured polyester jackets, large neck chains adorned with soft toys and calculators. Perfect long hair, more eye makeup. One boy wears an upturned *KFC* bucket as a hat, tipped at a jaunty angle. Shoes all shimmering hightops. Young girls jog past, dancing, little Bambis with flailing arms and legs, like newly ambulatory infants, all jittery and on the verge of toppling. Kids are so young they're bum-sucking their cigarettes, blowing the smoke back out quickly over their jutting lower lips. The more discerning have Jean-Charles de Castelbajac caps and bright-framed lensless glasses.

This is C A R T O O N country and I AM THE W A R R I O R WOMAN.

Lording over this scene is Namalee Bolle, in a yellow puffer jacket – fake fur lined – multicoloured tights, silver high-top Cons and star-print bikini. She stands to the side of the stage, holding a black plastic sceptre. Editrice of *Super Super* magazine, doyenne of New Rave, royalty of 2006/2007's most hyped youth cultural movement, she watches lovingly over her flock. Fashion tips in the latest issue of *Super Super* include:

– Ski jackets: "The nutter's equivalent of the navy duffel, a rrrave-ski is an absolute essential for a Super Super reader."

– Bright coloured wigs: "… if you are a newcomer to the wonderful world of wigs then cautiously wear it wivva hat the first time round…"

– Lensless glasses: "Spazzy Spex are probably the most exciting street trend to come outta the London Underground scene in like a billion years."

– Neck chains with pop culture pendants, like *Gameboys*, calculators: "… hang what you like from it… whether it be a plastic iron, cuddly toy, umbrella, or if you can, something ridiculous like a fridge!"

Namalee disappears back stage, as two rugged men in their late twenties, either A&R or journalists, pass by sipping pints.

"It's like they've all been dressed by stylists," one says in awe.

MYSPACE CONNECT the DOTS. Y O U made my top 24 friends list!!! WHO_IS_HERE_TONIGHT?

Standing by the side of the stage is Niyi, who produces some of Namalee's music, used to run a club, Gauche Chic, of genealogical importance for New Rave, and is a MySpace celebrity in his own right – 44,461 profile views, and 4,921 friends. *Real* friends, like he says beneath a photo of Namalee in his MySpace "About Me" box: "to those using MYSPACE ROBOTS :–(((((to get like 5 zillion friends, its so obvious, and so borrrrrrrrrring..... i do try and say thank you or SOMETHING for every request, to try and open the road of MySpace communication.... but they are getting to be more and more AND I DO IT ALL BY HAND, so dont get mad if it takes a week, or two, or longer, i will accept!!!!!promise xxxxxxxxxx."

His trademark look is a big red novelty top hat with "Bad Boy" emblazoned on the front, and a Costa apple juice carton on a thick gold neck chain. Tonight he also has a smaller, more discreet chain as accompaniment, with a miniature McDonald's drink container hanging from it. Two very young girls come up to Niyi, staring not at his face but at his juice box, the clubland motif on his MySpace profile and in all his press shots. One of the girls, with a dark mop fringe, yellow jumper and black leggings, reaches out, slowly, stops, then keeps reaching, entranced, and touches his fruit carton like it's a mythic talisman. Niyi remains unfazed as she turns and walks away in silence.

OUR c.r.e.w. was built on LOVE. THIS IS not IRONIC – This is SERRRIUZ.

On the stage behind Niyi, a band called Adventure Playground launch into a dancehall track while one of their MCs, Town Mouse Country Mouse, wearing a traditional Jewish dancing costume with a pencil moustache and long womanly hair in a loose top bun, climbs on top of one of the speakers. This is the cue for Jew D'Orange, on beats, to unleash a disco version of the secular Hebrew folk song "Hava Nagila".

"If you're young get lairy, get lairy now!" shouts the second MC, Mo Juiced, "And go to myspace.com/garmsoflondon. We've got shirts available on the first of March." He shows the audience his own T-shirt, pulling up his zebra-print hoodie. It says "ON ROAD", black on white. After a grime track with Nintendo samples, where the rhyming sort of falls apart for Mo Juiced, we all find ourselves in an a capella "Amazing Grace" singalong.

"Take your lighters out, put your hands up," Mo Juiced yells. Then it happens. Like the midnight spawning of Hawaiian coral polyps, or the blossoming of that rarely seen flowering cacti, the Nightblooming Cereus, the first glow stick I've seen all evening comes rising from the crowd, clutched in a sweaty pink hand. Others pop up, one, two, three, but then it stops, as if halted by some groupthink sentiment casting a dark shadow over the audience. Three is enough. Last year the floor would have been an Atlantic of pulsing fluorophors. But did you see that piece in the *Guardian/Independent on Sunday/Observer/Guardian/Independent on Sunday/Observer/Guardian/Independent on Sunday/Observer?*

EXPLODE. UPWARDS. OUTWARDS. There is no movement. New Rave is dead, long live Neon Pop. New Rave is alive. Relentless positivity. Evangelical O P T I M I S M.

The set ends and Town Mouse Country Mouse dives into crowd to wild applause, in amongst cries of "You're a wanker!"

In ecstasy, a boy throws his glow stick up into the light rig, where it stays. Another falls down from the upstairs balcony, landing on a photographer wearing one huge gold earring, who is shooting pictures of a tall blonde. Namalee has exited the backstage area, and is soon joined by Niyi and another acolyte. I can't recognise him, I haven't seen his MySpace yet. Pyjama pants, puma high tops, jacket with anthropomorphised popcorn and *Coke* bottles.

I follow them to the bar at the back of the hall, which is fully lit and hosts various packs of drunk and drugged children rolling around on the floor. The Van She remix of Klaxons' "Gravity's Rainbow" plays as I talk to Namalee.

NOTHING I DO MEANS NOTHING TO ME COS THIS IS M.Y. L.I.F.E!!

"With the colour, the clothes: you wear your heart on your sleeve. The kids are into it. I love it that anything goes," she says.

"This movement is all about being nice to your friends, about having fun."

Polite, softly spoken sentences, her gentle susurrations well-meaning, almost wholesome.

"I'm into cartoons and colour and art – the kids really get the sentiment. This is our first underage thing. I think these kids are our natural readership."

27 years old, in a bikini and yellow puffer jacket, with a plastic sceptre, reigning over a hall full of drunken 13 year olds dressed in psychedelic colours dancing and collapsing in great supple heaps of face paint and ski jackets to the sounds of a womanly Jewish rapper playing the mandolin. You cannot help but respect a woman capable of creating such a kingdom.

Late Of The Pier begin playing onstage, their lead singer, topless, drumming the slats from a futon bed hung off a mic stand, backed by arpeggiated computer games samples. Another band member, in a polyester ski jacket, dances next to a dining chair covered in soft toys harbouring a synthesiser, and occasionally reaches down to play handclaps.

Multigenre, multiracial, melting pot, eclectic, anything goes, cartoon couture, MySpace celebrity, MySexual, Raver, Quaver, Blaver, DIY, psychedelic, New Rave, Neon Pop, Fluoro Pop, optimism, euphoria, positivity. That's the idea. Party music. Like the next act, Brazilian MCs Bonde Do Role, who sound more like drunk karaoke than Baile Funk. Or another of tonight's performers, geek chic Grime artist JME, who lists faux-gangster cyber rules on his MySpace site, including:

"I do not allow HTML comments anywhere, so if i see you try

And HTML me, i will send you Sasser worm or Derkhead Trojan V1.3 And crash your server"; and, "If you post multiple comments on my page, or some long comment, as if I'm a doughnut, I will block you as if you are an original glazed."

Downstairs, on the street, the fracas is still continuing. None of the kids can get in, and they're all drunk. Crowding around a bottle of white wine, Bella, 14, red wool jacket, frizzy black hair and thick gold chain, and Hector, 14, tall, ginger hair, scarf, subdued dark cotton jacket and jeans, are feeling chatty.

They only came because they heard about it on MySpace, and all the right people with all the right MySpace profiles were going. One of Bella's friends told her to check out *Super Super*'s MySpace site before, but she ran out of time: "I was going to, I was going to but that doesn't mean I don't like *Super Super*."

"NO! ME!" screams one of Bella's friends, realising I have a Dictaphone in my hand. Other children turn around, twig. They start schooling around me like pelagic mackerel.

"We have a fashion label, go on 'I Stole It From My Sister' on MySpace, look it up," shouts Bella's friend. "I make bow jumpers. Who makes bow jumpers?! Basically, I get a jumper, and I make a big bow and put it on the front. Who does that?"

The other children start to join in, screaming about how they're the new face of independent film, about their bands, their art projects. I bring out a free copy of Super Super handed to me by a girl at the door, convening an impromptu focus group.

"It's so new rave. I love new rave, I love new rave, Hector loves new rave."

"Where are my glowsticks?!"

"This is shit, shit, look at her tits, this is not what we want to be an influence to young teenagers like ourselves!"

"Fred Pez, Fred Pez."

"I lick the magazine when I see Fred Perry boy."

"Look at that sexy mumma outfit, wouldn't you just go out every day in those!"

Everyone laughs... cackles... starts screaming again.

"How big is this magazine!"

"It's shit! Who wears an *Etch-A-Sketch*?"

"How much does it cost to print all those colours?"

"I think, OK look, thousands of trees are being burnt down, not burnt down but, well, cut down, for this shit."

"OH_MY_GOD, look at that dude, they go to our high school."

"And I was the first person who said I wanted to be in a band…"

"Look at her top, she's got a smiley face on it, she's blatantly new rave."

"Can I tell you something?" Bella butts in. "If you're going to print something, Fay, the lead singer, was the bassist in my band first," she says, pointing at someone on one of the pages. Bella's friend turns to the girl on the door, 20 yards away, and shrieks over the top of everyone,

"Look, they've spelt 'Nu Rave' wrong. Who does their goddamn English GCSE here!!"

Laughter and squeals come from all directions now. Their cachinnations grow greater and greater. They are losing control, screaming for me to go to their MySpace pages, where they have a music demo, or pictures of Turkish plimsolls they've painted in fluorescent colours. Eyes widening, bottles of pale white wine passed around in their pink little hands, they shriek in unison at the Dictaphone, everything flatlining into some desperate wailing expression of youth and alcohol, driven on by a scent that has permeated the whole evening of new and exciting things, and of fame.

Mini-Korg synths and beat led indie music, smoke machines and robot dancing. At the 13th birthday party of record label Fierce Panda, Joe Reeves from Glaswegian punk band Shitdisco tells me how he first became acquainted with the term New Rave.

"We did a photo shoot with the *NME*, and like Hot Chip were in it, Klaxons, and us. We were all in the same issue and they said it was going to be called 'Alt Disco'. We were like, 'What is it?' And they were like, 'Oh it's this movement that we think you and these guys and these guys are all part of.' It was quite good that it mentioned even the word disco, and we thought, y'know, it could help us that, and then about a month later it came out and it was 'New Rave', and we were like, 'What the fuck?'"

After three months of relentless press hype, the freaks started showing up. Suddenly Shitdisco were a New Rave band.

"You'd see guys walking around with paint all over their face at our gigs, or weird DIY clothes," Joe says.

"We totally embraced it," says Joel Stone, Shitdisco's bassist and vocalist. "We vibed off the audiences, and started getting more into it, more hyped up. I mean, life would have been much harder if we didn't."

'New Rave (sometimes referred to as nu-rave) is a style of music fusing elements of electronic dance music and rock, which developed in the UK in 2006,' reads the Wikipedia entry. 'Klaxons, Shitdisco and New Young Pony Club are generally accepted as the main exponents of the genre.' The next day cyberfans, or PR men engaging in some low-scale cultural warfare, have edited the profile: 'Klaxons, New Young Pony Club and Shitdisco are generally accepted...' In any case, the psychedelia has forgotten to show up tonight. The room is subdued: an indie crowd of blacks and blues, plimsolls. Briefly a young boy drifts past with glowing orange paint on one cheek, like some ethereal presence, the ghost of December 06/January 07, then disappears.

"I mean, we started seeing all this rave fashion coming in at the !WOWOW! squat parties we were playing 18 months ago, but it was more of an art scene at that point," Joe says.

"It was more just anything goes. There were glow sticks, but also like people wearing bin bags and weird stuff," Joel says. "Or like Farris Rotter from The Horrors posing all night on a dentist's chair, wearing the pointiest shoes you'd ever seen in your life."

"That was the first time we met the guys from Klaxons," Joe

says. "It's weird, because they obviously have kind of left that scene now, but at that point they weren't involved in it, or they were just beginning. Even though it was only kind of a year and a bit ago, you can see now that people had agendas or things on their minds."

The !WOWOW! parties are only one part of the heavily contested genealogy of New Rave, interbreeding with clubland: Nag Nag Nag, Kashpoint, Kashpoint II, Gauche Chic, Golf Sale, Family, Antisocial, All You Can Eat, Boombox, Namalee Loves Pop, and a raft of exponentially proliferating new club nights.

Jim Warboy has been there from the start, originally getting involved in Kashpoint, then Antisocial and now running All You Can Eat (AYCE) with Niyi's former creative partner K-Tron. He also produces some of Namalee's music with K-tron. Namalee occasionally plays at their club, and he's in the latest issue of *Super Super*. Matthew !WOWOW! was a resident at AYCE. Millie Brown, who works on the door at AYCE, a performance artists, was part of !WOWOW!. Warboy put on Yr Mum Ya Dad at Kashpoint, produced their music, and then was the resident DJ at their club Antisocial.

"Everyone keeps making new alliances, and nobody really falls out," he says. "I mean people do fall out temporarily, but everyone's OK with each other. It kind of just keeps splintering."

Warboy lives on an estate in Camden, in a boho apartment with wooden African masks and baking ingredients arranged neatly in jars on exposed shelving. The only visible reference to New Rave is "BIG DICK LOVER FUX MEN" in colourful plastic letters on the fridge, next to smiley faces placed in a circle around a diamante heart-shaped magnet.

"What am I being offered, what is anyone around me being offered? I mean, bugger all in my experience. Most people I know have got press books coming out of their ears, and earn very little money. And then you get flagship deals like the Klaxons, which is really not a kind of music that's pushing anything forward in any major way anyway," he says. "But we don't need that investment. We have our own computers, we can make our own music on them, we can make our own films on them, we can burn them off onto DVD or onto CD, we can start our own clubs, we can print our own magazines. We can promote everything through MySpace, find bands on MySpace, find visual artists on MySpace, socialise on MySpace. We've learned to keep it going on nothing. That's kind of what this movement is about, although the atmosphere is a lot more competitive now, because people know there's something to play for, and they want to get their stake.

"You know, people can get themselves in a position to become spokespeople or leaders or, you know, 'definitive' in their work. You've got people like fashion designer Carrie Mundane – Cassette Playa. She'll be brought in as a kind of 'creative visionary' to do looks. You know, not necessarily just for clothing but… I mean god knows, I don't know what she's been offered, but it's obvious that MTV or someone are going to ask her in to do like a New Rave makeover of their whole look.

"I mean, I've got a club, so my club could probably be doing more, it could turn into a much bigger brand if I just organised it more." AYCE is about to go to New York for the first time, and they've just launched All You Can Eat TV on their club's website – a showcase of odd short films that AYCE fans have uploaded. "We've had press for it already from the *Independent on Sunday*, even though we haven't really done anything yet.

"Last year we were handing out whistles and glo sticks. We were doing all these things that helped fuel that idea of a New Rave movement. Now we don't do that, we have girls doing body painting and stuff like that, it's a different kind of thing. So what is that new kind of thing? It's almost too early to name it – like in the 90s you couldn't have called it the rave generation very early on, that came later once there were like lots of little different things going on. There's definitely been a cultural shift in the way people are communicating, socialising, and no one's come up with a name for it yet. There's this new attitude to have fun. The idea of people being cool and stuff like that – that's kind of been really broken down, I mean that's out of fashion."

A week later at All You Can Eat, I can hear Sebastian, our photographer, screaming on the podium behind me:

"I want to fuck everyone in the room."

He taps stylist and celebrity clubber Jamie E17 on the shoulder and starts snapping his Day-Glo eyebrows, fake eyelashes, Day-Glo Hitler tache and lipgloss, and jump suit with neon panels – along with his trademark platinum bowl-cut wig.

A guy in a glowing smiley face T-shirt talks to girl in a Mickey Mouse shirt-dress with face paint. They're both wearing tights and he has a pacifier around his neck and a purple bum bag. There is butcher's paper on the walls, and paints available in Styrofoam trays.

Someone has written 'RAPE WITH KNIVES' in red paint on one sheet. On the next bit of paper 'Youth in Movement' is scrawled in blue paint, with 'Get involved' underneath in red as an addition. Basement Jaxx's 'Jump and Shout' plays as a girl picks up one set of paints and goes to the wall. She draws a circle, begins to turn it into a smiley face, but has the paints taken off her by a boy in white drainpipes, a yellow jumper, and red cap, who sketches some fusion of a piece of toast and a bear's head. There's a general warehouse rave atmosphere: chatting between strangers, and those lengthy, euphoric pick-ups where people flirt for hours before finally falling on each other like hungry vultures. Girls arrive at the wall dressed all in white. They start painting their bellies, shirts.

"Paint my back!" screams one at a passing guy.

She heads to the dance floor with her tray of paints, and someone upturns it on her head. In the unisex toilet, a Spanish girl with a yellow tow-along suitcase on roller blade wheels talks to a friend. She has a plastic iron around her neck on a piece of orange cord.

On the dance floor, some kid has painted *Youth in Movement* on his white T-shirt, like on the wall, maybe copying what he's seen: reciting some visual chant as part of the weird drug logic of the room.

Heading backstage, I pass Jim Warboy dressed in a giant skull shirt, black baseball cap with a yellow and black badge, 'Fashion Kills', 3/4 length black pants, white mid-tops and some gold carnival beads. In the small green room a boy with no top on, covered in paint, shouts over the music.

"It's just generic electro, there might be some pop later – or Matthew might play."

"Matthew !WOWOW!?"

"Yeah, he's gone to Peckham to see some band, he's going out with a friend of mine. He lives next door to me."

"Are you cold?"

"No, I'm fucked. If I was sober I'd be cold."

"I like your tweed," he says. "Where'd you get that?"

"Portsmouth."

His friends pull him away, whilst a couple paint each other blue, in front of a jaded mid-30s Goth in highsoled boots, black jeans and black singlet. A girl called Liz in acid-wash hotpants, a blue bra and black high heels comes and starts a conversation. She's promoting a night at the White Horse in Hoxton: there will be space hopper races, a 72 hour DJ marathon, a jumble sale room, and BYO booze. She hands over a flyer.

"WWW.MYSPACE/YOUTHINMOVEMENT" it says, drawn across the bodies of a pile of naked teenagers.

The Honeytrapper

Lauren Gard

The blue door opens just as I think my ass is about to permanently fuse to the wooden bench. I've been staring at this portal into a stately stone apartment building for four hours, willing a tall middle-aged man to step through it.

"That's got to be him," I tell my boss, Chris, whose thigh is pressed up against mine in an effort to retain some body heat. We're both underdressed for autumn in Scotland, and freezing. I reach into my back pocket and quickly unfold the snapshot I've studied a dozen times since our plane took off in San Francisco, 24 hours ago. The man in the photo, arm around our client, is indeed the same gent who just took a left out the door. A major relief: we'd been worried that his statuesque wife was wrong about him flying into Edinburgh last night. It would have been a shame for her to pay US $10,000 to find out if he's being unfaithful only to discover that his business trip to Scotland was utter fiction. During our two Stateside meetings she appeared to know very little about him.

"It could be another man, even," she suggested while counting out a mess of 20 dollar bills, extracted during numerous trips to the ATM, on our dark cherry conference table.

"We don't, ah – we're not intimate anymore. I can't even remember the last time…" She looked up then and offered a limp smile. "Can I write you a cheque for the remaining 2,000 dollars?"

"It's definitely him," I whisper to Chris as I leap off the bench. I'm sure Chris can hear my heart thumping, but I'm still new at this.

"Here we go!" Chris slowly rises, a chunky camera bag bobbing in his right hand. We give our guy a half-block lead, trailing him from across the street. We have to be particularly cautious with this one since we'll be following him on foot for four days straight. If we're burned today, we're screwed. He continues along the winding sidewalk towards a flashing red traffic light a few blocks away. He's oblivious – yet clearly on a mission. Chris stops and scans the street. Then he whips out his video camera and, without turning his head, barks a quiet command:

"Stay on him! And be careful – traffic's backwards here!"

Duly noted, although Chris is the one who has nearly been run down twice already. I scurry onward and watch our target approach the light, cross to our side of the street, and saunter out of view behind a thick hedge. Fuck! I make a mad dash for the corner, my heavy purse, a designer knock-off housing a hidden camera system, bouncing awkwardly against my hip. I careen around the corner.

"Shit!"

A split second later, Chris appears.

"Where is he?" he huffs. And then I'm forced to utter the three dreadful words that may one day get me fired:

"I don't know."

The street is nearly empty and our mark has vanished. We're in a part of the city known as New Town, but it's as though we've stumbled upon an 18th century village. Flowers spill from wooden boxes flanking brightly painted window frames. A bulbous black taxi toodles by. Off in the distance, a pristine white steeple splits a turquoise river. We soak it all in for 30 seconds.

The good news is there aren't many places our target could have ducked into. A chain supermarket. A sandwich shop. A dry cleaners. The sky, Disney blue just a few moments ago, begins to spit.

"Check the market," instructs Chris, camera still in hand. "I'll cover the rest of the block."

I breeze into the shop, tilting my head just so, nibbling my lower lip, and adopting a daft expression I hope reads, 'Now, why did I come here, again?' My eyes dart up and down the aisles, past a blonde woman examining loaves of bread and an elderly bald man lost in a cat food selection haze. I nearly jump when I see our target plucking a carton of milk from the dairy shelves – not in the least because he's unexpectedly dashing.

Not quite the Pierce Brosnan lookalike our client advised us to be on the lookout for, but then, I knew that from the photo she'd given us. Still, it didn't do him justice. Square jaw. Crinkly blue eyes. Plenty of stylishly mussy hair. Quite fit for 50. If we decide to sting him later in the week, it could be fun to play the part of decoy sent in to flirt with him. I spin around and make a beeline for the door, trying to suppress a jubilant grin, and give Chris a thumbs up at waist level as I bounce towards the other end of the street, where he's pacing.

"Got 'im," I announce. "He's buying milk!"

"What kind?"

The hokey smile topples off my face. I have no idea what kind. Was I really supposed to have gotten that close to this guy? I consider the question. He didn't look like a skim guy. More like a whole milk kind of bloke, the kind with a ridiculously high metabolism.

"I'm kidding!" chides Chris. "Excellent work. Now, c'mon, let's get out of the rain." We lie in wait opposite the market and when our target exits 10 minutes later, Chris's camera is rolling.

"Bet you 20 bucks he walks right back home," I challenge. I currently owe Chris about US $200 in lost bets.

"I'm sure you're right," he says. Darn – no bet.

"But you never know."

Ah yes, we never do. Even if Mr. Cute-for-50 returns to his apartment, what's not to say he hasn't just picked up supplies for a romantic breakfast with a lingerie-clad lover lounging in his bed? Unfortunately, there are certain things we cannot do. Not at this point, anyway.

"Don't go home! Don't go home!" I chant softly as we set out after him again. The last thing I want to do is spend the remainder of my first day overseas in forced communion with the bench. But a few minutes later, as the familiar blue front door slams shut, the seat, now dappled with raindrops, beckons. The sky has cleared, but the sun is still MIA and the shivering has begun again. A single syllable enters my mind: rum.

"We passed a liquor store about a block away," I inform Chris. He forces a dramatic sigh and, without a word, pulls a fat wad of cash out of his front pocket. The equivalent in pounds of the US $1,000 he exchanged at the airport, I'm guessing, which a mini-mart clerk has already suggested he never again whip out in public. He slips a £50 note from beneath a silver Montblanc money clip. I pocket the bill, drop the hidden camera bag on the bench and take off. Welcome to the thrill-a-minute world of private investigations.

If you'd asked me back when I was a nose-in-a-book kind of kid what I hoped to be when I was verging on 30, chances are I would have said a grown-up female version of Leroy "Encyclopedia" Brown, the precocious boy detective who was drawn to look kind of like me (gangly, glasses) and could always be relied upon to counter neighbourhood crime with nimble wit. That or Danielle Steel, whose scandalous sex-drenched books I'd sneak from my mother's bedside drawer and skim beneath the covers at night. So I suppose it's fitting that I'm now a professional love spy.

A journalist by trade, I was writing for a weekly newspaper in March 2006 when I tripped across an online Craigslist ad posted by Butler & Associates, a small agency owned by a former competitive bodybuilder turned rogue cop turned private investigator. (That'd be Chris.) "Private investigations firm is seeking undercover decoys, age 21–50, for select undercover assignments," the ad began. Last among a list of desirable qualities that included the ability to ad lib, to elicit information from targets and to remain calm under stress, flashed two words that really ignited my imagination: "BODY WIRE". As in, "the ability to perform the above tasks while wearing a body wire." I clicked on the link to the firm's website.

"Betrayed by someone you love? Deceived by someone you trust?" asked the page highlighting the firm's infidelity work. "For your peace of mind, let us uncover the truth." Ooh.

I picked up the phone.

"Sure," said Chris, who later admitted that he was wary of reporters but figured the publicity wouldn't hurt. "Come on in."

I approached the story like any other. I spent hours quizzing Chris, whose trilling *Blackberry* interrupted our chatter every few minutes. He explained that he invites client to call at any time, at no charge.

"Better to vent to me than to their husbands. I think of this job as investigator-slash-therapist. A lot of P.I.'s won't touch it – it's so emotionally charged."

He hadn't planned on tracking cheating spouses when he quit the police force after a decade. He'd advertised general investigative services in the phone book, and to his surprise anxious wives phoned in droves. Despite the rise of the Internet, he still believes in the power of the *Yellow Pages*, shelling out thousands of dollars a month for the ads. I sat down with Cyndi and Angelica, Chris's two full-time investigators. Affable, bright, and discernibly cautious, they'd been hired through decoy ads like the one I'd seen. Thirty-something Cyndi was a former prison nurse and competitive horseback-rider from Kentucky. Angelica, a newlywed, was fresh out of UC Berkeley and lived with her in-laws. She'd applied to be a cop but was told she needed more life experience. Chris invited me to tag along on a case.

One Friday night sting in a crowded pool hall was all it took to hook me. I went as a reporter but before I knew what was happening I found myself chatting up George Clooney's could-be cousin while the husband of Chris's client flirted with a buxom decoy. When I went out a second time Chris offered me a purse cloaking a hidden camera.

"Think you can do it?" he challenged as we raced across a mall parking lot.

"Do what?" I asked, trying to keep up

"You didn't think I was going to walk in there with a purse, did you?" He handed me the bag. I slipped it over my shoulder, screwed up my courage, and, a few minutes later, surreptitiously filmed an adulterous couple smooching near a turtleneck display at H&M. Although I had to genuinely repress my natural inclination to shop – an adorable dress sashayed on a hanger nearby – I'd never felt so alive. I whipped off an article for the newspaper.

"You totally crossed the line here!" my editor scolded me after I turned in my first draft. "You're supposed to report the news, not make it."

I blushed. I stammered. I shrugged. Then I quit my job and took my Toyota *Corolla* in to have the windows tinted.

Infidelity investigations comprise about 75% of our caseload. The rest of the time we tackle everything from tracking down runaway teens to performing surveillance for worker compensation cases. About three quarters of our infidelity clients are women. They arrive at our office, located in a lowslung beige industrial building in Concord, a suburb nestled 30 miles east of San Francisco, in varying states of shock and distress. Most can't quite believe their lives have come to this, that they actually opened a fat copy of the *Yellow Pages* long forgotten in a hall closet or googled "private investigator San Francisco" and wound up rapping on our locked, blacked-out front door. We monitor our small parking lot via video camera and have witnessed potential clients pull into a spot, only to speed away moments later without ever getting out of their cars. That way they can pretend they were never quite this desperate.

"I never in a million years thought I'd be sitting here right now," are often the first words that spill from their carefully lipsticked mouths as they reach into their Prada purses for *Kleenex*. (They tend to be a well-groomed bunch, able as they are to afford our US $95 and up hourly rates.) "I feel like I'm going crazy" is the sentiment that typically follows. Yet clients rarely seem crazy to me, even when they speak of steaming open their husband's credit card statements or sabotaging his cell phone by dousing the battery with drops of olive oil.

If clients share anything in common, it's that they tend to be very sad and, when we reach beneath the surface of their sorrow, very angry. One woman recently thrust a piece of paper towards me on which she'd provided the basics on her husband and his suspected lover, whom he had repeatedly denied being involved with. "My Husband" read the first line: "6 feet tall. Thin. Ultra marathon runner. White hair. Beard. White 1999 Volvo station wagon." It was what we required, in addition to a photo and a point of acquisition, to perform surveillance. Below it, she'd scrawled "WHORE", followed by a few mundane details on the other woman. My immediate, uncomfortable, instinct was to laugh. Chris sat across from me at the conference table, and I studied his framed P.I. license on the wall behind him as I waited for him to say something.

"How could she do this?" the client asked, cutting the silence. "We went to her wedding two years ago! Can you believe the Whore bought a house just a mile away from ours?"

She looked to me for affirmation. I shook my head slightly, studied the piece of paper she'd given me and gave a little tut.

"I want evidence that he's cheating on me, in case he tries to back out of the divorce agreement he agreed to last week." She paused. "He said he'd give me his entire retirement fund. Crazy, right?"

"You have to protect yourself," I replied. It was my multi-purpose line of choice. She was halfway out the door when she stopped and threw a question over her shoulder.

"You'll be careful, right?" She turned around. "I did notice yesterday that one of his guns is missing."

Most clients are less dramatic. "We've been married for 27 years and I feel like I barely know him anymore," they'll say. We routinely hear about husbands who claim to sleep at the office, creep out of bed in the middle of the night to feed an online porn habit, grow more concerned with the state of their pecs and their abs than that of their children, drive drunk more often than not, or spontaneously drop 80 grand on a sports car after spending 60 grand on one the year before. Cliché, cliché, cliché. But every so often we'll hear a truly jarring story, like the one from a woman who first found out about her husband's philandering after their entire family participated in a community blood bank donation for a sick kid in their neighbourhood. A few days later a letter from the blood bank arrived in the mail, addressed to her husband. She opened it: "Your request to withdraw your donation has been received and processed". The letter may well have concluded, "Thank you for informing us that you've had unprotected sex and that any number of nasty venereal diseases may be coursing through your bloodstream". Our client confronted her husband, who admitted he'd slept with a few prostitutes here and there. She forgave him, but never quite trusted him again.

I often have to stop myself from telling clients about a certain expertise I bring to the job: I've cheated. And I was remarkably good at it.

"Really?" I imagine they'd say, taking in my everywoman looks – the clear skin, minimal make-up, straight teeth, long dark hair and bangs. If I'm pretty at all, it's the kind of pretty that would never cause a wife worry.

"You must have had a good reason. Was it revenge cheating?"

"Oh, no," I'd reply. "No one's ever cheated on me."

I'd sigh then, that tiny waft of air propelling the client's gaze to the platinum wedding band circling my ring finger. I'd watch her watery eyes pop.

"I was just unhappy," I'd continue. "I wanted to – you know, feel the butterflies in my stomach again. To have someone touch me and not know what their hands were going to do for a change."

She'd lean in, successfully repressing the desire to say, "Yes, I've felt that, too." Instead:

"Did he catch you?"

"Nope. Although I told him everything, eventually. I'm too damn honest."

"But didn't you feel guilty?"

"A little. The first time especially."

"Oh. You did it more than once?"

"Uh-huh. I don't know how many times – I can't bring myself to count." It's true. I tried to make a list once but stopped when I couldn't conjure the name of a guy I met in a Tokyo nightclub. I did remember his bright orange vest, though, and the fact that it turned out he was a far better dancer than lover. "A dozen? Two dozen?"

A little gasp, then, in a voice buoyed by hope, "But you're still married? You worked through it?"

"Oh, no. This was before I met my husband," I'd say. Then I'd utter a conviction similar to that many of our clients' spouses have sworn, even when confronted with damning evidence.

"I'd never cheat on *him*. Never."

In my case it's true. Almost. Case in point: I'd been working for Butler and Associates for a month when a new client rang. She was a fast-talking neurologist who wanted to protect her kids from her alcoholic ex-husband and knock her alimony payments down a few notches. She painted him as a successful building contractor who lied to the court about his income and often knocked back a few pints before picking the kids up for his visitation. She wanted us to catch him on a DUI. Chris tailed him for several nights, hoping he'd get behind the wheel after leaving his usual watering hole. On one occasion he did – but then he simply drove a few blocks to his house. Not a chance the cops could nab him that quickly. Somehow we had to make him drive a greater distance.

The plan Chris orchestrated was beyond complicated, and involved my colleague, Cyndi, and I.

"Chat him up at the bar, watch him get sloshed, convince him to take a dip in your hot tub," Chris said, peering at me through his blue-tinted contact lenses, a small smile playing on his lips above a carefully manicured goatee. "The key is to act like he's going to get a threesome. No guy will turn that down – at least, no straight one." I rolled my eyes.

"I'll be waiting outside the bar. I'll call the cops the minute he gets in his car, and follow him. All you have to do is keep driving."

"You're just doing this because you want to see me and Cyndi make out," I told Chris. He denied this, failing miserably to keep a straight face.

"Just, you know, put a hand on her leg, run a hand through her hair – "

"Enough!" said Cyndi, who hadn't been shy about her burgeoning interest in tantra. "We know what to do."

"We've got it covered," I added. "So we'll just go to his favourite bar and hope he's there?" Chris shook his head.

A few days later, 5 pm. I'm pacing the kitchen of a house for sale, awaiting the grumble of a white pick-up truck pulling into the driveway. I'm wearing a low-cut jersey top that shows off cleavage I've artfully created with a mega-bra and bronzer, my favourite butt-hugging jeans and three coats of mascara. My purse is wired. Chris and Cyndi sit across the street in the sleek black Mercedes Chris's mysterious silent partner, whom we know only as "G", recently contributed to our fleet. They'll listen in, just in case our target's serial killer side emerges. Chris's realtor contact hooked us up with the house, and my fingers are crossed that no other realtors show up for a viewing.

"Hi!" I say, grasping the hand of the short, balding man in a polo shirt and khakis. "I'm Lauren." I've decided to stick with my real first name as much as possible in the line of duty. My memory just isn't that good.

"Hullo," he replies in a singsongy Irish accent, the one I found unexpectedly alluring when I left a message on his voicemail the day before. He quickly takes in my outfit. "Patrick McCauley. Pleasure to meet you."

I lead him into the kitchen, where his attention turns from my bust to the cabinets. The room is bright with the late afternoon sun so he doesn't seem to notice that the lights are off. Whew. I couldn't for the life of me find a switch that worked.

"You can see what I was talking about on the phone," I say. "The cabinets look like they haven't been touched since the 60s. The house just isn't moving, and my realtor thinks a quick makeover might help."

He tugs on a cabinet door and peers inside.

"Well, there's a lot we can do. All depends on how much you want to spend."

"Whatever you think will help it sell, and fast."

"It's your house?"

"No, it was my aunt's. She just died and I'm handling the sale for my parents, who live back East."

I step toward him and peer into his grey eyes. "You know, you look really familiar. Have we met before?"

"I don't think so," he replies. With a shock I realise that he's staring at my breasts. Has anyone ever been so fascinated with them before? Not that I can recall.

"Maybe at a bar? Yeah, somewhere around here. A place with all sorts of beer on tap?"

"Right, well, most nights I'm at Conlin's."

"That's where it was!" I exclaim. "Yeah, I think you were sitting up at the bar."

"Yep, that's my spot. On my way there now, actually." He glances at his watch. "Is there a light in here?"

I grimace. "Burnt out. Guess I'll need an electrician, too." I cross in front of him, lean over the stove and open a high cabinet. I examine it for no apparent reason – other than to "show the goods," as Chris so tactfully suggested. If only my women's studies professor could see me now, I think. Patrick pokes around the kitchen for a few minutes before reporting that for US $40,000 I can have a gorgeous new kitchen in just three weeks.

"Wow, so fast! You must work all the time." I bat my lashes a la Betty Boop. "When do you have time to drink?"

"I put in 14 hours most days," he says. Then, a chuckle, "but I make the time!"

"I bet you do", I think.

He proffers a business card and I tuck it into my back pocket. When we shake hands again I let mine linger.

"Thanks so much," I say, flashing him a coy smile.

"So… what time did you say you'd be at that bar?"

His eyes widen.

"Right," he stammers. "You should come join me for a drink. That'd be fun."

"A friend and I were planning to go out in San Francisco, but we might just come by on the way."

"Alright, then," he replies. "Goodbye."

From the door I watch him lumber toward his truck, and before I can even think about what I'm doing I'm back beside him.

"Oh, and Patrick," I purr into his car. "My friend just loves Irish accents."

It strikes me then that I sound like an underpaid phone sex operator, and my cheeks blaze. Fuck, I'm really, really bad at this. I dash back inside and hide until I hear him drive off.

"Who are you?" I ask my reflection when I pass a gawdy mirror in the entryway. If I were a spigot, Patrick would have drowned soon after stepping foot in the house. And yet he played right into my hand.

Four hours later, we're in a redneck bar where dozens of autographed cowboy boots dangle from the ceiling and so-called shots of lemon juice, sugar and vodka are served up in six-ounce glasses. I guzzle cocktails with Patrick while Cyndi nurses a soda water. After we'd ordered our first round a few hours back, she'd planned to stealthily slip the bartender a 20 and request that my future drinks be made virgin, per our usual drinking-with-targets protocol.

But it was a no-go – Patrick and the bartender clearly know one another well. In fact, he seems to know half the people in the bar. He turns out to be quite a charmer, with a gentle way about him and a self-deprecating Irish humour.

"I've never met a client for a drink before," he admits.

"C'mon," I retort. "You can't be serious!" I brush his knee with my fingertips. He leans in close.

"In fact, I haven't been on a date in 11 years."

He sips his drink and looks away. I run a finger down his cheek and shoot a woeful look across the table at Cyndi, who I can tell has become a bit panicked about my increasingly obvious state of intoxication. Poor Patrick! When I signed onto this P.I. thing, I never anticipated feeling sorry for the people we were out to sting. En route to the bathroom to phone Chris with an update, I whisper to Cyndi: "He's so nice! Don't you wish we could terminate now and get out of here?" She nods.

"But remember why we're here. If he drives drunk, we'll be getting someone dangerous off the road." Good point. And it's not like we'll force him into his car – he could easily call a cab. I return just as Cyndi knocks over my newly arrived gin and tonic. She meets my dazed gaze with arched eyebrows and embarks on a napkin search.

I plop into Patrick's lap. He wraps his arms around my waist. And that's the last scene I can recollect. I don't remember Patrick accepting Cyndi's invitation to take a dip with us in her hot tub. I can't recall the flashing blue and red lights atop the police car that pulled Patrick over, even after later viewing his arrest on video, as Chris filmed it. Nor can I summon up the memory of stumbling into our waiting room soon after midnight and collapsing in a chair usually reserved for forlorn clients. I come to briefly when my husband arrives to take me home, and again later when he tucks me in and brushes his soft lips against my forehead. The next morning I recoil at the site of a plastic sick bag in the kitchen wastebasket.

"You had that in the office, and the car," Adam reminds me as I fill a glass with water, a task that seems to involve 18 steps. Right. I call Cyndi on the way to work. I'm due to interview a decoy applicant at 9 am, with four more meetings to follow.

"Tell me I didn't sneak off to the bathroom and have sex with our target last night," I ask flatly when Cyndi picks up.

"You didn't!" She laughs.

"I'm serious. I blacked out, so I have no idea what I did. Adam told me the cops got our guy on a DUI. That's all."

"I'm sorry! I did everything I could think of to slow you down, but it was like the deck was stacked against us. When you ordered those lemon drop shots and the bartender – "

"Just tell me what happened." She has a tendency to ramble and my head is exploding.

"Well, you did kiss him." I figured as much. I hear a honk and realise I'm stopped at a green light. I step on the gas. "You sat in his lap for like, an hour. He was super into it and you were, too. I mean you were pretty much glued to him. You really don't remember this?"

I groan. I thought I'd kicked that old get-drunk-and-hook-up habit, and the fact that it happened in the line of duty doesn't make me feel any better.

"I'm so sorry. Must have been a blast for you!"

"Oh, I was fine. I just wish I could have done more to help. You seemed totally focused on the sting most of the night, and then suddenly you were just – gone."

I'm on the freeway now, on autopilot. In other words, speeding. It occurs to me that if I were pulled over right now, I may well get slapped with a DUI of my own. According to Adam, I registered a blood alcohol level of .16 on Chris's breathalyser test last night, way above the legal limit of .08. Seven hours have passed – enough time to metabolise all that alcohol? I slow down.

"What else happened?"

"We kissed, too," says Cyndi. "You and me, I mean."

Just the news I was hoping not to hear. I can't bring myself to request details and I'm grateful that she doesn't supply any. It's not the fact that I've kissed a woman, or her, even. What freaks me out is not remembering it. What if I said something embarrassing, or even worse, took it a step further? Sucked on an ear? Felt her up? All I can do is apologise.

"We did what we were supposed to do," insists Cyndi. "Let's just say that you were an exceptionally determined bait girl."

I'm not sure I believe her, but when I later search the term "alcohol blackout" online I come across an academic paper highlighting the fact that people who black out can indeed engage in goal-oriented behaviour. I print out a copy and save it on my hard drive. I barely make it through the decoy interviews that day, although my spirits do lift temporarily when an applicant shares a tale about appearing on the Howard Stern show. She claims she shed her clothes and asked if he'd use her bare bum as a set of bongo drums. He did. So I suppose life could be worse.

"Just be glad I didn't tape you last night," remarks Chris, who has been out in the field most of the day, as I leave to go home. He claims that he was watching us through the windshield of his mammoth black Chrysler, purportedly parked right in front of the bar. I'm not convinced.

"You know why I didn't?"

"Because when it comes down to it, you're not a total asshole?" I venture.

"Noooo," he smirks, his deep voice arching.

"Because if you saw yourself on video doing that, you'd never agree to be a decoy again."

Hah! As if I ever will. But my future role at the agency is the least of my worries. For starters, I have to tell my husband what happened. Don't I? Then there's the unnerving notion that Patrick will figure out he was set up and try to track me down. He doesn't know my last name, and the mobile number I left on his voicemail when I called him to set up the meeting is billed to our corporate P.O. Box. Our address is unlisted. Still, that night I take down my profile from MySpace and other networking sites, and enter what winds up being a long period during which I cannot glimpse a white pick-up truck without trembling. I suddenly long for the sterile cubicles and looming deadlines I used to despise.

A few more months on the job teach me that coming off a case feeling physically ill, guilty and fearing for my life is the exception. Instead, I grow accustomed to a quiet satisfaction that comes with empowering our clients. We give them information that helps them feel in control of their lives again – I can't think of any situation where the maxim "knowledge is power" is more fitting. Most of the time, the evidence we produce confirms their suspicions.

"How often are you successful?" Clients repeatedly ask. Chris will point out that success depends on their definition of it.

"If you mean, how often do we confirm clients' suspicions, then the answer is 99%, " he replies.

It's simultaneously what they want to hear, and not. They desire desperately to be validated, to not be wasting their time and money, and yet it seems to me that some small part of them wants to believe the lies they've been told. Under California's no-fault divorce statute, proof of infidelity rarely earns our clients a penny more in a divorce settlement. But that doesn't stop them from wanting evidence. Or, in the case of one client who requested 17 copies of a video showing his wife dining with her lover, from wanting everyone they know to see the evidence, too. Midway through an initial consultation, Chris usually asks a client: "Can you get his car and bring it here?"

"The reason I ask," he continues, "is because for many men, their car is their sanctuary. When they're in it, they feel invincible. Untouchable. They'll call a girlfriend from your driveway. Talk to their best friend for hours about their latest sexual conquest. It's almost – pardon my directness here – an extension of their penis." He reddens on cue here. The women almost universally love this part.

"Now, he's your husband, right? You co-own the car?"

Once a client establishes that the car is communal property –
and thus fair game – Chris suggests having us install a Global
Positioning System or one of the more sophisticated homemade
monitoring systems he concocts using old mobile phones. Once
installed, users simply log on to a dedicated Web site to snag real-
time and historical data about the car's location, and speed. And
if we need to pick up a car to start surveillance, or we've lost it in
traffic – it's rare, but it happens – we can get an immediate locate.
We call that a ping, as in, "Ping it!" This helps cut down on the
number of red lights we run.

Then there's the monitor. As far as Chris can deduce, few, if any,
other private eyes in California offer clients the opportunity to hear
what's going on inside their car as their husbands drive to work. Or,
as has been the case, bump and grind with a mistress.

Another option Chris tosses somewhat less frequently onto the
table is a sting. If a client suspects her husband is a player we'll
often test her theory using one of the dozen or two women on our
decoy roster. Sometimes a sting is as simple as sending two
attractive decoys – one known as "the bait", the other, "the
control" – into a target's environment to see how he responds.
Though bars are the norm, we've also carried out stings in
delicatessens, health clubs, office building lobbies and AA
meetings. There are few places we won't go.

The bait's job is to allow the guy to buy her drinks, match but
never exceed his level of interest, and allow him to take her digits
at the end of the night. We refer to this as a stage one sting. The
phone number she gives is for an agency-owned phone which we
set up in advance with her voice mail message. The woman acting
as control – the role I prefer to play –has a tougher job: to ensure
that her cohort is comfortable, and that the hidden camera purse
is positioned to optimise our footage. Chris is always present, too,
either observing from behind the scenes or right there in the mix
as the control girl's boyfriend who has – surprise! –wound up
getting off work early.

A stage two sting involves a phone call. If a target calls a decoy, our client can access his voicemail message and decide if she wants the decoy to call him back. If so, she'll give us questions to work into the conversation. ("Are you married?" is a popular one.)

If a client wants to go all the way to stage three, our decoy suggests a romantic dinner, which our client just happens to interrupt.

Of course, many stings are far more complex. Take the one involving our decoy, Jessica, who introduced herself to a client's husband via a casual sex personals site he'd recently begun frequenting. They emailed for six weeks: patience, we preach, is key. Then they met for drinks, which we caught on tape. At the conclusion of their second in-person meeting, Jessica left him, naked but for a heavy dousing of hickeys, chocolate sauce and whipped cream, tied to a four-poster bed in a 400 dollar a night hotel room. Last time I checked, his clothes, shoes and car keys were still in a bag in our office. Hey, don't blame us. Our client wanted to send him a wake-up call. All we did was deliver.

A chance to play decoy in Scotland never materialises. After hitting the supermarket that first day, our target stays home. Chris and I wait on the bench until 10 o'clock at night and then terminate. We stagger, exhausted, back to our hotel.

The next morning we follow our target, clad in a perfectly tailored navy suit, two miles to work. We take up post in a modern café near the sparkling glass office tower where he works. I read four different tabloids cover to cover. Around six we relocate to a stone wall across the street from the building.

"And we're off!" Chris says two hours later as I'm pondering whether smoking, a habit I generally despise, would warm me up.

We hurry after our mark – and wind up outside his apartment. We plop down on the blasted bench. I break out a small bottle of *Diet Coke* laced with rum that I've been lugging around all day. My stomach churns on contact, but it gets me through the next few hours.

The next evening seems to mark a turning point: our target leaves work alongside a handsome blond business associate. As the pair wind their way through the moonlit streets of old town Edinburgh, engaged in animated conversation, Chris catches sight of the castle perched on the hillside. "Lauren, look! It's Grayskull!" he cackles. I'm so intent on remembering the *He-Man* theme song that I nearly miss seeing our targets slipping into a bar. We huddle together in a doorway a few doors down and power on the hidden purse camera, then go inside. Perfect: they're at a small table. We choose one across the room, and Chris positions the purse atop our jackets on a chair so that the camera is pointed directly at them.

"He can't take his eyes off that guy," Chris comments.

"I don't know," I reply, trying to analyse the pair's interactions without actually looking at them. It's impossible.

"He could be gay, but is he really going to be having an affair with someone from work? Over here? When he lives near San Francisco, a virtual gay Mecca?"

Chris shrugs. They abruptly push back their chairs and leave, and we're on them from a distance through what seems like a mile of near-deserted streets. They finally alight on a section of the Royal Mile, and I sprint ahead of Chris and catch sight of them just as they disappear down a steep alley.

"Where the hell did they go?" Chris asks as he catches up, his chest heaving. "Don't tell me they're in the wind." We move together down the alley.

"They're here somewhere." I'm ever the optimist.

"We'll get 'em."

Chris eyes me dubiously, but before I can wager 20 dollars on my hunch, we round a bend and hit the jackpot: a tiny French bistro tucked away behind a tall stone wall. Candles flicker in its windows. I rush inside, nearly knocking over a harried server in the process.

"Excuse me. Uh, do we need reservations to dine here tonight?" I peer over his shoulder in search of our duo and spot them shrugging out of their overcoats at a table 20 feet away. Shit. Gotta get out of here. "Uh, I'll be right back!"

We dine *al fresco* on the chilly patio, Chris's leather jacket slung across my shoulders. Midway through the meal I make my way past the men's table to the bathroom, angling the purse cam to capture their image. A quick glimpse tells me they're sharing a bottle of wine – their second? – but there's no way to tell if they're also, say, stroking one another's legs beneath the table. When I ask Chris if we can bribe a waiter to do a bit of spying for us, he laughs.

"Too risky. Besides, the other guy could be a regular here."

Three and a half hours later the men emerge. They walk a few blocks, their pace more leisurely than before. Chris's camera is set to night vision mode. We're ready. They reach an intersection and stop. Our target lunges towards the other man and – clasps his hand in a firm shake. They amble off in opposite directions. Damn it! We shadow our guy to his apartment and wait an hour, thinking that perhaps he'll head out for a late-night reunion, or a taxi will glide up to the curb and his business associate will emerge, overnight bag in hand. But no such luck. One solid handshake is the most intimacy our client's husband displays in public during our entire trip to Scotland. But our work is not done. We're waiting by the baggage carousel in San Francisco when Chris's *Blackberry* buzzes. It's our client.

"I can get his car to you tomorrow," she says. "I want the GPS tracking thing, and that monitoring system. Because *something* is going on. I know I'm not crazy."

The Death Files

Laura Barton

Out on Borough High Street the day is in full swing: broad-bellied men in dark suits scuttling along the greasy pavement, Hackney cabs, pushchairs, London buses, rolling beneath a flat, grey sky. A few steps away, in the quiet enclave of Tennis Street, sits Southwark Coroner's Court, a low-lying modern building pressed up against the ungainly back view of a terrace. Its door swings quietly open and shut, and inside the air is calm, stirred only by the shuffled papers and muttered conversations of administrative duty.

On a Thursday in early November 2007, there are three inquests to be heard at Southwark Coroner's Court, the names of the deceased are printed on white A4 paper and pinned up behind a glass display case: Temur Sait, David Nicholas Lang, Heather May Phillips. A little after 10 am, the relatives of Temur Sait stand together in the foyer, before a long plateglass window that looks on to a small, damp park. They talk softly, wheeling to and fro a small child in a pushchair, until an official gently ushers them into the courtroom.

The room is painted a pale peach, and there are three tiers of wooden pews to the rear and two to the side, with red faux-leather seats, and red carpeting. On the two tables sit jugs of water and stacks of plastic cups, green paper towels and boxes of tissues. The court rises as the coroner enters. His name is John Sampson. He is a balding man in navy blue suit, white shirt, dark blue tie, and a red poppy pinned to his lapel.

Mehmet Sait sits in a pale grey suit, his limbs too long for the witness box, as the coroner runs through the facts of his brother's life and death: Temur was born in North London on 24th April 1967. He died aged 40 on 29th July 2007. His brother identified his body on 30th July 2007. He was Turkish Cypriot, and a married man. One of the strangest things about a coroner's inquest is to see a life stripped to the rafters; all the things that Temur Sait said and did and felt in his short life will not be made known, but in the following hour or so we will learn where he lived, the kind of lager he drank, how his fingernails were short and neat, he wore two gold rings, and his liver was heavy.

"Is there anything else you wish to tell me, Mr Sait, about your brother?" the coroner asks. Mr. Sait looks uncomfortable.

"He was mentally disturbed," he says, and his voice is thin and tired. "He was seeking help, but getting nowhere really."

Temur's wife, Sevilay, is in the front row, wearing black, her long, curly blonde hair tied back. Outside, it is their daughter in the pushchair. She does not look at the witness stand, or at her brother-in-law as he steps down and out of the courtroom, but at the table, at her hands.

The story that unravels, via statements from Temur's GP, from his psychiatrist, from a neighbour, from a friend, from Sevilay, from the London ambulance service, the police, another doctor, and a post mortem report, is one of a man who had spent much of his life battling psychiatric problems and substance dependence. His doctor speaks of long-standing addictions to alcohol, methadone and cannabis, of depression, bipolar disorder, a manic episode in 2006, admissions for formal detox.

Dr Kezia Lange, consultant psychiatrist at Greenwich West, tells the court that Sait had a history of opiate dependence, poly-substance abuse, hepatitis C, use of LSD, cocaine, glue, gas, heroin. He had been on psychiatric wards, in casualty departments; he had vomited blood, smashed windows, and heard voices. By the time his daughter was eight months old, he was drinking a bottle of spirits a day, as well as taking methadone and cocaine.

Temur Sait's final year began no more hopefully than any other: in February 2007 he visited his doctor and complained of feeling tearful, irritable, and of harbouring a passive death-wish. In March, however, events took an upward turn: he commenced a medically assisted detox; he also stopped taking lithium, which had stabilised his moods but also prompted considerable weight-gain. In May, he sought advice on stopping smoking, and at that appointment announced he would be going to Cyprus, to see his parents, for two months in July. But by early summer, though he was upset about his disrupted sleep, he seemed to have made some progress. It was the first time since he was 11 years old that he had been completely off drugs and alcohol.

There is always a feeling of hopelessness upon hearing a medical history like that of Temur Sait. The path of his life seems to have run perpetually uphill and, even when you learn of his period of abstinence, his progress and his pleasant demeanour, any faint optimism is always tempered by the knowledge that the person in question has died; we just do not yet know how. Sevilay Sait speaks awkwardly, her voice heavily accented and tearful. She grows increasingly distressed when she recounts how last summer her husband, though sober, grew increasingly depressed and unable to sleep, tried to seek help from his mental health team. The consultant, however, could not see him for two weeks.

"I knew he wasn't well," she tells the coroner. "He was suddenly crying, he wasn't making sense. I said to the doctor, 'that's not my husband.'"

Sevilay took Temur to the GP, who told them he had a problem with his thyroid, and prescribed sleeping tablets. Temur asked for something stronger, for temazepan, to stop his mind "shouting". The doctor told him he could not prescribe anything more until after he had seen the consultant. Sevilay remembers her husband was distraught.

"Did you think he would hurt himself?" the coroner asks Sevilay. She lifts her face, round and damp, up to meet his gaze.

"Yes," she says quietly. She recalls that in July the family went to Cyprus for two months, as planned, but just two and a half weeks into their stay, Temur announced that he had booked tickets back to London.

"And his Mother said 'Please stay, 'cos your dad is going to have an operation.'" Sevilay remembers, scrunching her tissued hand harder. "But he wouldn't."

After their return, Temur began smoking heavily and grew increasingly restless.

"He was in and out," Sevilay recalls. "He was in the bathroom, in the kitchen..." She shakes her head.

"What did you think he would do?" the coroner enquires gently. "Take tablets?"

Sevilay does not answer directly but recalls how her husband had once spoken to her of suicide, and that she had urged him then "to think of his daughter, to rest his mind".

By the middle of July, Temur had begun to drink again.

"Just one beer," Sevilay says, "not drinking heavy-heavy", and his behaviour was becoming increasingly unusual; one night she noticed that when she went to bed, he stayed in the sitting room and closed the door. It was odd, she explains "because in our house we keep all the doors open". At one point she went through to him, and he was sitting with the lights off.

"When I ask him to come to bed he says, 'I'm just going to sit here and think for a while.'"

Over the following days Temur's restlessness and his insomnia continued. On the Saturday before his death, he accompanied Sevilay to her hairdressing appointment. There, they met a friend who told him she would accompany him to see the mental health team on the Monday. Temur returned home later that day and drank two cans of *Special Brew*, ate nothing, took a sleeping tablet. Sevilay put their daughter to bed at around eight o'clock, and fell asleep next to her. When she awoke it was around 10 o'clock.

"It was the same," she recalls. "He had closed the sitting room door. I put my head in and said 'Can you not sleep?' I told him to come and lie down on the bed." In the middle of the night she got up and he was still lying there awake.

"He said 'My mind's not shutting.' And he went to the sitting room."

Mornings always began the same way in the Sait household. Their daughter would usually wake first, Sevilay explains, "and she would just come through: 'Mummy, Mummy, Mummy!'"

Sevilay could not see her husband at first. She called out "Tem, are you up?" and took her daughter through to the sitting room. He was not there. She checked the balcony, but it was empty.

"I pushed the kitchen door," she tells the court, "I couldn't open the door. I saw blood on the kitchen floor, by the fridge. So I know he did something."

Sevilay is crying in the witness box, breathing heavily. She takes her inhaler, tries to swab her tears, tries to catch her breath, and her friend slides out from her seat to give her tissues. Wailing, she is led away from the witness box.

The courtroom is full of her shallow breaths, the whispers of the court officer telling her "It's alright," the sound of her friend rubbing her back. After a few moments, the coroner speaks with gentle authority.

"If you want to take a break, just tell me."

Sevilay shakes her head, gathers her breath, and returns to the witness stand. She called for an ambulance. She ran to the door of a neighbour, Paul Vickery. She stayed in the bedroom with her daughter while he tried to open the kitchen door. She stayed in the bedroom when the ambulance crew arrived. He left no note. The coroner asks Sevilay if she has anything she would like to add. Her voice rises up full of anguish.

"I just want to ask the mental health team why when I ring them and tell them he is a state they don't send him to hospital?" she asks. "Why when I speak to GP and say I know my husband and this is not him they do not help?"

Paul Vickery's statement is read to the court.

"Tem was lying on the floor, with his back against the door, in his underpants," it runs. "He had a vertical puncture wound on his left breast. There was an eight-inch kitchen knife, and he was sitting on a rug, it was soaked with blood. Tem was cold. I pushed his stomach, got no response. Tem's eyes were partly open and I decided he looked dead."

A statement from the ambulance service follows, which recalls that at 7:01 am they received a call stating that a male had stabbed himself. "At 7:08 met patient's wife and small toddler. Wife was wearing a pink dressing gown and was very upset."

The report recalls how an ambulance crewmember squeezed around the kitchen door and saw Temur Sait, his chest covered with blood, the kitchen knife beside him. He picked up the knife with two fingers and placed it on the kitchen surface. It, too, was covered in blood. He moved Temur, pulling him by the ankles. There was blood on his stomach, his legs and his hands. There was a cut by his left nipple, no bigger than an inch and a half.

"By looking at him I could recognise life was extinct."

Statements follow from PC Lloyd who attended the scene, and from Dr Rachel Pickering, who states that she was called at 12:10 in order to confirm life extinct. She arrived at 12.30, attended the scene 12:40, and at 12.43 on 29th July 2007, the life of Temur Sait was declared extinct.

The post-mortem examination proves strangely soothing; a griefless description of a machine that has ceased to function. In this instance it notes that he was a well-built man, the fingernails, the rings, the faint purple bruise on his right leg and the graze on his left. His liver was heavy, his kidneys congested, in his stomach there was partially digested food and liquid.

It states that on Temur's chest, 7.5cm left of the middle line, was a gaping wound, between the fourth and fifth ribs; that the kitchen knife had entered the left ventricle of the heart, that the stab wound was entirely compatible with being self-inflicted, that the cause of death was 1(a) haemorrhage 1(b) stab wound to the heart.

The death of David Nicholas Lang was considerably less dramatic than that of Temur Sait, but the course of his life, too, had been directed by psychiatric problems. He was born on the 3rd October 1939 in Brighton, and died on the 28th July 2007. He had been a TEFL teacher and was a widower.

As with Mr Sait, this inquiry also began with a brother: John Lang is sworn in at the witness box and confirms that on the 1st August 2007 he identified his brother's body, two days after walking his daughter down the aisle. He tells the coroner that a few years ago, they had resumed contact after not speaking for 35 years. Although he had not seen David for two years, they had been in contact by telephone "often 20 times a week". They last spoke in the week before his death, and on the Thursday David left a message on his brother's answer phone. Their telephone conversations, he said, rarely touched upon personal matters but were generally occupied with word games.

Accordingly, he knew very little about his brother's health or about those missing 35 years.

"He met a Japanese lady in South Korea, whom he married," Mr Lang says, with only a vague certainty. "She died in a car accident somewhere, but it wasn't something he talked about. David was a loner, a travelling loner."

David Lang was a paranoid schizophrenic who lived in sheltered accommodation in South London. The report from his doctor, Justin Hayes, noted that though Mr Lang had been registered at his practice since 2003, his medical records went back as far as the inception of the NHS. There was a gap between 1962 and 1988, when it appeared he had lived abroad. He developed schizophrenia in 1990, while travelling overseas. The statement of Dr. Jonathan Beckett, consultant psychiatrist at Lambeth, reveals that Lang was in fact married twice and that his second wife died in 1989, after six years of marriage. Travelling in Germany in 1994 he suffered a manic episode, was hospitalised and transferred to St Thomas' Hospital in London. Travel, he said, had always been a coping mechanism. He first heard voices at the age of nine, and in adult life often got into fights because the voices were commanding him to attack. Dr Beckett noted that Lang's mental state was quite stable, but that he required 24-hour care. He was frustrated living in residential care and requested a move to warden care. He was a frequent visitor to the Efra Road Day Centre and the Mosaic Club, and attended church three times a week. In July 2005, Dr. Beckett recorded that Lang had told him he was depressed, preoccupied, thought a lot about his wife, and that recently he had bought 100 paracetamol tablets "just in case I decide to kill myself". He added that he would not commit suicide because of his Christian beliefs.

Over the course of 2007, Lang's decline was noted by the warden at his accommodation, who observed that his flat was increasingly untidy, he rarely wore adequate clothing, and seemed to have stockpiled a great deal of medicine. He often left his front door unlocked, and the warden was fearful that he might be exploited — he claimed, for example, that £6000 had been stolen from him by a friend of a friend. On the 28th of July he attended A&E at the Mayday Hospital, having collapsed in the street an hour earlier. He said his legs had suddenly felt weak. At the hospital they found no apparent cause for the collapse, but expressed concern about his mobility.

They referred him to St George's Hospital, but upon arrival Mr Lang was unprepared to wait and walked out.

To the witness stand comes George Omwuemezi, a friend of Mr Lang from the Efra Road Day Centre. He recalls how he popped by to see Lang at 4.30 in the afternoon.

"I knocked on the door," he says nervously. "There was no answer. I continued knocking. I went to look in the bathroom window. The lights were on and the window was ajar, I was able to see through, and I saw him slumped in the bath. I climbed through the window. He was looking like this," Omwuemezi slumps back in his chair, head rocked back.

"There was still water in the bath. It was very warm and the taps were still running. I immediately went out the door and called the police. I went to a phone box. No, I went to his friend's place."

The coroner asks if there is anything else he would like to add. Mr Omwuemezi raises his voice to the court.

"He was the most honest person I had ever come across," he says. "Truly just."

It is a strange moment of intimacy in an inquiry that has proved strikingly impersonal. The ambulance service arrived at 18:50. They found no pulse, no respiration, pupils fixed and some rigidity. At 18:55, Mr Lang was confirmed dead.

Police Constable Lawrence sits in the witness box. He has short black hair and is burly in his heavy police vest. He tells the coroner how he was called to Spa Court, and found the door to Lang's flat wide open. He knocked and shouted hello, and then saw the bathroom window wide open. He could see the deceased in the bath. The taps were off and the water had drained away. On his wrist was the hospital wristband from his visit to A&E. There was no one around, but he later spotted George Omwuemezi sitting nearby on a bench. They decided the scene was not suspicious.

The post mortem took place on the 31st of July at the public mortuary. It found that Mr Lang was a slender man, 1.6 metres in height with eyes that were slightly sunken. Internally his scalp was healthy, his brain slightly heavy and pale and soft. His lungs were very heavy, roughly twice the expected weight, and his pulmonary arteries were patent. The toxicology report found that his body showed levels of medication that were well within the therapeutic levels. He had died as the outcome of myocardial infarction and fibrosis: a heart attack. The cause of death, the coroner recorded, was natural.

Throughout the course of the inquiry, it becomes apparent just how little was known about David Lang. There was something substantial about the case of Temur Sait; from the fact that his wife always knew where he was likely to be, to his physical addiction to various substances, and even to the physically violent manner of his death. It is harder to put your finger on David Lang; he slipped out of his family's life, he slipped back in again, he told them little, his psychological problems were not addiction-related, the extent of his physical problems were unknown, and when he died it was as if he just unexpectedly slipped away again.

The court breaks for lunch. Outside it is threatening to rain; the trees in the small park cower a little. By the time the case of Heather May Phillips begins, the first drops are falling on Tennis Street, hitting the long, plate glass window in the foyer. Heather May Phillips, maiden surname Ring, was born in Malden, Essex on the 12th July 1949, she died on the 28th July 2007 at Queen Elizabeth Hospital, Woolwich, South London. Her husband, Anthony Phillips, identified the body of his wife on the 1st August. He sits, now, in the witness box, a solid man with tattoos on his forearm and half a finger missing, stewing with grief and with anger. He describes his wife's profession as "Carer".

"She cared for her father, she cares for two of my grandchildren," he says, inadvertently slipping into the present tense. "She cared for my father in law since his wife died 11 years ago. In her late life, she was more busy than in her own early life. But she loved it."

The coroner asks Mr Phillips if his wife was in general good health. He nods.

"Not the right thing to say," he replies, awkwardly, "but it was a case [with her] of you only go to the doctor when you're dying. You go through life, you suffer."

She had a body mass index of 28. She had smoked for most of her life, but had quit five and a half months before her death, in anticipation of the smoking ban. She was a social drinker.

"She liked to spend Saturday afternoons with her daughter-in-law," Mr Phillips recalls, "a drink and a cigarette, and they'd talk themselves to death."

Throughout the inquiry, Anthony Phillips never breaks down like Savilay Sait, but you suspect his grief is as keen. Instead of answering the coroner's questions, he sits in the witness box reading a lengthy statement about his wife's sudden decline in health, his complaints with her medical care, and ultimately, her death. At times he grows upset, pulling at his lower lip as he continues to read.

"Heather began being unwell at the end of June," his statement begins. "She had stomach pains, and when she went to the toilet, the diarrhoea had blood in it. Heather, she was a very private person. You had to prise things out of her. I managed to get her to see her GP on 15th June in Plumstead. He said her body's making too much acid and he gave her some medication tablets."

The tablets made no difference, and Heather Phillips' continued to be unwell. The doctor prescribed new tablets. The couple were due to go on holiday on June 29th, and a hospital appointment was scheduled for after they returned. She spent much of the holiday in bed.

"On holiday, you go on an all-inclusive, you think 'I'm gonna stuff myself to death'," says Mr Phillips.

"But she didn't. 50% of the time she was in the room… Took her to see the GP on holiday," he reads. "Paid the money, as you have to do [when abroad]. Examined my wife. Said she might have an ulcer. Gave her exactly the same tablets she had at home."

After their return on July 6th, Heather made the first of many hospital visits. She was still suffering from diarrhoea, still bleeding, and unable to eat or drink very much. Each visit brought tests, X-rays, tablets, each time it was observed that Heather had low blood pressure.

"On the 23rd July," he reads, "she got out of bed and had a fall… She fell onto the laundry basket. When I seen the injury, her left breast was black and blue and very painful. I'm not a medical expert, but the first thing that came to mind was a cracked or broken rib."

His pace is slow and steady, like a long-distance runner; his daughters sit in the front row of the court.

"At A&E they said she had a fractured rib and a tear in her lung. I don't know what the technical term is, but they had to put a drain in her side. They said it wouldn't hurt. But I know better." He pulls at his lip.

"I had to have a little word with the hospital, because her

brother was in that same ward dying of cancer. They put her in a different ward."

For the next few days, Mr Phillips and his family performed a routine of telephone calls to the ward and daily visits to the hospital. He recalls one such visit on July 27th when his wife, propped up on pillows, suddenly sat bolt upright, "and her eyes bulged from her head and she said 'Help me! Help me!' She said to the doctor 'I'm going to die aren't I?' And the doctor said 'No, what makes you think that?' She said. 'I know.'"

Heather Phillips died the next day. Anthony was summoned to the hospital on the Saturday morning and told that his wife had suffered a heart attack. By the afternoon she was on a life support machine, and he was told she was unlikely to survive.

"Being a man of the world," he tells the court, "you know what that means, once they're on a machine."

She died at two o'clock that afternoon. Between the end of June and her death, Heather visited her GP five times, and the A&E department three times. Mingled with Anthony Phillips' grief is a fierce indignation that his wife was not saved by the medical profession.

"You lose faith in the system," he says at the end of his statement, and shakes his head. The court hears statements from seven of the medical staff who treated her during that period – her GP, hospital doctors, staff nurses. The pathologist's report from Greenwich Mortuary notes diverticulitis, thickening of the bowel, heavy lungs, and a tattoo of a dolphin on her right shoulder.

The cause of death is given as a mix of natural and unnatural causes: 1 (a) sepsis arising from 1 (b) bilateral pneumonia, (2) complications from diverticulitis. The coroner records the verdict as accidental death.

The court rises as the coroner departs. In the back row of witnesses is one of the staff nurses who treated Heather Phillips. On the table before her lies a cardboard folder, stuffed with sheets of A4, and on its cover two words: "Dead File." She shuffles Mrs Phillips' notes and slips them inside.

Leave it to the Hand of God

Jack Roberts

Northern Iraq. It's 9 am and a white Toyota 4x4 *Landcruiser* hurtles down the road to Barzan. The driver of the vehicle, a bulky Iraqi Kurd called Bayard, is wearing dark sunglasses and a charcoal, short-sleeved shirt. He dips his head under the steering wheel, lights his cigarette, and presses his foot down on the pedal. The *Landcruiser* picks up pace and the speedometer clocks 120 kmh. In the lane ahead a slow moving car blocks progress; a Kurdish tribal flag billows out of its side window. In the left lane, approaching fast – less than 100 metres away – is an oncoming car.

Bayard is unfazed; he swerves from the right lane, overtakes the slow car, and then pulls back left. The hum of the oncoming vehicle, a dirty white 1970s Ford, buzzes in his ears. He jabs his horn as an afterthought. The speedometer rises to 140 kmh. A loose stone spits a small web onto the windscreen. There's a solid "crack". Bayard's nose twitches. 160 kmh. The car starts to shake as it loses traction with an uneven road. Sitting in the right passenger seat, I grit my teeth, hearing crackles as we skip and bump over loose stones on the tarmac.

Khasrow grips my shoulder from the back of the car. A wiry Iranian Kurd, 27, he is working as an interpreter for our film documentary team. He motions my eyes to Bayard's speedometer with bony fingers. The dial is hovering at the 180 kmh mark. Lifting his chin in Bayard's direction, he allows himself a nervous laugh.

"Crazy driver."

The dark glasses hide Bayard's expression. I notice he's not

wearing a seatbelt, but the large assault rifle by his right knee –
stood barrel-up and bouncing gently against the gearbox – is my
more immediate concern: it's pointed right at me.

"Is it safe to drive at this speed on these roads? Can you ask him
that?"

Khasrow asks Bayard. He slows to 140 kmh, fires back a
comment in Kurdish, and then laughs long and hard; a full body
laugh.

"What'd he say?"

"He say, 'You no worry: leave it to the hand of God.'"

I've been in Iraq four days now and the native fatalism – a
worldview encompassing both resignation and resolve – is
contagious. A safety belt? In Iraq historical events rain down at a
terminal velocity – too swift for Western newsprint, too brutal for
right-thinking comprehension. What's a loose safety belt in that
minefield? Why bother reconciling the cruelties of the past or
thinking too hard on the consequences of the present? Instead,
you "leave it to the hand of God", and when God moves, react
fast…

I'm working here as an assistant on a documentary that aims to
uncover what happened to a lost tribe of men who were abducted
by Saddam's Ba'ath government in 1983. The 8000 men from the
rural village of Barzan – tribal brothers of the famous Kurdish
leader Mustafa Barzani – were "disappeared" by the Ba'athi, and
are widely believed to have died in the southern deserts of the
country, near the border with Saudi Arabia.

The 1983 kidnappings are an important precursor to Saddam
Hussein's notorious Anfal operations of 1988, as they mark the
point when the dictator moved from isolated acts of brutality to
mass murder. Often described as the "Iraqi holocaust", the Anfal
was Saddam's punishment of the Kurds for their support of Iran
in the Iran–Iraq war, and involved state-sanctioned genocide on
an unprecedented scale. Over 100,000 Iraqi–Kurd civilians died

after they were subjected to chemical warfare, concentration camps, firing squads, and forced resettlements.

Those Kurds who have survived such abductions usually have horror stories to tell. Imagine the scene: you are forced to live in a single room with 250 people – newborn infants, 80 year old grandfathers, your mother, your brother. There are no toilet facilities; you have to relieve yourself in the corner of the room. At night, you sleep on a concrete floor, drink from a poisoned water supply, and seek sustenance in damp scraps of bread. You watch fellow captives drop dead from disease. Torture is common. Last week guards tied your brother to football goalposts outside the camp, leaving him in the midday desert sun. He comes back with a giant scar across his back, the mark where his molten skin was torn away from the post. You hear a lame man tell how guards beat his feet with wooden blocks. Another man can barely see after guards took turns to stand on his eyes, trying to blind him. One day you hear an old man scream as he is thrown off the two storey walls of the camp, then hear him scream again as he is picked up and thrown off the wall again, and then again. You will know the name of Saddam Hussein and you will bow.

There is no shortage of such stories in Iraq. One elderly man comes with us to a former prison camp near Kirkuk, where he tells us of his experiences at Nugra Salman, a desert prison camp in southern Iraq he was taken to 18 years ago. He was in his early 70s when he was taken from his wife and son. He has not seen them since, and he is in his 90s – coming to the end of his life. Trauma is etched on his face, carved like graffiti on wood. A broken man, he tells us; "Everyday I wake up and ask God why he did not kill me too."

Back then the international community largely ignored the Anfal. The British and American governments were so worried about the threat of the Ayatollah Khomeini's freshly Islamicised Iran that they happily provided Saddam with money and weapons. Having captured their old ally, and overseen his death sentence at the hands of an Iraqi court, they are now involved in a search for the mass graves of his victims, part of a farcical effort to justify their post-occupation strategy in Iraq.

Some people have simpler motives for wanting to see evidence of the mass graves. In the village of Barzan an entire generation of widowed women want to know if their stubborn hopes are true, to discover if their men found a way to survive all those years ago. They are resigned but defiant.

The journey to Barzan takes several hours, despite Bayard's maniac driving. I strike up a conversation with Khasrow. Why did he leave Iran to come and live in unstable Iraq?

"I had to leave because my life was under threat. Because I am a Kurd I was a target, and I was also active in student politics. If I go back to my home village I will probably be killed. I teach literature in Erbil now, but I may go back one day."

"That's a shame for them. I would have thought Iran needs young teachers."

"Teachers of Islam maybe. Remember that Kurds are not Arabs – we have a completely different history and culture. This is why we are persecuted. We are less extreme than the rest of the Muslim world – we have a separate mentality. Kurds who live in Turkey, Iran, Jordan and Syria are seen as a threat to 'identity' in these countries. Identity is political here, and this is why Kurdish autonomy – Kurdish identity – in Iraq is very controversial."

He laughs. "Life is different in the UK, no?"

We drive on. As we pass through a small settlement I see a large party of Kurds by the roadside, laughing and dancing in their traditional overalls and headdresses, preparing a feast. They are having a wedding ceremony; I've lost count of how many similar roadside weddings I've seen this past four days, but it has to be reaching double figures now.

I ask Khasrow why there are so many street marriages.

"Here, if you want to have sex with a girl, you must marry her first. Her family will chase you and kill you if you don't."

"No way."

"It happens all the time! That's why MANY people in the Middle East take more than one wife. It is the only safe way to have new 'experiences.'"

We drive on. After a couple of hours we approach a village settlement in a river valley.

"This Barzan," says Bayard pointing his finger at the windscreen. The river glitters in the beating sunlight; its inclines are flanked by sporadic, mossy grass.

"!!!!!!! Murkthalabai!!!!!!!!!!! Hiiiiiiii!!!!!!!!!!!Aiaiaiaiaiaia!!!!!!!!!!"

Bayard's phone jangles with the polyphonic rendition of a strings-heavy Middle Eastern pop song. He flips it open to his ear, bellows down the phone, and then kills our speed. We park beside the main village thoroughfare and wait for the rest of the Toyota convoy to catch us up. Spindly boys surround our car. Before opening the car door, Bayard taps me on the knee.

"Mr Jack. Look."

He hands me his mobile phone.

"Look."

A technicolour animation plays on its screen. A wild-eyed cartoon Saddam is trapped in a hole, his long beard poking out of the ground as George Bush, in full US marine uniform, prods his face.

"Funny Mr Jack!"

I smile.

"Ha, ha. Yes, Saddam stupid. He kill many people. Now he is in hole."

The rest of our convoy arrives and I help unload the film equipment from the back of the second Toyota. The burly, bespectacled figure of Dr Mohammed Ihsan, the Kurdish human rights minister, emerges from the second car; he will be conducting today's on-camera interviews. Imp-faced young boys arrive to help us carry the equipment, but we lug the cameras ourselves. The older tribesmen keep their distance at first, watching the scene impassively. Their heads are dressed with red and white dotted scarves, the pattern of their tribe. As soon as they recognise Dr Ihsan, they bustle forward to give his hand a hearty shake. They seek our hands next, locking their steely eyes on each of us as they do so. The other members of the documentary crew have arrived in a third Toyota; the filmmaker Gwynne Roberts, co-director John Williams, and a Sunni Iraqi cameraman called Khoutaiba al-Janabi.

We are ushered into the outside veranda of a single floor house. The tribesmen have decided that the interview will take place here. Over the next hour we set up tripods, mics, cameras, and lenses as a group of at least 20 women, all of them hooded in ink black robes, seat themselves in a square formation. They look anxious. There is a buzz of noise around the periphery and the young boys raise fingers to point and laugh at each other.

We are ready to start filming, and after a word from Khasrow the tribal elders demand hush from the youngsters. Dr Ihsan has perched himself on a stool in the centre of the square of cloaked women. Nearby, John watches intently as the rushes of the interview are relayed on a portable monitor. Khasrow translates for him as Khoutaiba squints by the camera's viewfinder and readies himself to film. Dr Ihsan talks to the women casually, explaining what will happen. Then John's voice rises above the rest.

"ROLLING! 3 – 2 –1."

Under the glare of the camera, Ihsan turns to the oldest woman in the group. She has the look of a fairytale hag, curling bark skin betraying a life chastened by ill fortune. In her hands she holds a framed picture of the men she lost, a digitally manipulated image of her husband, Marku, and her five sons – "Othman, Abdullah, Karim, Awni, Aziz", she lists – who were also taken. Khasrow later translates her answers to Ihsan's questions, which she delivers with an indignant, staccato passion.

"What did you witness on the day when they took your men away?" Ihsan asks the old woman.

"I was at home and it was early in the morning when the army surrounded our village. They asked our men to return all their guns and everything they had left over from the the their time serving the national army. We had no impression that something bad would happen. The men followed their orders. Then helicopters flew over our village, opening fire at us."

The old woman shakes her head. Next to her, a woman of middle age is weeping bitterly. The crying spreads from woman to woman like a plague.

"What do you think happened to the missing men? What are your feelings on this?"

"Those responsible should be put on trial for what they did to us. They denied us drinking water, food, and they took our men from us. Whenever someone died, us women had to prepare a grave and bury the body. There are 8000 Barzanis missing. This is not a joke. It is a fact."

"Do you think they are still alive?"

"God willing, I think they are. I have always waited for their return. We have not received any proof that they are dead."

The other women are sobbing loudly now, a black mass of teary widows.

"Cut," says John.

The old woman puts aside her picture and urgently grabs Ihsan's hand. She speaks quickly in Kurdish, her voice rising until she is practically wailing at him.

"What's she saying Mohammed?" says John.

"She says they are alive. She wants us to bring the men back. Can you believe this? She believes we will find them and bring them back. After 22 years."

But her faith is misplaced. Her men were sent to isolated death camps over 1000 kilometres from their home. They lived with thousands of others under the blistering desert sun. Those that were not given amnesty by Saddam Hussein died of disease or were murdered: pushed into holes in the ground and drilled with machine gun fire. There was no chance of escape by foot in the southern deserts. But still her hope rises like an air pocket in water, irrepressibly seeking a path back to the surface.

"Once we find the evidence of what happened to these men we will come back, and we will bring these women answers. They need to know the truth," says Dr Ihsan to the camera.

As the afternoon continues, we film interviews with several other women, all of whom give variations on the same story. Like the first old lady, they saw their men snatched by Ba'athi, they will not outwardly speculate on what has happened to them, and they refuse to believe that they could be dead. Their attempts to form coherent chains of words are often foiled by the cold hand of memory. Looking at these women it strikes me that they have a collective quality; they share physically hard features, pained expressions, and similar stories, all of which are expressed simply to each other; hymns to a defiant, transcendent sorrow.

We finish filming and pack up our equipment. A small group of young boys play on the veranda as I unplug the boom socket from the shooting camera. A few of them approach me. First amongst them is a little boy, smaller than the others. He has tiny bright green shoes on his feet. In his right hand is a Glock handgun. He stares right through me with dark, bottomless pupils, standing there for a few seconds – his expression unchanging – before his father approaches him. He gently strokes the crown of his son's head with his palm. The father is a Kurdish Peshmerga, dressed in full guerilla uniform. I pick my camera up from the floor and take a picture of the Peshmerga boy. His father smiles and gives me a conspiratorial wink.

I later discover that "Peshmerga" means "those who face death". It's clearly a proud tradition.

The next day we are back in Erbil, the oldest continually inhabited settlement in the world, a setting that has witnessed humanity develop for over 9000 years. In the 21st century, the Mesopotamian city is abuzz with construction sites, half formed building structures, disorderly traffic, and the hustle of street markets. The ubiquitous Wahabi mosques – beautiful mosaic towers financed by Saudi money – blare out Islamic incantations via loudspeakers. Sitting high in the centre of the city is the Qalah: a fading citadel, the scene of myriad past conflicts, now inhabited by squatter families. Towards the outskirts of Erbil the grey concrete walls of government compounds have been repainted with brightly coloured graffiti – images of swans and galloping horses.

These signs of redevelopment and economic regeneration are at odds with the sectarian chaos in the rest of Iraq. The relative stability has allowed the Kurdish authorities to consolidate their long-held ambition of autonomy. Despite the British and American refusal to publicly discuss federalism, it is rapidly becoming the only practical solution as Iraq slides towards bloody civil war. These are high times for the long-oppressed Kurds, but they come with risks, as diplomacy with hostile neighbours Turkey and Iran will not be easy. The Kurds have come far though; 20 years ago they were guerilla fighters, hiding from Saddam in the mountains. Now they are the power. Things have changed.

Our four-man documentary team waits in the lobby of our heavily guarded high-rise hotel. We've spent several hours sitting on sofas, drinking sweet tea from small cups, waiting for a driver to pick us up. I pick up my half-read book *Cruelty and Silence* by Iraqi dissident Kanan Makiya and seat myself by the hotel reception desk. Five American GIs emerge from a nearby elevator. I recognise them from when they booked their rooms a few days back. They were in full camo uniform and looked like freshly cut bionic factory products; giant, close-cropped hunks of meat, their large assault rifles held out for all to see. Now they're off-duty in their casuals: oversized T-shirts, low-dipping baggy shorts, headbands, wrist sweatbands, and Air Jordans. They look like suburban mall punks en route to a hip hop concert. There can't be one of them over the age of 21. A young, square faced

GI with a rigid, straight-backed posture approaches the Kurdish reception clerk.

"Hey buddy, where's our guy?"

The clerk introduces him to their Kurdish guide – moustache, floppy black hair – who has been asked to give them a driving tour of the city.

"You are ready?" asks the guide.

"Yes."

The guide stares hard at one heavyset soldier in the group; he's decked out in a black T-shirt with a giant white American eagle printed on its front, and "OPERATION IRAQI FREEDOM" in X-large letters on the back.

"You sure you're ready?"

The American GI looks confused. His colleagues are fully dressed, and good to go with their bumbags, digital cameras, and shiny personal music players.

"Hell yes we're ready. Let's roll out."

The guide turns to me, shrugs, and then laughs as he leads the GIs out the door, off on a welcome tour of the city streets of Northern Iraq.

What the hell? You leave it to the hand of God.

New Orleans Lost and Found

Sarah M. Broom

"I decided to return here because I was afraid to"
– James Baldwin

It is a hard and treacherous thing sitting here trying to call up the right words for how your family is running from water, for how your family is fighting drowning even on dry land. So you tend toward forgetting. Your search for a haven finds you in Massachusetts, then Turkey and Berlin. It has you wishing you had the time and money to go farther. Papua New Guinea or South Africa, even. When books come out with such titles as *The Place You Love is Gone* and *Come Hell or High Water*, you sit them piled in your bedroom. You do this only for yourself, so that every now and then you can look toward that stack and practice saying "later" to it all. I never cared much for nostalgia, and so naturally would like to jump to the story's end, daydream this one to perfection. I want to write something less painful, fend off the return back there, to New Orleans, make this a piece about conquering this or that philosophical thing, but that city always begins any story I start to tell, and so I must go back there now, in memory, 10 months past the storm – and solidly so.

I. Memory

When you come from a huge, wild New Orleans family (a clan, really) and realise that your city is underneath so much water it cannot breathe, and when the other thing you know is that two of your hardheaded brothers are somewhere *in* all of that mess, you simply try to get your legs to carry you through the way they did before: easy and glide-like.

In the day-to-day, you neglect serious consideration of any newspaper or broadcast except to scan names and faces of the missing – Broom, Michael, Carl, my brothers. Three full days past Hurricane Katrina and it was a Harlem summer day. On this kind of day when the humidity hangs low down to the ground, and the windows are up as far as they can go, when your loud-mouthed neighbors are out, and there is music touching air and those same neighbors are dancing happy on skinny sidewalks – on a day such as this, I can imagine being in New Orleans. Except that here in New York, trees blow back and forth with only innocent fury.

I sit cross-legged watching CNN on mute. See a headline underneath a picture of storm evacuees that reads "REFUGEES". It's a strange word. I wonder whether state-to-state moves will now be called immigration.

Right before my eyes a brown-skinned man wearing white boxers and with bare feet gets lifted from a roof. He twines chicken legs around the rescuer's bulk.

"It's Carl," I yell.

"That doesn't look anything like your brother," a visiting friend says. But I kept faith in that lanky man in boxers until the next day when there was no phone call. I spent the next nights watching again for a skinny man who maybe had a dog with him.

Imagine this being all you can do.

It is as paltry as it sounds.

The day before the storm came, my mother, my sister Karen, her two teenagers, and my brother Troy packed a bag apiece and drove to Hattiesburg, Mississippi. In the rush, my nephew forgot his eyeglasses. As they were leaving town, I sat wearing a wide brimmed hat in a New York park listening to jazz. While I was tapping my foot, my brother Carl gathered up his family to go to a shelter. He had his green motorised boat with him in the back of his pickup. At the shelter, Carl told them to go on in, said, "I'll be all right," then turned around and went back home to wait for the hurricane.

Something to know about growing up in New Orleans: during the months of hurricane season, you might evacuate three, four, five times for naught. You'd pack your most important possessions and drive as far as gas money would carry you. When you've lived this way for most of your life – every single summer thinking, "Is this the big one?" – you forget the wrath of Hurricane Betsy. You get careless.

When I called my chef brother, Michael, to make sure he was leaving, he claimed he was crossing the Texas border at that very moment.

"I'm out of there, baby," he said to me.

This, it turns out, was the lie you tell your nosey younger sister who you know would come straight through the phone and strangle you if you said the truth.

Carl and Michael swam for their lives in Hurricane Betsy, the 1965 storm – a lady compared to Katrina. But Carl, who loves fishing – especially at night – never demonised the Mississippi the way I did. I never trusted it. It was and still is a mean, ugly river that only pretends calm; growing up near it made me dislike big bodies of water, made me terrified of waves – even at the beach, with sand and all.

I think about the Hurricane Betsy stories we tell at Christmas when we are together. Everyone was asleep. Someone yelled, "Get out of bed." My oldest sister, Deborah, put her feet on the floor and felt water. Mom yelled, "Get the baby."

Everyone remembers charcoal blackness and the rush of water into the house. They swam through live wires and snakes to get to higher ground.

The dogs swam too.

My mother calls from Hattiesburg on Monday – the day Katrina hits – and says, "Water is coming into the house. We're calling for help." The phone goes out right as she's talking, so that's all I have to go on for three days. Those two lines keep replaying in my head – during half-sleep, at dinners where I appear to have it together, at each and every still moment.

This is all I knew about my mother, Ivory, and the six of my 11 siblings who called New Orleans home.

Still no word from the boys, but it is early on and phone lines are out. When your mobile phone rings, you sprint from wherever you are to answer, and when it's a friend "just checking in", you are mightily disappointed.

On the Wednesday after Katrina, my mom calls and says she's safe. The water had buried her car, but she and her group were okay. By Friday, they are in Dallas. On Saturday, they fly to Vacaville, California, where my brother Byron lives. This is the first time my brother Troy has flown, so we have to talk him into it.

I leave New York for Vacaville, where on the first night Herman, a 34 year old who lived next door to where we grew up, and whose feet are swollen up from dehydration, has a house-waking nightmare.

Herman's dreams are scary because during the storm he sat one whole day on the second-storey roof of my childhood home until it split in two under him.

Herman-the-storyteller swears he saw Carl in a boat helping people near the Superdome.

This sounds like exactly the kind of thing Carl would be doing, so most everyone believes him, except for me. I keep saying I need to hear from him. Whenever Herman repeats his Carl-the-rescuer tale, I look to him angrily, stone-faced.

Neighbours have brought over piles of used clothes, and so my family, whom I have never seen ask for a thing, slowly look for things they like, though it is mostly about need now. They are a prideful people, but when you have one pair of pants to your name that is no longer a trait you can rightfully claim. My mom was going around in a pair of uncomfortable gold shoes. When I asked her why, my mom, in her soft voice, said, "My good ones got messed up in all that water." Those were brown suede, and her favourites. So there are these moments that poke fun at what little your family has now – and all of a sudden! And that leads you to think of your two brothers you haven't yet heard from. You hope that the water has not had its way with them.

There are 10 of us in this three-bedroom house. When your displaced family is not stocking up on underwear or acting like clowns to help the forgetting, you are all watching news and yelling curse words at the TV. Attitude helps you through. Or you eat red beans and rice with smoked sausage. I imagine that for Troy, who until now has never left New Orleans for more than a day or two, this blue California sky must seem strange. I notice too that my niece and nephew have the knowing eyes of grown people now.

Exactly one week after Hurricane Katrina, we hear from Michael. He's in San Antonio with 15 others. He calls New Orleans during Hurricane Katrina "a disgrace to humanity". Says he will never go back, and this hurts my heart because Michael has always loved the city with all his might. He was the one to show it off to me, the one who helped me fall so deeply in love with it. But I believe him because I do not hear any play in his voice.

Two days later I am driving my mother to the grocery store, where we have come looking for coffee and chicory, when, like a good rhythm, Carl calls. I yell his name in a drawn-out bayou drawl.

I am sappy; my words run off without me.

Carl starts talking nonstop:

"I fell asleep, and when I woke up water was coming through the doors quick. The front yard looked like a river. I got up in the attic with a meat cleaver and knocked out a hole in the roof big enough to get my shoulders through at an angle.

"The dogs beat me out. I was on the roof for three days with two gallons of water – I'd pour some on my head when it got too hot. You couldn't stay in that attic. It felt like 200 degrees in there. Mostly I was sitting on tarpaper. When people saw that water, their eyes started getting big, they started sucking on five, six cigarettes in a row. People didn't think that thing was gonna do what it did. Nobody had a chance."

Carl remembered the life jacket in his boat, but that was underwater with a shed atop it. He dove down twice for the jacket and then used its reflectors to signal a rescuer. Which is how he got off the roof of the house with his two Pekingese dogs, Mindie and Tiger. Later, from the convention centre, he and "some dude" struck out on their own in a paddleboat, heading toward the interstate. But the paddleboat only got them so far because of the downed trees. They had to swim 30 yards through debris and dead bodies until they got picked up and taken to the airport. "There was so much despair in that place," Carl said, which is why he left and walked the miles to a cousin's house in Kenner, Louisiana, where he slept for three days straight.

I'd never heard my brother Carl say *despair* before.

II. Movement

When each and every one of your 11 siblings are accounted for – and no second earlier than that – you let yourself mourn the city of your birth.

I was in New Orleans two days before the storm. I sent bragging, languorous emails to friends: "I am at an outdoor café drinking *café au lait*. A brass band has just gone by me."

Even when you have left New Orleans for better things, the city does not let go of you, so when you're back it feels as though you are returning to an old lover, the one who always takes you in no matter how far you've wandered.

I wish I could help you understand what it means to feel homesick now. I do not yet have the kind of imagination I need to understand this violation, all the world watching as my city drowned. I have known New Orleans in the same way I've known my name. I have loved it hard, the hardest of any one thing outside of family – and fanatically. I couldn't help it. My grandmother Beulah was a tough Creole woman who spoke

French. My father, Simon, played the banjo and the trumpet in Doc Pauline's brass band. You learn to move around the world in a certain, wide-eyed way when you are born into all of this richness of spirit.

In quiet moments, you wonder about those street musicians you came to know with their voices of gold. Theirs was an audience of passersby, and you paid by dropping a dollar or two in a hat. I am remembering one trombonist who had the eyes of my brother Carl. He looked like a hard man, looked as though he could fight for his life. But for those eyes and for all that he put into his horn, I gave him 5 dollars. And the man in the wheelchair who, when there was a citywide blackout and you were stranded together on the sidewalk, took out his lighter, pretended it was a flashlight, and sang the blues to calm your nerves. You hope he made it out.

I wish you could hear the sounds our brass bands make, wish you could know the kind of drumbeat that sends you dancing exuberant midstreet, sends you strutting and second-line dancing so hard, you start to believe your life depends on this movement.

And perhaps it does.

Now, these many months past the storm, I have only three immediate family members in Louisiana: Mom, Carl and Eddie. They are half an hour from New Orleans.

To get there via highway you have to first drive down a narrow swamp road where if you had to describe the mossy water on both sides, you would say it looks like the ancient trees rose from the water to do an emphatic jig, then collapsed, every which way, in exhaustion.

I wish I could write the sound of deep sadness in voices of grown men I've known all my life.

Carl wakes at 4 am every day now. Once, when I woke then and stumbled to the bathroom, I caught him by surprise, and he acted like he was cleaning up. One day I watched him in the backyard sitting on a swing. Alone. Quiet.

Carl the grown-up-fisherman is now living at my grandmother's house after his own was destroyed; when we tried getting him a FEMA trailer it turned out to be too long to fit on the property. Michael is still living in San Antonio, Texas, where he's signed a one-year lease and had a cooking job that he quit after too little pay. He tells me it is still "a much better life". Says next time he's in New Orleans he will flee at the hint of rain.

The California group is still out there. Troy is unloading boxes from a Wal-Mart truck for US $8 an hour after building furniture most his life. Another sister, Valeria, is in Alabama starting anew. Working at Burger King. Beginning again at 50 years of age.

We are everywhere and *nowhere* together.

This Thanksgiving, I called my mom in California close to 15 times. "I could just sleep all the day," she said. Carl cooked fried chicken and eggs for his holiday dinner.

There is, you see, no neat ending to a story like this. And that would not feel right anyway.

The Broom clan may be a displaced people with far fewer possessions than before, but wherever there is ground, there can be dancing. We don't even need a drum; we've got our hands for that. And a wild, big New Orleans family spread out around the country is a dangerous and wonderworking thing to behold – like our city itself. New Orleans will resurrect, it will, just as all mighty things do, but it will take its own sweet, slow moving time. Just the thought sends your legs moving again, gets your heart burning hopeful the exact moment you think it.

Young Republicans in London

Jean Hannah Edelstein

Parliament Square is packed with a rabble of protesters – wrapped up in woolly hats and duvets masquerading as outerwear, chanting and shouting and brandishing handmade slogan posters – registering their disapproval of Tony Blair's renewal of the Trident nuclear weapons system.

The queue for security at the St Stephen's Entrance to the Houses of Parliament, however, is silent. I am in an orderly line of middle-aged men and women clad in black and grey overcoats and sombre suits; the women have accented their outfits with pearls, while the men's necks are ringed with subtle ties. I am wearing my own version of a conservative outfit: a plain black dress with opaque tights and high black heels.

En route from Covent Garden to Westminster, fearing that my dress was a little too trendy, I picked up a scarf at Accessorize, which I've knotted around my neck in the style of an air hostess.

My companion Christiane and I have talked over our outfits for this evening *ad nauseum*; she's also sporting a black dress, and a circlet of plastic pearls. But despite these efforts, we're just not sure that we are going to pass at this evening's cocktail party, an affair jointly sponsored by Republicans Abroad and Conservatives Abroad.

According to its official website, Republicans Abroad (RA) is an international organisation that "mobilises the support of Americans overseas to support Republican candidates in US elections".

It's a surprising political cause, given that absentee ballots are rarely counted in US elections. The way that American electoral districts are drawn up, it's never likely that a handful of votes from overseas will make a difference, and even in the battle between Gore and Bush for Florida in 2000, thousands of absentee ballots were never opened and were destroyed. Yet this doesn't seem to deter ex-pat Americans, with RA represented in 54 separate countries. Democrats Abroad is similarly well subscribed, but Democrats Abroad I can understand – I mean, of course unhappy Democrats leave the US all the time. Many who I have met – from my occasional attendance of DAUK meetings since I moved to London in 2003 – are folks on the far left side of the Democratic Party. They often hold events at Conway Hall or at the LSE, creating a safe ex-pat haven where it's okay to believe, if only for an hour or so, that the world really is a left-wing paradise where John Kerry was a serious contender for President. Before the 2004 election they even organised teams of members to stand outside London tube stations, handing out 'Vote for Kerry' cards: that's how much they believed.

In popular myth, however, Republicans are associated with the kind of rampant patriotism that contributes to the statistic that only a quarter of Americans own passports. So I am mystified by what kind of person chooses to live outside the US but to actively engage in support of the G.O.P. (Grand Old Party), especially given the rest of the world's less than enthusiastic support for Bush's governance.

Of course, I am also mystified because, just as I have never given a thought to having three arms, I have also never dreamed of being a Republican.

To my knowledge, everyone in the American side of my family votes Democrat, unless they're being crazy and voting for the Green Party. One time my brother phoned me in London from California and mentioned that he was thinking about voting for Bush in 2004. I hung up on him. I have no close Republican friends, and I'm pretty sure that I could never really be attracted to a man who is a Republican. For that matter, I couldn't be attracted to a man who doesn't think that *All the President's Men* is a really exciting film.

"You're not liberal," Christiane says when I tell her this, very quietly, in line. "You're left-wing and narrow-minded."

Tonight's event is co-sponsored by Republicans Abroad and Conservatives Abroad, but it's not clear how many people in attendance really are "abroad". Many are sporting parliamentary ID badges. As we circulate trying to find some fellow Americans, we're enveloped by a cacophony of British voices.

Small-"C" conservatives seem to share some universal traits, however. As far as I can see, only two people in the room aren't white, and one of those people has a cloth draped over his arm and is passing canapés. When Christiane tries to intercept him for something wrapped in puff pastry on the way to the ladies, he refuses. A well-coiffed middle-aged lady nearby who overhears this chases after him.

"You *will* give this lady a canape!" she bellows.

While Christiane and I stand in the middle of the crowd, wondering how one approaches people at a Republican party, a hereditary peer sidles up to us. He's a big supporter of the peerage, he explains. The House of Lords is much better for law-making than the House of Commons, what with all the debate and wrangling they have to go through. The House of Lords, he seems to think, is frightfully efficient.

"How did you get involved in politics?" he says.

I choose my words carefully.

"Ah, well," I say, "I suppose my parents were always very political. I guess... I never really had a choice as to whether I was going to be involved in politics."

"*Much like you,*" I think.

He spots someone more interesting to talk to.

"Keep voting Conservative!" he purrs, and is gone.

Police boats are circling in the Thames next to the Terrace Pavilion where the party is being held. It's really like any other Westminster drinks party: there's a choice of red or white or orange juice; people stand around in clusters, speaking in jolly, self-aggrandising tones, forcing out short, barky laughs in the interest of political networking. The word "likeminded" is tossed around a lot, as in "it's wonderful to meet likeminded people," which I think is a euphemism for "correct, unlike those pinko Democrats."

There are several other parties going on this evening in rooms along the length of the Pavilion. The one next door looks more fun: the people are younger and more attractive, less starchy, and seem to be having a much better time.

"Democrats have more fun," Elizabeth, a thirty-something Parliamentary researcher from Texas, laughs dryly, when I ask her why RAUK doesn't have a stronger youth movement. For a moment, I consider vaulting over the flimsy divider and looking for folks closer to me on the ideological spectrum.

Then the evening's hosts take to the centre of the room to give the obligatory welcoming speech, recounting a litany of the accomplishments of the right, with enthusiastic references to Margaret Thatcher and none at all to John Major.

The assembled guests form a semi-circle on the luxurious scalloped Parliamentary standard-issue carpet and sip their drinks, waiting expectantly for someone to sum up the reasons that we're gathered here this evening.

I fiddle with my nametag. "Jean Hannah Edelstein, Republicans Abroad", it says, with a small picture of an elephant on it. I feel a little claustrophobic.

Conservative MP Liam Fox gives the keynote address, starting with his reflections on the Trident vote.

"We had almost 100 Labour rebels on that particular vote, and I reckon we added a few just at the very end by reminding them that the Cold War didn't just end, the Cold War was won. And the Cold War was won by strong political and moral resolve. And in fact just invoking the names of Margaret Thatcher and Ronald Reagan probably guaranteed that we had 100 Labour rebels going into the lobby against the government. So great politicians have their uses for a very long time."

The crowd dissolves into giggles and applause at the mention of Margaret and Ronald.

"We have always maintained very strong links with the Republican Party: there's so much that we share together in terms of our commonalities of views. And we're going to face a great challenge in the years ahead to stick with resolve to those views, and in particular as we face some of the difficulties in the international security picture, which I believe is deteriorating at the present time.

"We have to understand that you can't take and apply a Jeffersonian model of democracy onto broken countries in five years."

It's a bold criticism of Bush. There's applause, but it's robotic, rather than raucous; everyone seems a little bit confused about the way forward from here, which is perhaps in keeping with the general state of Republican politics.

After the speeches, wading through a crowd of young Conservative researchers milling about enjoying the free drinks, I meet Frank T. Brooks, who is running to be a Tory councillor in a village near Leeds. He looks like he was born to be a Tory councillor, which is maybe why he's running unopposed – I can't imagine that anyone would want to challenge a man who wears a double-breasted suit so well at 27.

Frank has travelled down to London especially for this evening's event. As he's not an American citizen, he can't actually join Republicans Abroad, but, he assures me, he wants to do everything he possibly can to support the Bush administration – he is, he says, a huge Bush fan. He also seems to be a particular fan of William Hague; after we meet, he adds me as his friend on Facebook, where his profile features a photo of him with William and his wife Ffion. He lists his "interests" as "Doing the Right thing by annoying the Left!"

So I ask Frank why he admires George W.

"After 9/11, America needed a strong leader," he says. "From an outsider's point of view, America was – it was almost a Pearl

Harbor. I believe that Bush showed strong leadership right after 9/11 happened, when America was very uncertain about the future. Had there not been a strong leader at the time, there could have been a strong downturn in the economy because of Americans not feeling good about themselves; everyone needs to feel good about themselves for the economy to tick over. There could have been a serious global recession. I think Bush showed true leadership, and surrounded himself with the right people like Colin Powell, Condoleezza Rice. Like Donald Rumsfeld."

True, Americans seem to have retained high self-esteem, but the dollar has tanked since

9/11, as any bargain-hunting Brit on a shopping trip to New York would attest, and the Bush administration appears to have been powerless to stop its decline.

Furthermore, Frank believes that the influence of the United States on global politics – his is a unipolar perspective – means that the UK must defer to Bush's policy.

"As far as defence is concerned," Frank continues, "I believe that we are now reliant on the US for our strategic defence purposes. We could have made a big fuss about Iraq, but at the end of the day we are reliant on the US. That's fact. I don't think Blair had any choice but to go into Iraq. I don't think it's done Blair any good, being so close to Bush, because Bush is such an unpopular person."

So I ask Frank why he thinks that Bush is so unpopular.

"Maybe his lack of understanding about the rest of the world?" he responds, laughing.

At the time of our conversation, Tony Blair has not yet announced his resignation, but Frank is already firmly fixed on the vision of a post-Blair world, which, to Frank, won't be about Gordon Brown – who he thinks will be a temporary blip of a PM – but rather about the comeback of the Conservatives. Frank doesn't see Conservative leader David Cameron continuing the Blair/Bush relationship along its current lines.

"I think he would probably be more openly critical of the Bush administration, but the historical link between the Conservative Party and the Republican Party would still remain very strong. And I think some form of criticism of Bush on the global scene is actually quite healthy to a relationship. I crave for the Thatcher–Reagan days again."

"You were pretty young during the Thatcher–Reagan days," I say. "Do you remember them clearly?"

"Ish," he says.

A week later, I meet up with Elizabeth to chat more about what it means to be a Republican Abroad. Elizabeth is really, really nice. It surprises me how struck I am by this, as she leads me through the maze of corridors that lead from Westminster Palace's Central Lobby to the leafy atrium of Portcullis House. My memory of her from the party was of a woman who was serious and imposing, even though she was six inches shorter than me. Republicans, I clearly think, are not nice people.

It's Friday, the first day of the Easter recess, so she's in jeans and a cardigan and half-rimmed hipsterish plastic glasses, which makes me feel fairly stupid in my latest overwrought Republican costume: another demure black dress accompanied by a string of pearls that are faker than my right-wing beliefs. Elizabeth is smiley and gracious – she offers to give me a tour of the Chambers, pointing out the features of the building as we walk past. Elizabeth drinks full fat *Coke*, which is, in my opinion, a sign of a girl with her head screwed on. Elizabeth and I, it occurs to me, could really be friends if we never spoke about politics.

Elizabeth moved to the UK in 2004 to study for a master's degree; she'd done public relations and political work in the US for years, including a stint working as part of the communications team for the Bush campaign in her home state of Texas, where, she tells me, she once saved the day by reminding the people in charge that they'd failed to arrange for the broadcast of a key political advertisement on the largest Spanish language television channel. She has also been part of the team that worked for Tom DeLay, the one-time House Majority Leader who was indicted on criminal charges for the violation of campaign finance laws. Now, she is a researcher for a Conservative MP who, among other things, leads a parliamentary group that campaigns in "the fight against political correctness".

Elizabeth didn't exactly feel welcomed as a Republican when she first arrived in England; this was shortly before Bush's re-election. Whenever she admitted her political affiliation, she says, "You were hit with this flood of hate beaming toward you."

It wasn't, necessarily, that this was the first thing that she told people about herself, but "since I was doing a masters in International Relations, it was going to come [out] in conversation anyway.

"With the election going on [in 2004] people were just naturally asking every American that they would run in to, 'What do you think about President Bush?' And I would say, 'Well, I'm quite happy with him,' and people would say, 'Oh.'"

She utters this last syllable with a note of crisp English horror.

"And a prime example," Elizabeth continues, "is a friend of mine: we had a party at our flat the day after the election. He walked in the door, someone heard his accent, and said, 'What do you think about the election?' and he said, 'Well, I think it's a good outcome.'"

Elizabeth's friend found himself trapped in the foyer, compelled to defend his political beliefs without even the aid of a beer. After 20 minutes of interrogation, Elizabeth says, "He goes, 'Oh, by the way, my name is Oscar,' and [the other person] went, 'I am so sorry.'" Elizabeth smiles wryly. "But that was the treatment you got, you would be cornered... and if they hear that you've worked for campaigns [the reaction is] 'How dare you!?'"

Elizabeth's beliefs haven't been eroded by her experiences abroad, however.

"Actually, I think it's probably strengthened my conservatism," she says, "and [sense of] being a Republican. Especially being in the UK, which is supposed to be, you know, this first-world country, highly developed, it should be the equivalent to US as far as accessibility to things, and it's not. And the prime example I would say is health care. The health care is substandard in my opinion, and I would say in most Americans' opinion.

"When an American comes over, they expect to get the same treatment that they would at their doctor. But NHS doctors have seven minutes per patient, and that's all they're allowed. I think it's the little things like that which have actually made me more conservative. I really have to question Americans who come over and don't convert a bit more to being conservative – because of the taxes, and the health care and the education system.

"I will never, ever complain about taxes again."

She also thinks that there are some very key philosophical differences between the way

Americans and Brits view their governments.

"In the US, we have more of a feeling that I am my brother's keeper, not the government. Whereas here, the government is supposed to provide for you throughout your life. In the US people say, 'It's my responsibility to make sure that I am taken care of'. I think it's changing here, to become more like that."

I ask Elizabeth if she's been a lifelong Republican.

"Well, I'd always been interested in [politics]," she says. When she was small, living in a little town on the outskirts of Houston, Texas, Elizabeth remembers campaigning with her family against the incorporation of their town by the city.

"I remember helping my parents make signs for the yard – 'Vote NO' – I didn't understand really, why we'd want to vote no, but you know, I remember making signs for the yard."

"Hey, you're just like me!' I want to say, because one of my earliest memories is of sitting in the back of my mum's car, debating the merits of Walter Mondale over Ronald Reagan in the 1984 presidential election (I was born in 1981) with Emma, the daughter of family friends. I wonder whether if Elizabeth's parents had adopted me, and vice versa, I would now be working for a Conservative MP spearheading "the campaign against political correctness."

We finish our drinks and Elizabeth escorts me, through an underground tunnel, out of the shiny new surroundings of Portcullis House and back through the limestone passages of the House of Commons.

"I think political correctness is much worse here," she says. "Because what they've done is they've actually tried to regulate it a lot more. It's something that people in the States have done a bit more voluntarily. Here you can't say 'lady', you have to say 'woman'. And certainly, I am a lady."

Undoubtedly.

Russ Thwaite is a master's student at the London School of Economics in European Politics. The LSE is not exactly known for being a hotbed of right-wing politics, and indeed he estimates that he's one of only three Republicans there, despite the college's substantial population of Americans. He's from Missouri – very tall, with the solid build of an ex-military man and a neat, close-cropped haircut to match. Russ is wearing a suit because he's working as an intern in the House of Commons. His face is open and friendly and trusting: Russ is a real all-American boy, like a figure in a Norman Rockwell painting.

Or maybe I'm just saying that because I know that before coming to the LSE, Russ was living in Italy, where he was stationed on an American army base, following his tour of duty in Afghanistan. I don't come across ex-military Americans very often in London. Or anywhere, for that matter: I'm realising just how the circles I move in, both socially and professionally, are distinctly separate from those populated by Republicans.

"I arrived in September, I came directly from Italy," Russ tells me, when I ask him how long he's been in the UK.

"It was kind of odd because I made the transition from the

military life to civilian life with just the stroke of a pen: on the 20th I was signing the paper [to be discharged from the Army] in Italy and on the 21st I was registering for classes at the LSE."

His course focuses on the European Union, which seems a slightly surprising choice, to me, for someone who professes right-wing views.

"What do you think of the European Union?" I ask him.

"Enh," he says, sending my eyebrows flying up to my hairline – why spend a year of your life and £10,000 studying something you're indifferent to?

"Especially leading up to the Iraq War, definitely… I came to the LSE because I wanted to better understand why European politics worked the way they did on a lot of issues. Really I was kind of sceptical about the whole European Union project, and to be honest I'm still kind of sceptical. I think its major achievement is that it's prevented Western Europe from going to war with itself.

"It's a system that would never happen in America – or in North America – though. To think that legislation could be passed in Ottawa or Mexico City that could affect me in Franklin County, Missouri – it just blows my mind."

Russ's classmates are not always very impressed with his military pedigree, but he's not bothered when they challenge him.

"I really take the gloves off, I don't mind defending the Republican position or the position of the US in general. I've received some hostile, anti-American views and so on being thrown at me: no one can tell me anything new."

Perhaps it is eight years in the army that have given him the stiff upper lip. He joined as an undergraduate at university in his home state of Missouri; after completing the student training corps (ROTC), he was committed to four years of active duty in return for the sponsorship that he received for completing his degree. After being posted to Italy, where he worked as a police officer on an American base, he was sent to Afghanistan.

"My official title was Detainee Operations Officer in Charge," he explains, which included "coordinating missions from

Afghanistan to Guantanamo, releasing them if they're coming back, and also I did take part in a lot of projects to improve the well-being and life of the detainees in custody."

"I never wanted to make a career out of the army," he says. "It was something that I always wanted to do growing up," even though he didn't come from a military family. But then Russ seems to be a bit of an independent thinker. "I'm the only Republican as well."

He's also the first person in his family to go to university.

"I have to say, growing up you kind of follow your family. I sort of had these Democratic – Democrat tendencies."

So unlike Elizabeth and me, Russ is going against the grain with his politics. But he's not convinced that the rest of his family is really that different from him – their politics, he explains, are rooted in their careers in car manufacturing in Missouri.

"The thing with being a Democrat in my family, is that if you gave my family members a checklist without any title, Republican or Democrat... they'd be Republicans. But, I'm the first male in three generations not to work at Chrysler, in the factory lines. So with unions and everything else – just automatically, you had to vote Democrat, because they're in your best interests."

Not that his parents were particularly politically active, anyway, he says "They voted, but that was all of their political activity."

So what spurred Russ on to break the mould? The military, for one thing.

"I think it was a big influence. It helped bring it out," he admits. "Whereas my parents thought Democrats best represented their views in light of working at Chrysler, as an army officer I thought the Republicans historically and presently take better care of the military. I just think they're better looked-after under a Republican administration."

Furthermore, however, leaving the US was what really cemented Russ's identification as a Republican, having to defend his views to non-Americans.

"I think that when I really found out that I was a hardcore

Republican was when I studied abroad in South Africa," he says.

That's not to say he doesn't relish an international experience. Rather, Russ sees himself as something of an ambassador for Republicans.

"I think that it's a very good opportunity to show people abroad something about Republicans," he explains to me. "I bring something new to the table, maybe what a real Republican would look like – how they talk, how they behave."

It's all a bit zoological.

"Usually the average person comes across two types of Americans in Europe. One, I call 'the apologetic American' – they're sorry for everything that America's done. And then you have 'the stereotypical American', over here on vacation, and they're loud and obnoxious and they expect ice in their drink."

Russ is drinking a pint of chilly lager. So what does he think is the point of Republicans Abroad, anyway? Russ tells me that he's only just recently signed up, but he's excited about it, and not just because it gives the opportunity to get the vote out to the enfranchised overseas constituency.

"At a minimum it's a good opportunity to bring likeminded people together. One of the reasons that I live abroad is that I want to meet new people and learn about different places. But once in a while it is just nice to be around fellow Americans, and talk about American things."

But what about the actual political role of Republicans Abroad, I wonder. Really, what's the point?

"It definitely has a role because, of course, we're still enfranchised abroad," Russ says, positively.

Even though absentee ballots are rarely counted? Russ raises an eyebrow when I point out that absentee ballots weren't even tallied in the contentious 2000 presidential election when it all came down to a handful of voters in Florida.

"Well, I mean generally speaking, there was a lot of attention focused…" he says, "… it was probably because Gore realised that a lot of military personnel have their home of record in Florida. So a lot of absentee votes coming into Florida are from the military."

It's an interesting argument, and I'm surprised how much I sympathise with Russ. I rather admire him. On the way to the tube, he asks me what my political orientation is. I don't want to be dishonest, so I admit it: I'm a hardcore liberal, with a dogged commitment to social progressivism and the need for everyone to look after those on the margins of society, which is why I am quite OK with high taxes. Russ doesn't seem too bothered that I'm not, in fact, a likeminded Republican. He smiles down at me.

"But don't you think they're lazy?" he says.

"No," I say, but I can see why a man who got himself out of Missouri on the strength of his solitary Republican volition might think so.

It's my weekly Sunday phone call with my parents, who are back in Baltimore. I tell them about my adventures with Republicans.

"I realised," I tell them, "that the only reason I'm so left-wing is because of you. If I had different parents, I could be a Republican too."

I swallow in fear.

"There but by the grace of God go I, you know?"

They laugh, kindly.

"Nah," says my dad. "We're not that left-wing. I'm quite socially conservative, you know."

I do know, of course. My dad used to get in trouble at his office for questioning policies meant to enforce political correctness and sent me into paroxysms of teenage mortification by delighting in referring to parking spots for the disabled as "crippled spaces". But I very much doubt that dad has ever voted for a Republican. I doubt that my mum has either.

When my far-flung family gets together we tend to gather around the kitchen table, drinking tea and setting the world to rights for hours. We invariably conclude that President Bush is a very bad guy, that Iraq is a terrible problem, that we need a nationalised health care system, that we're excited for the 2008 election. We like Obama. Then we go over the points again. For much like Elizabeth and Russ, we're typical Americans: unlikely ever to change the party that we'll vote for; certain that we're right and the other, non-likeminded faction, are certainly wrong.

I thought that Republicans who went abroad and held on to their views were narrow-minded, ignorant, maybe a little crackers. But living outside the US for the past eight years hasn't caused me to change my mind. If anything, it's just made my political attitudes toward the US more firmly entrenched. If exposure to the world outside the US borders hasn't caused my opinions to metamorphose, why did I expect the opinions of lifelong Republicans would? Especially when most arguments they encounter from Brits abroad consist of the question "Did you vote Republican?" followed by an uninformed 20 minute diatribe about globalisation and Iraq that has little at all to do with the essential core values that drive America's robust two party democracy. I think if I was cornered by one poseur American politics buff after another, forced to stomach the same broadly drawn insults at every student party and gathering I went to, my political views would strengthen to the point of becoming radical. In that case, Russ and Elizabeth seem surprisingly calm. More like stoic political martyrs than deluded right wing nut jobs. I am unnerved.

"You," my mother says, with affection, "are a Fascist on the other end of the political spectrum."

Over 4,000 miles of phone line, we laugh.

Bobbies in Jamaica

Martyn McLaughlin

The killing began on Black Ants Lane. 90 minutes after the first shots were fired a sleek Mercedes saloon, the dawn light gleaming off its waxed black bonnet, arrived from nearby Kingston. The car came to a halt outside the victims' small concrete house, and Leslie Green – a stumpy, middle-aged Scot – stepped out of the passenger door. Flattening a plain navy tie against a crisp, white shirt, he made his way inside the house, taking care not to place his polished brogues in the dark, vermilion pools that licked their way across the floor.

The first victim in the house was no older than 30, lying bloodied and lifeless against the bathroom wall. Nearby, another man struggled for breath, his hand clutching a deep neck wound. Spent AK-47 shell cases scattered the ground like confetti. Blurred figures moved back and forth through the house, some in militaristic uniform, barking in confusion at one another. The house had yet to be cordoned off by a panicked police force. Taking control, Green hastily reminded the officers under his command they now occupied a murder scene.

As the yellow tape went up, Green walked through the building, discovering the victims for himself. Recognising their faces, he knew a long weekend lay in wait. The dead man, Richard Francis, was a member of the Park Lane gang; the survivor, still gasping for oxygen, was Cleveland "Cassie" Downer, its leader.

A day later, early on Monday morning, the screaming of the newly widowed let the people of Common, Jamaica, know revenge had visited them. A fierce current, taking hold of the

Caribbean basin, lashed rolls of thunder and heavy rainfall down upon the tough uptown community's ramshackle buildings. Flyposters – advertising reggae dancehalls and erotica clubs – grew soggy and limpid, giving way to graffiti tags sprayed on the walls underneath. Dirt and leaves clogged the strip of potholes and fissures that passes for Red Hills Road. A lone jerk vendor, braving the elements, hurriedly tethered a goat to his makeshift stall.

Not even the downpour soothed the pain of the reprisals. Events had quickly spiralled out of control since the first shootings: the death toll had reached five, with a further six people shot and injured, and several houses razed to the ground.

The latest fatalities – Ezra Patrick, Tyrone Ashley, and brothers Anthony and Everton Simpson – were mostly men with young families, but more importantly, members of the Hundred Lane gang, Park Lane's bitter rivals. Their deaths, it was later alleged, resulted from orders handed down from Cleveland Downer's hospital bed. Now, as midday approached, a dozen forlorn figures sat hunched in a shambolic tenement yard, casting lighthouse glares over a charred metal pile where their homes had once stood. A slender woman bawled with grief, a young boy huddled quietly by her side.

"They nu come nuh, they nu come nuh," she shouted. "They gunmen, they kill a sumaddy father. For wha'? He nuh have no papa."

In 2005, Jamaica endured the highest homicide rate in its history, with 1,674 murders, the equivalent of a life taken every six hours. Since gaining its independence in 1962, promise and opportunity have been sullied by a culture of political tribalism. For years inner-city garrison communities, ruled by crime "dons" such as Downer, have aligned themselves with mainstream political parties. Their gangs – whose members have sometimes yet to reach teenage years – defend the ideological and territorial front lines of these garrisons behind blockades of tyres and the husks of burnt-out cars.

The roots of Jamaica's omnipresent gang culture lie in the political patronage of the 1970s and 1980s, when elected representatives established armed gangs to intimidate their opponents.

Though some outfits now consider themselves politically ambivalent, thanks to the economic self-sufficiency afforded by drug trafficking, gunrunning, protection and extortion, they constitute a minority. The long-running enmity between Park Lane and Hundred Lane – respectively siding with the Jamaican Labour Party (JLP), the main opposition party, and the People's National Party (PNP), in government for 18 years – is more indicative of the rivalries being played out across Kingston.

Police sources believe the Red Hills Road murders of November 19 and 20 – five of some 14 murders in Jamaica that weekend, and 37 over just one week – stemmed from a dispute over a lucrative government contract for gully cleaning work in the parish of St Andrew. The parish is represented by a JLP member of parliament, and so it was Cleveland Downer's Park Lane gang that received the contract: a partisan decision that appears to have precipitated the slaughter. Karl Samuda, the Labour Party MP in question, denied any political links to the killings when confronted with the allegations by the Jamaican press.

"Cleveland Downer has been instrumental in ensuring that the [gully] project delivered value for money," he insisted.

Certainly, it would not be the first time Downer's name has been smeared in cold blood. Several murder trials over a 2002 massacre which saw two men, three women, and two young girls from a Hundred Lane/People's National Party domain shot dead, have been repeatedly postponed; not only have numerous witnesses changed their accounts or failed to show, but so too have judges.

Carolyn Gomes, executive director of Jamaicans for Justice, a domestic human rights watchdog, articulated the saddening ordinariness such incidents have come to assume.

"If you're part of a gang, [then] depending on your political allegiance there are politicians you can go to to help make bail and ensure the police are sympathetic," she explains. "But there are relationships between the gunmen and the politicians which go beyond begging for bail."

It is into this violent stalemate that Caithnessborn Leslie Green has volunteered himself until 2009. For close to three decades the 48-year-old Scottish Highlander served with the Metropolitan Police, rising through the ranks to become a detective chief inspector overseeing major investigations. Jamaica though, has been on his mind for the past decade.

In London, Green held a key detective role in Operation Trident, a Met initiative set up in 1998 to curtail the escalating numbers of "black on black" shootings and murders in the capital's Brent and Lambeth regions. The targets of this investigation, some 40% of whom were Jamaican nationals residing in Britain, were heavily involved in the burgeoning crack cocaine market. Through his contacts with both customs and immigration officials and the Jamaican authorities, Green was among the first to draw attention to the growing numbers of Jamaican drug mules traversing a 5,000 mile journey to Aberdeenshire, where they mined a client base by enticing the north-east's heroin users with free rocks of crack.

In October 2004, Green was seconded to Operation Kingfish, a joint British–Jamaican police operation aimed at flushing out cocaine traffickers in Kingston's sprawling ports, where around 20 tonnes of the class A drug are shipped to Britain each year. Working undercover and providing technical assistance to the venture, Green anticipated returning to London before long. But the Caribbean connection was to continue.

For the past year, he has occupied the third highest rank in the nation's policing body, the Jamaican Constabulary Force (JCF). As assistant commissioner responsible for serious and organised crime, he plays an integral part in Jamaica's endeavours to rid itself of gang crime.

Over coffee in a modest café near the JCF's Hope Road headquarters in Kingston's commercial district, Green offers a relaxed and forthright account of his time so far in the Caribbean. Though a seasoned detective, even he has been taken aback.

"The crime scenes are unlike anything I've seen in Britain," he says. "In some cases there's hundreds of shots that have been fired in the one incident, and at a lot of scenes I'll find as many as 12 or 13 guns have been discharged in the one house. There is a viciousness to the criminals here.

"It's indiscriminate. I've seen armed men running out of houses under siege holding a baby over their chest with one hand, shooting at police with a pistol in the other."

Like Gomes, he acknowledges the dark, nebulous relationships that bind the island's democratic elect and inner-city garrisons.

"Of course, the gangs are directly linked to the political parties. It's like Northern Ireland in that respect. If your community is in support of the People's National Party it'll get more government funding."

Jamaica's social environment, Green reasons, actively encourages young men to lead a life of crime. The country is economically stagnant, with high unemployment (around 15%), and the national minimum wage barely exceeds £30 a week. For many, gang life is predestined.

"There are gang members with a lot of influence who are held up as icons," he says. "It subverts the structure of normal society. Criminals openly flaunt their assets here. You see the Beamers and the Mercs coming from the inner-city garrisons, going home to sprawling mansions. The government has to ensure people are employed and paid to a reasonable standard."

The task facing the Jamaican Constabulary Force, however, is made even worse by a chronic lack of resources for the police force. Last autumn, security on the island reached crisis level after nearly a third of the JCF's officers called in sick as part of a wage dispute. Moreover, around seven out of 10 police cars are over a decade old; some of those officers with automobiles, meanwhile, cannot afford fuel to run them.

Green openly acknowledges the fact that gangs find it easier to obtain weapons – mainly AK-47s, Glocks, Browning, and   M-9s – than the police, and indeed, use them in regular coordinated ambushes of security patrols. Only a select band of officers are armed, while there is a wider shortage of protective helmets and body armour.

"They can't do their job, let alone offer the public reassurance," Green confides. "It's immensely frustrating."

Unsurprisingly, the JCF's rank-and-file have come to exercise a precarious neuroticism in their daily work. Confronted with a better-equipped criminal element, they are seldom able to control volatile situations, leading to what Green describes as "sledgehammer-style policing".

Over the past seven years, some 1,066 lives have been claimed by fatal police shootings, placing the nation among countries with the world's highest rate of killings by security forces. Those officers who are armed carry M-16 assault rifles, a weapon of poor accuracy that, particularly in urban environs, increases the risk of injuring civilian bystanders.

To blacken the picture further, Amnesty International's most recent annual report on the island notes that the police killed at least 168 people in 2005, yet not a single officer was convicted.

"Many of the killings," it adds, "were in circumstances suggesting [the victims] were extrajudicially executed."

Such clandestine behaviour is indicative of a grave immorality lurking within the JCF. Last May, a special task force on crime – comprising members of the judiciary, church leaders, and civil rights monitors – compiled a document entitled "Road Map to a Safe and Secure Jamaica". Its contents made disconcerting reading for those at the top of the constabulary.

Corruption across the paramilitary-style body, the report

concluded, is endemic and institutionalised, prevalent not only among street officers, but in the air-conditioned offices of senior officialdom.

Arbitrary practices deemed widespread include contract killings, extortion, the sale of arms and ammunition on the black market, the provision of bodyguard services for dons, the removal of evidence from crime scenes, perjury, and advising criminals of planned police interdictions. Given this catalogue of misdemeanours, the public's opinion of the police ranges from distrust to violent hostility. Nowhere is resentment towards the JCF more acutely felt than on the streets of Kingston's downtown fiefdoms.

After meeting with Green, I decide to visit Rema, a poor area in the Trenchtown neighbourhood, and ask the locals about their experiences of the JCF. This is where national icon Bob Marley spent much of his youth, waging an articulate revolt through his music and political campaigning that remains as relevant today as in his 1970s heyday.

An anxious taxi driver ferries me westbound through the city's heart, as the sense of poverty grows: the houses and shops visibly deteriorating with every corner turned. The traffic is thick with mini-vans and buses, young men dressed in green hanging from the windows, hooting and hollering.

It later transpires they are on their way to the National Stadium for the Jamaican Labour Party annual conference, a rumbustious affair where the politicians will enter the hustings dancing to their individual theme music, beer and marijuana will be widely consumed, and a gaggle of overenthusiastic JLP supporters will loot the stadium of computers, stationery supplies, and even sinks and urinals.

Finally, we arrive in Rema. After a five-minute canter, I see a wiry, sullen teenager clad in white shorts and T-shirt perched on a twisted metal stool outside one of the battered street bars ubiquitous throughout Jamaica. He sups from a bottled beer, his dark mocha eyes probing each passing car, seemingly content to allow the day to fritter away before him.

After some remonstrance on my part to disassociate myself from the police, he introduces himself as Clinton, and begins to open up about the JCF's standing in Rema.

"Dem dangerous to yute lek me," he says in a gruff patois. "I seen police shoot bwoys first plenty time, shootin' nine, 10 time, mashin' up the place. Dem plant stuff on yu too... yu no trust de police here, if yu want to live, bredda."

The unemployed teenager says he is part of a gang known as Fatherless, a group of disenchanted youths who have lost their fathers through violence or imprisonment; in a country where 80% of births are outside marriage, and 70% fail to record the father's name on the birth certificate, the rudderless family is all too familiar. Clinton's own father, a taxi driver, was just 34 when he was gunned down five years ago. The killer has never been caught.

At 18, he already has a three-year-old boy and an infant girl. His first family though, remains the gang. Born and raised in Rema, he became involved with Fatherless at just 15 ("I was man nuff"), looking out for rival gangs and JCF police patrols in and around Trenchtown. A year later, he received his first gun from a local don. Clinton will not say whether he has killed anyone, but refers to having spent several spells in the city's Hilltop juvenile correction centre. Now he is a man, devoted to the tribe, and prepared for the consequences such loyalty may hold in store. He lifts up his T-shirt, revealing a squat silver Ruger automatic pistol tucked into his waistband.

"I'm a soldier, dat's the way tis," he says through a wry smile.

As resentment of the JCF becomes the norm for a generation of young people in the inner city, an international recruitment drive has begun to bolster the upper echelons of Caribbean police forces across Jamaica, Trinidad & Tobago, and St Lucia with senior foreign policemen. To date, Leslie Green is one of four Brits on long-term secondment in Kingston, a move funded partly by the UK Department for International Development, and worldwide private sector consultants such as Atos Consulting and Memex, following discussions between Scotland Yard, the Foreign Office, and the Jamaican Ministry of National Security. Gilbert Scott, permanent secretary in the national security ministry, describes the Brits' arrival as the "infusion of a body of talent to help speed up a process of modernisation".

Another recent arrival, John McLean from Glasgow, has been appointed assistant commissioner for community safety. He was working as the head of the Scottish Criminal Records Office (SCRO), when he saw a vacancy published in a specialist policing journal. He visited the island four times before making the leap with his partner, Caryl Jackson, former head of public relations at Glasgow City Council. It was not his intention to flee Britain.

"I'd only joined the SCRO when [the vacancy] came up, and I wasn't actively looking for another job," he recalls. "I just thought, 'Here's a chance to make a difference.' And the sunshine helped too, of course."

On an overcast Kingston morning six months to the day since "trading the Scottish midgie for the Jamaican mozzie", McLean entertains me at his home in a gated community in a suburb of Kingston. His neighbours number among the nation's influential and wealthy, including Gordon 'Butch' Stewart, head of the Sandals hotel chain.

In his new life he finds himself rising much earlier in the morning, at four or five, a time when ordinary Jamaicans think nothing of turning on their boomboxes. He likes to eat a fresh fruit breakfast and read British newspapers online.

"You don't have the same freedom we take for granted in Glasgow," he says. "You don't have the same chance to just pop out and go for a walk in the street."

It is the 51 year-old's responsibility to ensure the JCF engages with normal Jamaicans. McLean, who spent three years investigating the Lockerbie bombing, confesses the job involves starting at the beginning.

"It's obvious to a blind man that [the JCF] is too militaristic, and stuck in a bygone age," he admits.

"There needs to be a strategic review of the force. Force is the optimum word when describing the Jamaican police. Their style of law enforcement is 30 years out of date."

He too shares grievances over the scarcity of resources available. Despite signing a contract with the JCF last February, he has yet to procure either a permanent office or staff. His arrival also fostered resentment among Jamaican-born senior officers.

"They felt threatened. I'm not naïve enough to think some people will not dislike us and the reason we're here," he says.

Known as a tight-lipped authoritarian amongst his former colleagues in Scotland, McLean dismisses the notion that his secondment has evangelical undertones.

"We're here to help bring law and order," he stresses. "It's a country of stark contrasts. It has the highest ratio of churches in the world, yet also among the highest murder and illegitimacy rates. To me, it's immoral, but then that depends on your classification of morality. If we can crack the crime and corruption, though, Jamaica will be one of the best places in the world to live."

Already, a halting progress is being made. The day I meet Green and McLean, they have discovered the most recent murder statistics. Showing some 1,070 killings as of mid-November, it remains an "appalling rate", according to the former, but nonetheless represents a decrease of 300 deaths compared to the year before.

Furthermore, early autumn heralded the introduction of new technology to assist the JCF, an automated palm and fingerprint identification system that, in its first four weeks, brought 150 "hits." Previously, only 15 to 20 identifications were made annually using manual techniques.

Improved ballistics identification techniques too, will hopefully bring swifter prosecutions, and ultimately, an element of deterrence, though the JCF's claim that the Pakistani Cricket Coach Bob Woolmer, who died in Kingston of natural causes at this year's Cricket World Cup, was strangled, did little to engender confidence in its capability for rigorous forensic investigation.

A modernised JCF, of course, cannot act as Jamaica's lone saviour. For the first time in years, the PNP's dominance is under serious threat from a reinvigorated JLP, whose manifesto focuses strongly on rooting out corruption. By the year's end, a new government may be in place. Increased resources for the police force and a concerted effort to aid, rather than sustain, garrison communities such as Common and Rema, can bring peace to parts of the country where it has been absent for decades. Perhaps then Jamaicans will be able to find solace in politics for the right reasons.

Moscow is Broken

Max Wheeler

"The first thing I remember is being naked in a hospital bed," says Harry Glazebrook. Dazzling July sunshine finds him much the same as ever – a state of flux – hair dishevelled, clothes hanging baggy on a tall frame. He's trying to tell me a story, hindered only slightly by the shuffling hordes of apprentice glitterati who convulse around us – devoted style soldiers in the great, shrieking fashionista vortex we call Brighton. Amidst the frenzy of trucker-hats and tinted "fuck-me" shades, Harry seems the only one not in search of a photo opportunity. Despite his deadpan intonation, I feel that bizarre journalistic glee that accompanies a truly grim tale – a predatory reflex no doubt seen in the watery eyes and foam-flecked mouths of unprincipled hacks everywhere. I ask Harry to stop, call the other protagonist, and let me get this kaleidoscopic yarn down on record. Harry's friend, Joe Hart joins us in the quiet backroom of a North Laines bar and they tell me the following story.

"So... the first thing I remember is being naked in a hospital bed," Harry reiterates. A Moscow hospital bed. He has no money, his passport is in tatters, and his travelling companion, Joe, is gone. Worse, he has no clue what in the abstract Christ he is doing here. His wrists, feet and neck are lashed to a bed with torn up strips of dishrag, and he watches as his blood pumps onto the bed sheets with every passing heartbeat. A badly inserted saline drip and the spreading pool of crimson fluid at his elbow are, however, only some of his major concerns. Harry does not speak Russian, and a growing crowd of doctors struggles to interpret his unintelligible screams.

"They just thought I was completely crazy," he remembers, laughing.

I ask how the story starts and Joe, smaller, neater and closer cropped than Harry, but tuned to the same lo-fi frequency, tells me, "We were on holiday... but when we got there we realised that we should really be getting out."

Moscow, they discover on arrival, is no relaxing summer destination – stifling despite its frosty caricature. Something seems wrong, even on their first trip into the city.

"We got this really cheap taxi ride in a Lada," Joe explains. "There were no seatbelts, and I think he was listening to trance or something. Quite pumping trance music. Just driving, and the way you change lanes..."

Harry interjects, "... across three lanes at 80mph, y'know, undertake a bus."

They speed through a vast forest of decaying tower blocks and stray dogs, before heading on into the city itself. Once in Moscow they are struck by a sense of desperation.

"In an army surplus shop I saw a complete Russian cosmonaut outfit for about 160 quid," Joe says, "with all the pipes and stuff so you can piss in the suit."

AK-47 assault rifles are available from wall-mounted racks at a similar sum. I picture a reluctant cosmonaut, glassy eyed, pushing this bright orange relic of the once renowned Soviet space program across the counter of a city centre pawnshop.

On the streets, the main form of recreation is now the 'test-your-strength machine'; "They're everywhere," says Harry.

Big men with their girlfriends, mobs of teenage boys – everyone considers these old-time carnival attractions a key feature of an evening's entertainment. The drink of choice for this activity is "gin and tonic in a big beer-sized can." I recoil inwardly, picturing gin-crazed men in black-market *Levis*, hammering the living shit out of antique fairground machines as their girlfriends holler pro-capitalist slogans. In my mind Moscow is now a kind of colder, meaner version of Blackpool, all canned gin and former astronauts freelancing on street corners.

On their second day in the city, Harry and Joe visit V.K.M.D. Park, "a monument to Soviet success", which Joe compares to Nuremberg.

"You're just supposed to feel belittled," he says.

Gigantic but dilapidated communist-era statues flake titanium, deflating the Red Menace in ways Reagan never dreamed of. The atmosphere is bleak. The word "broken" is settled on as the right adjective for this Cold War graveyard, and by extension for a Moscow which they find shot through with an all-pervasive sadness. They decide to leave for St Petersburg that night.

"A Dostoevsky by moonlight kind of train ride?" I ask.

"I even had *Notes from the Underground* with me," says Harry.

"That got nicked later," Joe notes.

They go to a café for a meal of sausage and beer, hoping to kill time until their train arrives. The place is a Russian greasy spoon, which they share with a mother and a kid – enough to establish it has family credentials and is a good place to "keep our heads down and just wait a couple of hours, without getting in any trouble".

The café is in Moscow's travel epicentre: a maze of railway tracks and addiction that Harry later learns would give most prizefighters nightmares. Joe recognises the dead end he sees here, people with "nothing to do, no money – they just go and hang out".

They are both glad to be leaving, and consider this meal a farewell to Moscow. Their dinner is disturbed by a huge man whose T-shirt, apparently the brutal product of some thriving cottage industry, depicts the cartoon character Taz tearing someone limb from limb in a shower of blood and innards. The man is a 6 ft 6 blond "giant" who proceeds to show Harry an extensive collection of tattoos, covering a large part of his upper body.

"He pointed at my tattoo," Harry explains, "just pointed at it, and put his arm around my shoulder in quite an intimidating way."

Although Harry is himself 6 ft 3, he feels threatened by this man, who has noticed a sole tattoo, a poignant rendition of an exploding planet, on Harry's forearm.

"He put his arm around me, then he got out his papers, his passport, and he showed me a picture of him in military uniform."

This giant, Harry learns, is currently serving in Chechnya and is "really, really proud of it". He belongs to a group consisting of a Siberian who doesn't speak, and a small man of whom Joe opines, "He looked like he'd seen some horror... he had that stare. He'd been in Chechnya."

Harry feels it is best to "be nice to them, they probably won't kill us". He offers to buy a round of drinks, and the barwoman weighs out vodkas, bringing them over a tray from which everyone takes a glass. They wash these down with a bottle of sweet, fizzy orangeade, which Joe does not particularly care for.

The blond giant then disappears and returns with his girlfriend who, Joe says, is "just in a fucking bad way". She is one of Harry's scant memories of the café, an unforgettable riot of "bleached blonde hair, smacked up to the eyeballs". She is laughing at them, but they don't understand why.

Their conversation is surprisingly educational. These men, it transpires, are big fans of Roman Abramovich, the surreally rich owner of Chelsea Football Club, and one of a small band of oligarchs who, with Yeltsin famously drunk in command, took control of Russian industry at fire sale prices, often dumping their profits straight into foreign bank accounts. The Soldier and his friends are also fans of a Muslim-free "Russian" Chechnya, and injecting heroin.

"They all had track-marks up their arms," says Joe.

At this point I recap briefly: a giant Aryan soldier in a T-shirt depicting a brutal cartoon murder, his smacked up moll, a quietly brooding Siberian, and a man who has "seen horror".

In addition to this fully ticked-off checklist of things to avoid at all costs when travelling, these people display a near religious appreciation of intravenous hard drugs, coupled with a fairly hardline Russian nationalism.

Harry and Joe admit that they are wary of their new friends; but far from being uncomfortable, they are by this stage enjoying themselves.

These people are *interesting*.

It's at this point that Harry loses all memory of events. Confusingly, however, he continues to play an active role in them, still in possession of basic motor skills and the faculty of speech. Joe remembers that Harry, "seemed fine, y'know, as he is now".

As Harry puts it: "I can remember being there for about half an hour and then I woke up in hospital."

Feeling what he assumes to be the vodka announcing itself, and perhaps sensing impending doom on a molecular level, Joe makes their apologies and leaves with Harry, for the train station. The soldier and his friends continue to knock back shots, apparently unfazed by the sudden exit of these two brief acquaintances.

Events now take on somewhat cosmic overtones. What seems like a half hour journey takes them only 20 metres from the café. Joe's legs begin to feel heavy, and he rests, leaning against a pillar for support.

"It was raining, and in every shadow was like these really dodgy looking people, but I didn't, I didn't care," Joe says.

He closes his eyes and drifts away, only to be awoken by three unexpected and painful blows to the head. This is their first encounter with the Moscow Transport Police.

Joe tries to explain to the heavily armed traffic warden that Harry and he have a train to catch, but in his efforts to escape he falls into the street, landing heavily in the gutter with his rucksack. This doesn't impress the lawmen, and both he and Harry are led to a waiting room furnished with nothing but plastic chairs. They are then questioned briefly in fragmentary English, and left alone. An hour passes, and Joe realises their train is due. Noticing that, oddly, an unlocked door opens directly onto the street, he tries to leave.

He is then thrown roughly to the ground and put in a nerve-submission hold by a large policeman.

"You know, like, when you're round your friend's house and his bigger brother wants to prove a nerve grip on you, and it really fucking hurts," says Joe. "He was really enjoying it."

Satisfied that Harry and Joe are not leaving, the policemen bring one blanket and one pillow, instructing them to sleep in the cell. Without being formally arrested or allowed a phone call, they have no choice but to sit in their plastic chairs, guard their bags jealously, and wait. Joe fights the urge to sleep but eventually succumbs to a series of lucid waking dreams; improbably, he is at a music awards ceremony, taking place outside the police station. Harry and he have backstage passes to "the Russian MTV awards, I really don't know why".

Coming to, Joe thinks, "Shit! Where's that backstage pass gone?"

He turns to ask Harry but finds his companion's chair now contains a small Russian woman. Harry, along with their luggage, is nowhere to be seen. In addition, Joe finds himself surrounded by fresh pools of his own vomit – he has been violently ill throughout the night – and is inexplicably missing a tooth. This must have happened during "either the nerve grip incident, or when I fell over trying to walk away from the police".

Joe tries to get the time from the woman in Harry's chair, but she is hostile, assuming he simply wants to steal her watch. Joe now thinks that he has "ruined everything", resigning himself to the fact that he must have gone on the mother of all drunks, thereby destroying the holiday. He is also, for the first time in his life, hearing strange voices – even holding entire conversations with Harry, who by now is in an entirely different part of Moscow. Sensing that his situation is fairly dire, and that the police have apparently lost interest in him, Joe releases himself; he waits until there is no one around and wanders off through the unlocked door.

Although their baggage has disappeared, Joe has a washing machine tablet bag containing around £30 worth of roubles and a credit card, safely stashed in his boxer shorts. He searches for Harry, whom he assumes must have taken their luggage to a nearby hotel. Joe thinks Harry has left him to sleep it off, angry at him for failing to hold down his vodka. Still vomiting regularly, Joe retraces their steps, looking for his friend in a city he doesn't know.

"I just had no idea at all. I was sick on the tube a couple of times, at one point I had to get off the tube and be sick on the platform."

Eventually he accepts that he will never find Harry by himself, instead locating the British Embassy with the assistance of a cab driver. Knowing Moscow, the embassy does not share Joe's certainty that Harry is safe and well. Joe is stripped of his soiled clothing, and sent home first class, wearing an Umbro training top and skintight white *Kappa* trousers.

When Harry regains consciousness it is still dark: by his estimate around four in the morning. He left the café roughly six hours earlier. In his words this period is a "complete black hole". Upon waking, he claims, "The first thing I remember is being naked in a hospital bed, like, shouting for Joe, completely out of my head... not knowing where the fuck I am."

Harry is delirious for a long period, like a feverish child, "in and out of hallucinating, in and out of sleep, unconsciousness".

He is apparently naked because upon admission his clothes were soaking wet. He has no idea why this might be. He has no idea, in a more general sense, what the raging fuck is happening. He remembers being determined to find Joe, and demanding to be released. It is this sense of urgency that gets him tied down.

"It wasn't, y'know, like I had the strength of 10 men. It would have been quite easy," says Harry. It soon becomes clear why the doctors thought him mad. He was, at least temporarily.

"At one point I thought Joe was in the same ward as me, a few beds down, and I was trying to shout across the ward to him."

The doctors ask who this mysterious Joe character is and Harry exclaims, "He's that guy right there!" He is, however, pointing at a Russian man who he has never met. Harry is then sedated.

A hospital staff member dresses him in a misshapen shirt with no buttons and a "pair of corduroys with a really wide waist so I had to hold them, but really short, so they only went up to the middle of my shins".

For three days his diet consists of porridge and stale bread twice a day, washed down with water and more sedatives. He befriends a Russian man in the next bed, who takes to waking him up for mealtimes. Despite being hospitalised with a chest condition, this man smokes relentlessly, sharing his tobacco willingly. In the absence of television, radio, reading materials or any other entertainment, Harry sees patients wander aimlessly around the hospital, which he claims "looks like the NHS circa the 1960s".

Whilst hospitalised, he passes the time with around 10 "old people who looked like they were straight out of Tolstoy, old men with really long beards just sitting and chain smoking in the toilets". This, it seems, is the sole entertainment available for invalids in the care of the Russian state.

Harry is kept in the hospital for three days, from early Monday morning until Wednesday afternoon, during which time he isn't allowed to make phone calls or communicate with the outside world. Following a refusal to allow him contact with the embassy or his family, he asks for access to the Internet. The doctors laugh, believing this ridiculous request shows he is definitely under the grip of some fairly heinous drugs, or simply mad in a more conventional sense.

"They got in this special Russian psychiatrist," Harry remembers. "I think he was actually just one of the doctors, I don't think he was really any different from anyone else. But he came and he just sat down and he kind of... really patronisingly asked me to write my name again, and my address, and then kept asking me about Joe, as though... I really got the feeling that he didn't believe this Joe person existed at all."

Eventually the embassy tracks him down.

"I thought they must find me eventually," Harry says. "I was probably the only English person that night who'd been admitted in a state of madness."

It later transpires that the hospital have summoned them, deciding that Harry is now well enough to rejoin civilisation. I ask Harry what goes through his mind during this stint in the ward.

"I really thought Joe could be dead," he remembers.

By this point he must be terrified, I think. I would be. Hospital staff have told him he was found "in the street, in the pouring rain, in the middle of Moscow", but this is all they tell him. At this stage he knows nothing about the holding cell or the police. He only recalls half an hour of what went on in the café. He must be beginning to wonder if this hospital ward is his new life. The first concrete news he hears is when the Embassy finally reaches him by telephone, telling him that Joe is safe, well, and in England.

"I was like, 'That fucking bastard, I'm gonna kill him.'"

"You thought I'd left you for dead Harry," says Joe.

Safely reunited in Britain, conversation turns to what in the gyrating hell these men actually ingested. Methadone seems a possibility to Harry, but rohypnol or some variant sounds more likely. Joe is adamant that it is something the soldier and his friends were drinking recreationally, most likely in the orangeade chaser. By the looks of them, Joe guesses they would keep any methadone they had well to themselves. Both suspect Joe fared better because he threw up most of what he drank. In a letter to his insurance company Harry writes:

The verdict of the doctors in the hospital, and of the two embassy doctors who examined me on the Wednesday, is that my drink was spiked in the café, either

with rohypnol or clonidine. All of this is detailed on the accompanying forms,
both from the hospital and the embassy.

In retrospect it is clear that they were slipped a fairly ferocious
mickey of some description, and whilst under its influence there
was no shortage of people prepared to commandeer their
possessions. The surprising detail is that both are equally adamant
it was the Moscow Transport Police who took their luggage,
belongings, and money while they were drugged and unconscious.
More seriously, they also seem to have sought no medical attention
for Joe, and dumped Harry unceremoniously in the street –
leaving him for dead. Harry sustained cuts and bruises on his
elbows, back and head, "as though I'd been dragged".

The police may have called his ambulance – he isn't sure – but
this doesn't especially endear them to him. He simply assumes
that, as in Mexico City, the Russian police earn so little that "the
only way they can possibly make ends meet is to take bribes, and
that's pretty much accepted".

We discuss the possibility of collusion between the police and
the men in the café, but the only thing we agree on is that there
was some element of opportunism, borne largely of necessity.
This sense of opportunism is reinforced by Joe's *Lonely Planet*
Russian phrasebook, whose first suggestion for dealing with the
police is the Russian for "Can I pay an on the spot fine?"

According to Joe the police in Moscow won't give reports for
stolen objects, so if the police rob you, well, just chalk it up as a
loss. He relates the major points of a story that exposed a yet
darker side of Moscow's law enforcement. In April 2004, a student
was mysteriously shot in the head twice with his own gun, after
working to expose a rape ring among the Moscow Transport
Police – a notorious group known as the "Werewolf Police", with
alleged victims well into the double figures. One of the first things
the embassy doctors asked Harry was if he himself had been
raped, and this shows that the story could have been far more
serious. In fact, a constant undercurrent of relief, and of gratitude

towards the staff of the hospital and embassy underpinned everything Harry and Joe told me.

The British Embassy in Moscow was unable to speak on the record, for various reasons, but my unanswered question, "Does this kind of thing happen often?" is probably not one those in Russian tourism are keen to see answered any time soon.

On balance, it's no surprise that interference in Russia's economy and the consequent grand scale corruption has finally come back to haunt the humble Western tourist. What this corruption means for Russians, however, is a darker story. What would have happened had Harry and Joe been tourists from a country less well represented: neighbouring Georgia for example? Would a Chechnyan Muslim have flown home first class? Would they have even received an ambulance?

When I ask Harry if he is planning a return to Moscow he insists mysteriously that he isn't unless "I've got full... protection".

We all agree that if they had picked up the cosmonaut suit and an AK-47 when they could, then maybe none of this would've ever happened.

"Have you ever tried to mug a cosmonaut?" Joe asks. "It's impossible, you can't get your hands anywhere."

He later sends me a poignant story from the Moscow paper *Moskovsky Komsomolets*, concerning Colonel Magomed Tolboyev, who was stopped by two police sergeants for a routine document check. The paper states that: "After the law enforcers saw the Colonel's name, which suggests he is of Caucasian Muslim descent, they started beating him up."

Colonel Tolboyev, it later transpired, was a decorated Russian cosmonaut and one time commander of Russia's first and only space shuttle – bearing the country's top title, "Hero of Russia". No one is safe, it seems, cosmonaut or otherwise. I wonder to myself if they drugged him first – if that's how the spacesuit got to the pawnshop in the first place. Maybe it was taken from his back with a nerve grip and a slug of rohypnol.

Of the corrupt police, Tolboyev himself said, "There are tens of thousands of them, nothing can be done anyway."

The government claims to be cracking down on police corruption, but the escalation of the conflict between Chechnyan separatists and the state, which culminated in the death of hundreds in the Beslan school siege, indicates that the state of Russian law enforcement, civilian and military, is dire. The chaos seen at Beslan, beamed live across the world, and subsequent stories of police bribed by hostage takers, and journalists drugged by authorities on their way to cover the story, bear unsettling similarities to Harry and Joe's accounts.

Whilst Russian state power grows ever more draconian, and Russian billionaires grow even richer, the police seem less and less answerable to anyone – busy supplementing their wages by taking bribes, robbing tourists, committing rape and beating cosmonauts with Muslim-sounding names.

Interview done, I wonder if the police are enjoying Harry's copy of *Notes from the Underground*. Maybe it's on a separate rack, in between rocket launchers made from Sputnik components and T-shirts of Mickey Mouse committing hari-kiri with a boathook. I feel like knocking off someone's trucker hat. A can of gin is what I need.

Maybe there's a test-your-strength machine down at the pier, I think to myself. The night is but young.

Sex 2.0

Daniel Stacey

SEX. HOT SEX. CUM SHOT. VIRGIN GETS ANAL THEN CUM ON FACE. TEEN BLOW JOB. BLACK COCK IN ASIAN SLUT. HOT BOY 19 MASTURBATES. LESBIAN COLLEGE GIRLS PISS PARTY IN SHOWER.

The ubiquitous language of online porn: sexual caricature, writ large in capitals with phonetic spelling. Threaded through with a slimy, pulsing vein of misogyny and brutal, basic gratification. A reduced language of taboos, of one-dimensional adolescent fantasies. A language stripped of romance to raw physical description.

Online porn. School computers, home computers, wireless laptops. 12 year-olds with eyestrain who've seen more pornography than their parents have in a lifetime of "cheeky" adult shop purchases. A generation whose sexual fantasies are shaped by their voyeurism, their onanism, and others' exhibitionism.

BEARDED DADDY LIKES REAMING TWINKS. NASTY BLONDE TAKES HUGE...

Big black overcoat, designer specs and blue jeans. A man in his late 30s, resembling a fusion of Matrix era Keanu Reeves and your regular trench coat flasher – future-tech meets dildohead – looks down from the mezzanine level of the Sheraton Hotel in Sydney. His hands jab at a *PalmPilot*, while he gestures his head towards me.

"Daniel?"

"Yes, hi. Mark?"

Ascending the curved staircase, I meet Mark Semaan, General Manager of RedHotPie.com (RHP) – Australia's third biggest online dating site. We lead each other through a large open plan café and bar area, almost completely deserted on a weekday morning, past an abandoned child playing Deep Purple's "Smoke on the Water" on the hotel's grand piano.

Semaan runs what is euphemistically called a "sexy dating" site. Unlike most dating sites, which target the mainstream population looking for relationships and soul mates, RHP targets people looking for fuck buddies and casual sex, orgies, swinging and everything in between. The strange thing is though, his audience is looking more and more like the mainstream every week: his site now claims over a million users.

He's excited because not only has he grown this business from a garage operation four years ago to a million dollar enterprise, but he can feel the future. RHP has always built itself on the idea of being an interactive community site. It encourages people to post photo shoots of themselves having sex, engage in sexy webcams with each other, write stories about sex, chat about sex in forums, post questions, and organise orgies at their suburban villas ("free drinks and lube, 8 pm–12 pm"). It's user generated, and it's a community, and right now that means buzz. Giant, cosmic oscillations; sleepless nights, visions of rapid expansion. He's found himself a bit part in the Web 2.0 bubble. He can feel it. Three months ago he went and saw Shawn Gold – CMO of MySpace – talk at an ad:tech conference. He felt at home, amongst his own. A Sex 2.0 start-up entrepreneur, mining gold at the nexus of online porn and social networking.

He's also excited because he's about to launch RHP in the UK. The global online dating industry has traditionally been dominated by safe, relationship-oriented sites. That was, until the American based FriendFinder Network – led by sexy dating leviathan AdultFriendFinder.com (AFF) – began trouncing competition globally. AFF now claims 18.4 million unique visitors a month, 13 million more than its nearest competitor Yahoo!

Personals, and in the UK has four times the audience of its closest rival LoopyLove (Nielsen NetRatings: June, 2007). In Australia AdultMatchMaker.com (AMM), RHP's only major 'sexy dating' competitor, stands second on the national league table of personals sites (Alexa Ratings: 2007). But unlike AMM, RHP was started by hobbyists with no seed capital.

Semaan met his business partner Max at a dinner party in Perth, Western Australia, in 2003. Max, who worked in marketing, had an idea for a more risqué dating site, and Semaan, who was implementing software for the world's largest mining company, BHP Billiton, had the technical knowledge.

They launched a beta site of RHP in late 2003, and within three months they had 25,000 members. There was no marketing, the name just caught on. By the end of 2004, they decided to take a risk – they filmed a television ad using a handheld camera and a team of friends acting out a wild party scene. It cost them a mere AUS $5000 (approx. £2000) to run, late at night on Channel 7 in Perth, and immediately the site exploded. Both partners quit their jobs as the site outgrew Perth's population of 1.5 million, and focused on marketing to east coast users, filming their commercials in front of iconic landmarks like the Sydney Harbour Bridge to convince people RHP wasn't just a local site.

Now, with the money coming in, Semaan is growing messianic.

"We are the MySpace of the adult community in Australia," he says, soft voice quivering and eyes lighting up.

Like all dating sites, RHP tries to increase the ease and efficiency of meeting new people; they're not so much greasing the wheels for love and relationships, as marketing hyper-promiscuity. Most members' profiles contain nude pictures – blurry images of bums and breasts and penises, with bedroom mirrors reflecting camera flashes. Part of the sign up process involves listing the sexual activities you're willing to be involved in: anal play, mutual masturbation, MFM threesomes. They're soon to introduce location based searching using mobile phone WAP technology and the software platform Twister. RHP members will be able to track other users to within 100 metres while they're out at bars and clubs, view each other's profiles on their phones, then suggest an "instant date". It's not new technology, but it's effective.

Their Datefinder feature – where members post their availability by time and date for casual liaisons – is already attracting thousands of listings a week. Semaan's other push is for more user-generated content.

"You see sex on porn websites, you see it in magazines and you fantasise about it, and you think – is that real? Is it only professionals that do it?" Semaan says.

"When you go to RHP you find that you're not the only one, everybody's doing it, and that you can be your own star. We get people who post photo sets on a monthly basis, and if they take a break everyone will say, 'Hey what happened?' Members become used to them putting up photos; they get a following."

About 50 full photo sets are posted each month, but it's growing. With the introduction of WAP technology people will also be able to upload pictures from their phones.

"A bit like *Girls Gone Wild*," says Semaan.

He's also about to introduce a video upload feature, something which has proven phenomenally popular on a site called YouPorn, which within the last 12 months skyrocketed from nowhere to become one of the top 100 global Internet sites (Alexa Ratings, 2007). A lascivious simulacrum of YouTube devoted to user-generated porn, it has a facility to post comments below videos creating community involvement.

In one video on the site a young Belgian couple, particularly in sway with this community spirit, have filmed themselves interacting with a message board during the act of coitus. A fan asks whether the woman is capable of fellating the entire length of her partner's penis. She reads the post from a nearby computer screen and accepts the challenge, before the couple engage in a prolonged fit of rapturous lovemaking.

In another film, entitled simply "train station", a blonde wearing a puffy black polyester jacket to protect against biting winds perches on the stairwell rails of a German train station, receiving cunnilingus from her female lover while a stream of startled onlookers walk in parabolas of disgust and bemusement around them. An early morning commuter train arrives just as the blonde unleashes a stream of urine into the mouth of her willing accomplice.

Enthusiasm for user-generated content, says Semaan, is not a problem, and sometimes needs to be reigned in.

"Allowing people to explore their sexuality and fantasies you sometimes reach a dangerous point," he says.

"There are a few girls having fantasies about being raped for example. They can talk about it, but once we realise they're actually getting two girls to act out a rape scene and they've asked some guys to come along, this could cause problems and we shut it down."

As Internet users become accustomed and addicted to the varying forms of minor celebrity offered by Web 2.0 applications, sexual exhibitionism has begun to make intuitive sense to a lot of people. Browsing the profiles of RHP members presents you with an infinite gallery of middle aged men, bored wives, insecure teenagers, engineers, accountants, skinny hipsters and permed spinsters, all posing in varying personal interpretations of "sexiness", privately undressing and assuming libidinous gestures in front of their cameras. Many men opt for a muscle flex, fighting through layers of fat to reveal forgotten abdominals. Or they look over their shoulders, cheekily pulling the top of their pants down to offer the viewer vision of their arse cracks. The women bare their breasts but hide their faces, or lie face down on their beds, poking their buttocks skyward and draping their hair along their backs.

"I want to suk and fuk your big, thick dik all night long."

Earlier this year Californian sex therapist Michael Simon, in an article by the Associated Press's Martha Irvine, reported a large spike in the number of teenage girls placed in therapy after being caught undressing or masturbating in front of web cams.

"Instead of pornography or performative sexuality being one

choice among many ways of being sexual, it's essentially become the standard of sexiness," said Simon.

Semaan sees RHP more as a healthy way to overcome sexual isolation and explore fantasy and taboo.

"We know for a fact that everybody thinks about sex, that everybody has their fantasies. And rather than feeling – 'Hey, are we the only ones or am I weird thinking like that?' – they realise there are a lot of other people, and that they're not freaks, they're just normal. I mean, we have a million plus members who are over 18, in a country where there's 20 million people – and if you take the older people and the under 18s out, you realise 20-25% of the population are using a site like RHP. It astounds you.

"We try as hard as we can to make people feel it's not something creepy, it's natural. If you think it's natural, and everyone is enjoying it, then people will like it. I think we find the right balance between talking about sexuality without feeling sleazy."

To reach this balance they have tried to tone down their opening page. Whilst the market leader AMM, with its imagery of naked women and slogan "Explore your naughty side," is angling itself towards the taboo obsessed American public, RHP have focused on peppy, cheeky copywriting, and images of laughing, smiling couples. They offer two dating options: "Singles Dating", a traditional dating network, and "Original Uncut", a sexfest.

The "Original Uncut" section is overwhelmingly more popular, but having the two options creates the impression of a normal dating site… with a deep end.

They've also eschewed the slightly disgusting requirements of their Australian competitor AMM, who ask new users to list the dimensions of their genitals and their pubic hair grooming habits. They've been clever and subtle, and so far it's been effective. And in their latest initiative to sanitise the site, as they prepare to move further into the mainstream, they've hired the prominent Australian sexpert couple Bessie Bardot and Geoff Barker to become the public faces of RHP.

Bardot and Barker are part of a strange tribe of entertainers with a sanitised erotic edge, appearing frequently on radio and in magazines in Australia to discuss sex and relationships, and recently hosting *Erotic Star*, a cable reality TV show that repackaged *Pop Idol* for pole dancers. Cheeky, platinum smiles; bedroom tips for mums and dads.

Arriving at their Woolloomooloo apartment, overlooking the Domain Parklands in Sydney, I'm greeted by Bardot, who takes my umbrella. Her British husband Geoff Barker, aka Commando from the mid 90s Australian TV series *Gladiators*, walks into view from the back passageway. Strings of glass beads that hang from the roof move aside for his bulky frame as he enters the living room, which is a shrine to the female body. One corner of the room is covered in a collage of swimsuit shots cut from magazines; on another wall is a giant Pirelli poster featuring an oiled model whose breasts poke out the bottom of her bikini top.

Bardot, 29, blonde, is made up perfectly, clothes perfectly arranged and adjusted. Former body model turned entrepreneur, her look is something like "sexy secretary" – hair styled immaculately to the point of looking like a wig, tight knee length beige skirt, bust elevated but cleavage covered by a spotless white vest under her armless top, snakeskin stilettos.

They're just back from Iraq, where they were MCs on a concert tour for Australian troops.

"There are male and female troops there, so they brought Geoff along as some eye candy," says Bessie from the kitchen, making a cup of tea.

I sit across from Barker, 37, on their leather couches.

"Yeeesss, I did my best," he says, stretching back into the couch smiling, unconsciously flexing his pectorals, his silk shirt, unbuttoned at the neck, spreading apart to reveal a leathery, tanned chest.

In February this year they were approached by the RHP team.

"They contacted us one day and said, 'Look, we're interested in you doing some dating advice, and it would kind of be nice to have you guys as a bit of a husband and wife team,'" says Geoff.

Bessie leans forward: "When they came to us, I personally really liked the fresh look of the site, and the fact that there are so many different options for women. Some of the other sites can look a bit 'dark', and this had a really good feel to it."

"It's very progressive. It's a fascinating world really, it's fabulous," Geoff says.

In a recent article the couple published on RHP, they answered a member's query, asking how best to entice their partner into swinging:

"The best trick is to play fantasies together," they wrote. "Over time bring the subject of real people into your discussions and pretty soon you'll be talking about all sorts of semi-real life fantasy situations, like imagine when that hot pizza guy came around, or if that sexy clothing shop girl had walked in the changing rooms, etc. Next discuss what you like and want from this and get on RHP and explore the feeling of actually talking to real people."

Bardot, Barker and Semaan all talk about a large user base who play online, without necessarily needing to follow through with actual sexual encounters. It's a gradual process, they say: people test the water on the site for a while as a free member, then sign up for a paid membership to get better privileges and become more a part of the community. They chat online, perhaps use the webcams, and then maybe, as their confidence grows, start physically exploring their sexuality with real members in the real world.

"It really helps women explore their sexuality, because we're conditioned as we're young to think that we shouldn't actually be interested in sex, we shouldn't even be that interested in flirting, and that we should let people come to us," says Bardot.

"So for a lot of women that then becomes their sexuality for their whole lives. And there's a huge proportion of women who at 60 are only really discovering who they are. Online this whole new side to your personality can come out which is a little bit cheekier. Women especially can find that they kind of tap into their inner vixen."

"I think the owners of the site were determined to be able to provide a service that made everybody feel comfortable," says Geoff, "whether it was a young innocent Christian virgin who wants to find the man of her dreams, or someone who likes to get together with 10 people in their home and get naked and rub baby oil all over each other."

The diversity of sexual offerings is a feature RHP shares with the world of online porn; like the web itself it has tried to remain general and unthemed, a place where you can lose yourself amongst a cornucopia of different sexual images and ideas.

It's a theme Sean Thomas explored in his 2006 book on Internet porn and dating, *Millions of Women Are Waiting to Meet You*. Online porn, he said, revealed to men "that they have peccadillos aplenty, hidden in the cellar of their libido". He found he had a strange fascination with dental themed lesbian porn, and Russian spanking; trawling the Internet awakened fetishes and desires hitherto unknown to him.

"I hear a lot of people say, 'I came in here wanting to find the man of my dreams,'" says Barker, "And of course, curiosity killed the cat: they suddenly have a little peak into the more risqué parts of the site. Because everybody wants to indulge in a little voyeurism, to have a little peek at what the other half are doing, and then they go, 'Oh these people aren't so weird, they don't have big gold chains on.' Well, not all of them anyway." He starts laughing.

"Geoff's got his on under his shirt," Bessie says. Barker unbuttons his silk shirt further, revealing a thick gold chain. When asked in 2003 whether theirs was an open marriage, Bardot replied, "We have fun here and there, so do many people."

Happy to partake in anything that keeps them smiling, and dispensing simple, pragmatic relationship advice through their many self-help books, they're homely sexual liberationists on a suburban crusade: stiff hair products and perfume, and a sunny, pants down attitude.

"Why don't other sites do this?" I ask.

"Aside from AdultMatchMaker the other ones try and stay very far away from it, because they... I don't know why to be honest, because of the social taboo," Barker says, sounding disappointed, deflated, and slumping into the couch, then sitting back up. "But I think that's ridiculous. I think people should be able to do whatever the heck they want.

"And they're doing it with class too, they're not doing it in a smutty, sleazy way, they're doing it in a way which is totally up front. The way that RHP merges swingers sites with straight dating sites makes everyone feel like they're just people."

Not everyone feels normal on the site though. Steve, a 28 year-old electrician from Perth, was turned onto the community by some miners he met at a bar, who were in town from the remote Nifty copper mine in northern Western Australia. They used RHP to tee up casual encounters with women when they came back to the city on their weeks off. He thought he'd give it a try.

"Basically, it seemed to me that there were just hundreds of guys on the site, and the girls got hammered with desperados. Lots of psychos are just hitting them up for sex straight away. I remember MSNing a couple of girls on the site, and they were telling me about how they were bombarded by nude pics of guys – photos of their cocks – and then they got off the site because it was getting ridiculous."

A quick survey of RHP's Datefinder option, where people list their availability for sex by day and time, reveals overwhelmingly more men posting dates, with names like yeahbaby69er2005, throbbinghelmet and Can_You_Imagine. Trawling through these profiles there is an eerie sense of having cast off into a deep, dark psychic space, peopled by the desperate and aggressive fantasies men have of themselves and their "seXXyness".

...
*A slut or sex slave will do mee nicely. I don't
want anything complicated*

...

Dare to fullfil your SEX fantasies with me!!!

...

Sex like the porn stars... thats what I'm looking
for!!!

...

dont b shy sexy lady call me and w hook up
2day im very openmind ladys so dont b shy hear
from ya soon

...

Other users complain of a variety of scams – especially phantom
profiles set up by the site's administrators to lure new paid
members.

One systems analyst from the American website Scam.com
devised a simple test for RHP called "Hunky Guy v Geek Man".
He made two new profiles: one an attractive, successful man, the
other a "40 year old virgin who still lives with his mum".

"What you'll notice is that EXACTLY the same chicks look at
each stooge's profile," he says. "Whether he is God's gift to women
or the dork who works in the IT area, they get visited by the same
babes."

Worse, when he sent messages to these "babes" from both
Hunky Guy and Geek Man he received the "same reply flirts at the
SAME time."

Prognosis: automated sex bots.

AdultFriendFinder.com has even been accused of placing hired
plants in their chat rooms, who seduce first time users into buying
memberships. RHP, AFF and AMM all work on a subscriptions
revenue model, where the more expensive the membership you
buy, the more you're able to send messages to other members. Most
women end up having free profiles, which cannot be messaged
from other free profiles, forcing the men to buy memberships so
they can initiate chat with women on the site – a bit like buying a
girl a drink in a bar. My free profile was immediately contacted by
"kinkynhot", a cartoonishly attractive free member, who sent me a

professionally lit picture of her spread buttocks as she lent over an apartment balcony.

Semaan says that a lot of these fake profiles are SMS scammers – people who ask you to message them on premium rate phone lines, and initiate a text chat that costs about AUS $5 (approx. £2) per message. RHP has a security team that weeds out these profiles by looking for multiple identities set up from the same IP address.

The main problem for sexy dating sites though isn't scammers, or members accusing the company of setting up automated sex bots. It's much simpler than that – WOMEN.

Whether it's because promiscuity has typically been glamorised for men and used as a slur against women, or because most women are looking for more than just physical gratification, marketing casual sex to a broad female audience is difficult, and takes inventiveness and intelligence.

Witness European dating site Meetic, whose new ad campaign works with the slogan "Same Game, New Rules". Their French TV commercial promotes the idea of women as the new sexual predators: they ask their male workmates for condoms before a date and they fall asleep after sex while their male companion waxes lyrical about how great it was. In one scene a man hops on the back of a woman's scooter and indecisively moves his hands around in front of her, trying to work out where it's appropriate to hold on. She grabs his hands and places them decisively on her breasts.

"Sexy dating is a little bit threatening for women," says Semaan.

But he's confident about RHP's launch in the UK. Meetic, who bought the UK's third biggest dating site DatingDirect.com in February this year, are so large and mainstream that they can't risk moving into "sexy dating" without alienating their customers, Semaan says. He also sees a point of differentiation from AFF in the UK, as they are marketing themselves like a porn site and are accused of having an incredibly low female user base.

"They have community features on their site, but they're not a community," he says. AMM's UK site is little more than a shell, and the other players in the British market are small and disorganised. He plans to use word of mouth amongst the massive Australian diaspora in the UK to launch the site, as well as offering free memberships and getting his own localised PR team to make RHP UK feel like a genuine British community site.

"Peter André and Jordan?" I suggest.

"Maybe," he says, smiling.

Semaan can smell the potential for this, as a generation becomes accustomed to social networking. He can smell the mainstream, and mainstream dollars: money tremulating along the electric tangents of computer lust, resonating, amplifying into a roaring flood of cash. Various, the parent company of AFF, are now worth US $200 million (approx. £100 million). RHP has one twentieth of their user base, but is growing rapidly.

With growth comes rebranding, and a drive to sanitise his company. I ask him about the inspiration for the name Red Hot Pie.

"Red is the colour of passion, hot is the sensation of passion."

And pie? He pauses, visibly racks his brain, searching for a re-explanation for this most obvious of sexual euphemisms: a warm, carmine pink, vaguely circular thing that may in certain situations be tasted, licked or "consumed."

"The word pie is based on the concept of a community, and you being in a Web 2.0 user environment where you can put in your share. You are actually one piece of the pie, the pie being the whole community. You are a part of it, other people help make up the pie."

Blood In, Blood Out

Billy Briggs

The ambulance arrives, siren wailing, and a team of medics run to the entrance of Accident and Emergency. Doors burst open and a trolley is lowered down, a young man lying on it groaning. It is 2.19 am. Gersen Armando Ramirez Santus, a tattooed gang member nicknamed Lucifer, has just been shot twice in the chest on the streets of Guatemala City.

He is wheeled into San Juan Dion Hospital followed by a paramedic filming the scene on a camcorder. Startled onlookers watch as Lucifer is rushed past them, frantic medical staff barking orders to each other in Spanish. In the emergency treatment room Lucifer is stripped naked by a team of young medics. A catheter is inserted into his penis, a drip into his left arm. He twists and moans as a doctor presses his chest. Lucifer is the 10th shooting victim to be brought to the hospital in as many hours, alongside a taxi driver who'd been macheted across the face, and a patient wheeled in with his intestines piled on his stomach. His clothes join others strewn across a blood-stained floor, the ward now resembling a field hospital. A row of fearful, wide-eyed patients, suffering from a variety of gunshot, knife and machete wounds, watch as doctors try to stabilise Lucifer. The smell of sweat, fear and death permeates the room. Lucifer lifts his head slightly.

He is drugged, bemused, an anaesthetic bringing a sense of calm to his chaos. These are his last moments alive perhaps. Two holes where the bullets entered Lucifer's chest are clearly visible, pock-marking his tattooed torso. The wounds make his brown Latino skin look strangely like rubber or plastic. He is staring at me. He stretches out his hand and speaks in English, surprisingly with an American accent.

"Can I use your phone please, Sir? I have to phone my brother…"

A couple of young female nurses are examining his body. His torso, legs, and arms bear dozens of tattoos. One of them, XV3, on his back, denotes his gang loyalty: Mara 18. One girl laughs, covers her mouth with her hand and points. Lucifer has numerous sexual positions from the *Kama Sutra* inked onto his skin: entwined erotic figures about one inch high. I smile too.

"Can I use your phone please, Sir?" Lucifer says again, his voice jolting me, while his tattooed arm stretches out towards my pocket. The medics look at me. I stand, stare back, and say nothing. Arcane thoughts run through my head. Everything seems to slow.

"Give him the bloody phone," says Angie, the photographer, exasperated, dropping her camera from face level.

Everyone is still looking at me. Waiting for my line.

"But what if he uses up all our credit?" I blurt out, inexplicably. What I mean is that I'm bloody petrified of being stranded here with no credit left on our only phone, and trying to flag down a taxi while dodging muggers and rapists. He's not exactly going to run off with it though, is he?

Alberto, the senior doctor in charge tonight, nods his head and beckons me to come closer. Lucifer stretches out an arm and takes the phone. He grimaces, carefully punching in a number.

"Romeo, they shot me. If I don't make it… goodbye Romeo." Lucifer hands back the bloodied phone and lays down his head.

"I can't believe you said that," Angie says the next morning over brunch.

"Neither can I," I mumble.

"Do you want to go and see if he's still alive?" I say.

"Why don't you just call his friends and find out?"

"What do you mean?"

Then I realise that my phone, like millions of others, has a redial button. I pick it up and call the number Lucifer had keyed in the night before.

"Hello," the voice answers in an American drawl.

It is Romeo. After I explain who I am, Romeo informs me Lucifer is still alive, and is actually doing OK.

Next morning, after breakfast, we decide to go and visit him, back in San Juan Dion Hospital. After two hours of trawling through unsanitary wards, which stink of urine and excrement, we eventually find Lucifer, who is attached to a drip and hobbling back from the toilet. He sees us and breaks into a smile.

"I remember you guys," he says.

Holding his left arm to his chest, he slowly sits down on his bed, clearly in a lot of pain.

"The doctors said I died twice after you left but I'm going to be OK," he says.

We get a distinct feeling Lucifer feels indebted to us in some way. His very last words before we left the hospital the night he'd been shot were:

"Please don't leave me, the doctors won't treat me because I am *maras*."

Perhaps the presence of journalists had helped his situation in A & E. The *maras* are responsible for much of the extreme violence in Guatemala, and are despised by the wider population. It's rumoured that some of the hospitals refuse to treat them.

We talk over the events of that night, which he can remember clearly, despite his trauma. He was returning from a party in a taxi, when his driver suddenly pulled over to the side of the road.

"The driver said there was something wrong with the taxi and got out. These four men appeared and demanded money. I don't take no shit from anyone, so I fought with them and then ran."

It was after he'd escaped his would-be robbers that he was injured.

"I got away and was still running, when the police appeared out of nowhere and shot me… I suppose because I have tattoos."

At that point in Guatemala City, relations between the numerous local gangs and the police have escalated into a small-scale war. A few days earlier, the authorities had stormed Pavel Prison, a local jail under control of the drug cartels, shooting seven gang members dead.

"Why don't you report it – press charges?" I ask.

"It don't work like that here. The police are as bad as the gangs. I know who set me up, so I could get him killed, quite easily. Friends from LA said they'll come down," Lucifer says, fixing me with a stare.

His family moved to Los Angeles from Guatemala after his father was killed during the 36-year civil war. He points to a tattoo that reads "Rest In Peace Elizardo," and then to another in Spanish that translates as "Many Men Wished My Death".

By the age of 10 in LA he was running with the notorious Mara 18, quickly earning the nickname Tas, short for Tasmanian Devil. It was an accolade bestowed by older gang members because of his stature and violent temper. Joining the gang had been tough. Initiation rights included being beaten to a pulp by fellow members, and then being forced to dress as a tramp, walk into enemy territory, and let rip with an Uzi machine gun.

"Did you kill anyone?"

"I don't know. I didn't stop to see. I ran like fuck."

By the age of 14 he had graduated to the moniker Lucifer, and at the age of 15 was given a life sentence for murder. He ended up in Pelican Bay Prison, California's highest security institution.

"On my third day there the homies told me to whack someone. I was a bad ass and I even slashed my cousin inside, because he disrespected the gang," Lucifer says.

His expression can change in an instant, boyish and charming to cold and savage. I picture some poor guy sitting in a prison canteen shitting his pants and trying not to watch as Lucifer sharpens the blade of a knife on his pearly white teeth, while drawing an index finger slowly across his neck.

Lucifer is no longer in a gang, though. He was released two years ago on appeal in the wake of the Rampart police corruption probe, an LAPD scandal where almost 100 wrongful arrests were overturned on the evidence of disgraced officer Rafael Perez.

"When I was released I cried all the way back to LA. I believe that God has given me another chance, so I am finished with gangs," Lucifer says.

Deciding that enough was enough, he left the USA for Guatemala to start a new life. He chose to come to Guatemala City because he has a sister and stepsisters here. Does he regret his past life: the violence and killing?

"I have no regrets. My life was my life and has made me who I am today. It was good, but it sucked at the same time. I have learned my lessons."

Three days after being shot twice in the chest, and against the doctors' advice, Lucifer left hospital for home. Angie and I call him and are invited to his girlfriend Margarita's house to take some more pictures. It takes about 45 minutes in a taxi to drive from the downtown to the suburbs of Guatemala City, and on the way we pass through an infamous area called the *barrancos*, whose gorges are a favourite dumping place for bodies. Unnervingly, vultures hover above us in an azure blue sky.

Margarita's home is in a poor area, with narrow, dusty streets lined by single-storey concrete buildings, with cracked walls and flaking paint.

As we alight the car, faces stare at us from every doorway. I'd called Lucifer from the taxi and, right on cue, he appears at the door of one of the nearby houses, greeting us with a smile. Dressed in white jeans and white vest, he looks like he's just stepped off the set of *Miami Vice*.

"I'm in so much pain today, so I can't talk for long," he says, furrowing his eyebrows.

We are taken into Margarita's bedroom, where cuddly toys sit on a bed beneath a poster of Winnie the Pooh.

"Would you like some *Coke?*" Lucifer says, motioning to Margarita to go to the kitchen. He picks up the remote control for the TV and VCR, and turns on a violent action flick.

"This is my favourite film. *Blood In, Blood Out.* It's about gangs in prisons," Lucifer says, increasing the volume.

The three of us watch the screen for about five minutes in silence. Lucifer is transfixed.

"'Blood In' means you have to spill someone else's blood to join, usually murder. It's so undercover cops can't infiltrate gangs, as they won't kill," he says.

"'Blood Out' is when you try to leave the gang. Some gangs will beat you up or even kill you. I was allowed to leave my gang because I was moving to Guatemala."

Margarita appears with three glasses of *Coke*, sits on the bed and puts her arms around Lucifer's shoulders. He winces in pain as she kisses him on the cheek.

"Is this Mara 18 territory?" I ask.

"No, this is Salvatrucha territory. But I don't get no bother from them as they know I've left the gang. I even do tattoos for them," Lucifer says.

He motions to Margarita again and she goes to the corner of the room, retrieving a white Tupperware box. Inside, there is a homemade tattoo kit with inks and needles.

"I did most of my own tattoos using a mirror. In prison I did all the guys too. I charged US $25 for the *Kama Sutra* figures. I even did Margarita's tattoos," he says, pointing to her face. Her lips and eyebrows have pencil-thin tattooed blue outlines. Lucifer tells us his artistic skills are inherited from his late father who was a graphic artist.

"I'd like to teach art but no-one will give me a job because of all the tattoos I have… because I was in a gang. That's the way it works here. Once a gang member, always a gang member," Lucifer says.

"I'm trying really hard to sort out my life but it ain't easy. I just don't want to fall back into trouble – trouble seems to follow me about.

"I have the same dream all the time, where I am baptised, and when I come up from under the water all my tattoos have gone."

Margarita kisses him again and he grimaces once more. Concerned, she leans over and whispers something to him in Spanish.

"She's telling me off for not resting. I should really be in hospital. I only have paracetamol for the pain, so I'm not so good today. I should sleep," Lucifer says.

"We should get off, we have a plane to catch," I say, nodding to Angie.

"I'll phone you a taxi," Lucifer says, pausing, "but, then again, maybe that's not such a good idea."

The three of us burst out laughing.

CULTURAL REVELATIONS

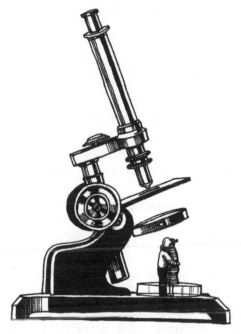

Specialise In Something Until It Specialises In You

London Quiz Mafia • Hard Drive Enema
Cricket Life Metaphors • Günter Wallraff
Gourmands vs. Foodies • Dubai Sex Traffic

Put Those Hackysackers on a Rocket and Blow Them All to Hell

Chris Flynn

Anyone who has ever stayed in a youth hostel, guest house or camp ground knows that you are bound to encounter at some time or other a juggler, fire-twirler or hacky sack player. Whether or not we are supposed to be impressed by their amateur clowning, I am not sure.

Fire-twirlers raise an eyebrow on me at the most, as it is, after all, fire they are playing with, and there are a lot of combustible dreadlocks in the mix. There's always a chance you might witness a self-immolation.

Jugglers, on the other hand, are scum. No human being in sound mind should ever attempt to juggle, unless they are wearing a red nose and size 16 shoes, and even then it should only be done to stop the whining of small children.

Which leaves hacky sack players. How does society deal with these show-offs? Are "hackytration" camps the solution? You put 500 hacky sackers together, the smallest ones roll up into balls and the others toss them over the razor wire, neutralising the guards with some 80s robotic dancing. Next thing you know, you've got a horde of crazed escapee hacky sackers roaming the countryside in packs (hacky packs), devastating crops and raiding new age stores, your country ends up with a chronic shortage of incense, your economy collapses, the World Bank and U.S. Marine Corps move in to restore order, hacky rights abuses are committed and your society circles the drain.

This bullshit is all leading somewhere, should you be wondering.

Sitting on the steps outside a goof hostel in Montreal, enjoying the morning sun and waiting for my ride, my reverie was broken, nay shattered, by the emergence of an individual of unmistakably Scandinavian appearance, who proceeded to reverentially produce a battered, brightly coloured soft ball from his pocket, hefting it suggestively.

"Is that a hacky sack?" I winced, knowing it was.

"Yes," he smiled. "I always practise in the mornings when no one is around. Do you mind?"

At least he was polite enough to ask.

"As long as it doesn't end up in my tea," I warned him.

Something about what he had said rankled me though.

"You always practise in the mornings?" I queried.

He looked surprised.

"Of course. I have to practise every day, and first thing in the morning is best to get me in a good mood for the day ahead."

I nodded sagely. "I prefer masturbation myself, but each to their own I suppose."

I glanced at the time on my phone, wishing the two Dutch girls who were taking me away from all this madness for a few days would come careening around the corner before he started. I had no real urge to witness the hacky sack version of having a wank.

Nonetheless, it seemed I was to be privy to this private act of hack-onanism. He began his idiotic leaping around, whilst I safeguarded my tea. I tried not to look, preferring instead to stare at the gutter, which was infinitely more interesting.

The pat-pat-pat of tiny beans rolling around inside a woven sack continued for several minutes, boring into my brain. My only consolation was the beeping horn of my beautiful Dutch saviours as they turned the corner and sped down the street to meet me. We exchanged hugs and greetings, and I was just about to launch into my, 'Boy, am I glad you're here' speech when Sophia – tall, ash blonde hair – exclaimed, 'Ooh, hacky sack!'

and promptly began ignoring me in favour of the monkey-like antics of my nemesis.

"Wow, you're very good," she told him.

Without missing a hack, he smiled and said cryptically, "Not good enough, perhaps."

"Good enough for what?" She inquired.

"I'm in town for the World Championships," he announced casually. "And I'll have to keep practising if I'm going to defend my crown."

At this point I felt compelled to intervene.

"Come on Sophia, let's go, it's getting late, I'm very keen to make a start towards wherever it is we're going."

Sophia, whose grasp of English was not as complete as Lonneke's (small, short blonde hair, prime subject of onanistic fantasy), was confused by his expression.

"Defend your crown?" She looked to her companion.

"Are you the current World Champion?" Lonneke asked him, my heart racing at her cheeky expression, suddenly wishing I was current World Champion of something, then remembering the only thing I was really good at was spilling other people's drinks.

"Yes, but I won't win this year. There are a couple of guys better than me now."

Magnanimous prick.

"Wow, you should come with us. We're going to see a ghost town!" Sophia jumped around in excitement.

Without skipping a beat, the dude caught his hacky mid-spin and climbed into the back seat of the car. I watched in astonishment as the girls took their places too.

"Is this strange guy coming with us?" I asked Lonneke, hands indignantly splayed on hips.

"We only met you the day before yesterday," she reminded me.

"Yes, so that's two full days you've known me. That's 200% more getting to know time than this guy. Plus, he plays hacky for god's sake."

"I know. He's the current World Champion."

I raised my hands in deference to his superior status.

"Fine. Fine. Just don't blame me if something goes badly wrong. It's always a risk with their sort."

We finally found our ghost town – called "*Esperance*" or some such pioneering nonsense – after much map consulting and retracing our steps down back roads, driving into town a little after noon.

"It's eerie," I whispered to Lonneke, who agreed, rewarding me with a shiver. The other two did not know what the word meant, so I resolved to use as many obscure phrases as possible to establish my superiority over Lens ("Your parents named you after part of a camera?" I had scoffed, trying to embarrass him. "Yes, that's right!" he had replied enthusiastically, apparently glad I had understood correctly).

"What do you think happened here?" asked Lens as we climbed out of the car into the dusty street.

"Probably just smallpox," I opined. "You've been inoculated though, right?"

His brow furrowed. "I... I think so."

"Well, we'll soon find out, eh?" I replied heartily, giving him a friendly slap on the back. Lonneke approached one of the houses, peering in through a cobwebbed window. I followed her, the pit of my stomach heaving as I pushed the front door.

"You two coming?" I asked Lens and Sophia.

"Noo, no," Sophia stalled. "I'm going for a walk down the street. It's a bit scary for me."

"Uh, yeah, I'll do that too," Lens gulped. Pussy.

The house was dimly lit by thin beams of light coming through the cracks in the walls. Butterflies swooped around my stomach as we walked slowly up the creaking staircase, careful to test each step for safety first. We came to a big bedroom with bay windows, only a few panes broken. Disengaging her hand from mine, Lonneke crept quietly to one wall, examining the mark left where a picture had once been hanging.

I watched her run her fingers over the rectangle shape, and for a moment as she turned her head sideways to look towards the windows I thought I was having a vision of some sort. She looked extraordinarily beautiful and my legs buckled slightly at the knees. I thought I was going to faint.

My body was telling me to walk quickly to her, put my arm around her waist and meet her lips as she turned to embrace me, but my foolish, boyish mind was sending out a different message.

'What if she doesn't want to?' it was bleating. 'You don't want to embarrass yourself, do you?' Ahh, the vagaries and uncertainties of youth.

Voices from outside ended the moment, and we both moved towards the windows, affording us a view of a small, pebbled beach next to a breathtakingly large lake. To my surprise, Sophia was in the process of taking off her bra. She looked up at us and gave us a wave.

"We're going swimming," she yelled. Lens was trying to pull his combat pants off next to her, a little too eagerly I thought, but in that pleasingly clumsy fashion men fall into when they sense the prospect of sex.

"We'll be right down," Lonneke called back, pulling the bay windows shut again.

"Come on," she urged me, skipping quickly out of the room and down the stairs, dust motes scattering in her wake. I followed slowly, nervously. The prospect of watching her undress next to me was almost too much to bear. By the time I got there, she was walking naked into the cold, clear water, her back to shore. I shook my head, muttering under my breath to calm down. Lens knew he now had the upper hand. He stood up in the shallows, his ripped, tanned body and ample leathery penis mocking me.

"Come on man, it's freezing but it's good!"

Freezing, eh? Then why isn't that serpent the size of a walnut?

"Oh, I'm not a very good swimmer," I protested pathetically, nervous about the inevitable comparison of assets.

Lonneke emerged from below the surface of the water, gasping for air. She smiled at me and stood up, droplets shimmering in the sun as they leapt off her body.

"Come on," she shivered. "I'll protect you."

Postscript:

It was not until four years later when Lonneke and I spent a single week together, touring vineyards and small, intimate hotels in the Champagne region of France that the love that had been bubbling under the surface all those long months finally saw the light of day. I never saw her again, and now, when I recall those seven days in each other's arms, something I don't know how to describe within me aches just a little.

Moral Lesson:

Years later, after much trawling through the lists of results at footbag.org, and other sites for this disturbed community, I discovered Lens was not only not the reigning world champion, but he failed to place in any event at the Montreal 1996 Worlds. The four-time hacky sack Men's Overall World Champion from 1993–1996 was Allan Petersen from Denmark, a pioneer in the – ahem – "sport" and designer of his own line of sacks (or 'footbags' as he so quaintly called them). Petersen was renowned at the time for his boofhead of curly locks. Lens had short hair and a goatee. He was simply an impostor, an also-ran footbagger, laying claim to the title to get into the knickers of backpacker chicks. This discovery devastated me, primarily because I did not think of it first.

After all, there was a Sean Flynn competing, I could have been him.

The Quiz Mafia Muscling in on *Millionaire*

Alyssa McDonald

The evening Chris first brought Olav Bjortomt to the pub quiz at our local, I arrived late, just as the first round was about to start.

Quiz night is always a busy one at the George, an East End boozer replete with stuffed birds in glass cases, four-inch thick mahogany bar top and a life size bust of Brunel. The place starts filling up early, and by five to nine drinkers are jostling to buy their beers, get their answer sheets and lay claim to the last few empty seats before the music is turned down and the questions begin. Amidst the clatter of scraping stools, raised voices and the dying strains of a David Bowie track, Olav, slight and younger-looking than his 28 years, sat quietly in a fug of fag smoke with his head down, one thumb positioned on the corner of the answer sheet, waiting. He didn't even look up when I introduced myself. While the rest of our team drank pints of overpriced Czech lager, chatted over the quizmaster's tinnily amplified questions, and muttered uncertain responses in undertones, he devoted his energies in joyless silence to the quiz, calmly filling in each and every answer. When the time came, he acknowledged his inevitable win with a slight nod, shared his £20 beer token with Chris, then went home.

Olav, it turned out, is a quizzing master: a European and World general knowledge champion and esteemed runner-up on such daytime TV mainstays as *15 to 1*. I made a mental note never to go to a pub quiz with him again, but, somehow, the thought of hardcore trivia devotees was intriguing. I emailed Olav, and received a surprisingly friendly invitation to a meeting of the Quiz League of London, a collective of game show luminaries who meet each week to pit their wits against one another. It promised to be a good game: the league's top two teams were competing, and if Olav's side won, the season title was theirs. But he thought I might be "bored senseless"; this kind of quiz could be silly and parochial. The questions were largely about history, literature, and science: pop culture was resolutely shunned.

"I've heard of outrage over questions about things like *Seinfeld*," he said. "Quizzing is truly a middle-aged man's game. With really bad sweaters."

In the basement of The Old Star in Westminster, a cove had been reserved for this top-of-the-table QLL fixture – Olav's team, Broken Hearts, vs. Allsorts, captained by Kevin Ashman, winner of just about every TV and radio quiz going and a man whose name is intoned, in certain circles, with more than a little reverence. Jenny, Broken Hearts supporter and the match's only other nonparticipating attendee, nodded her approval:

"Yep, this is a perfect quizzing venue."

At first glance, the cove didn't strike me as a perfect venue for anything – small and cold, its ceiling dripped water and the adjoining nook appeared to be hosting the Bellowing League of London. But being unfamiliar with the QLL quiz format, I'd overlooked its major advantage: a long central table with bench seats on three sides, so that the two teams of four could line up facing each other. The Question Mistress, Phillida, sat at the end of the table exuding steely poise.

The players were indeed all male, well-spoken and mostly middle-aged. They squeezed into their seats, flicking obscure questions and titbits of trivia back and forth between themselves like schoolboys pinging rubber bands across a classroom.

"Which Viking king did Alfred defeat in 878?"

"Gudrum."

"No, *Guthrum* – the 'D'-like symbol is a Norse letter pronounced 'th'."

"And what's its name?"

"It's 'eth'."

"Pronounced the same as 'thorn', the *other* uniquely Norse consonant..."

With everyone seated, the players fell quiet. Phyllida combed her hair back one final time. The game began.

The questions had a definite arts degree bent, covering Titian, medieval kings and English heraldry (twice). Sport was barely touched upon, and the science questions were high school standard, on atomic weights and the like. As Olav had predicted, the few pop culture questions were scoffed at: when a player correctly answered two questions about *Little Britain*, his teammate admonished him with a teasing "shameful!"

So far, so Radio 4. The QLL takes its cue from all those long-running quizzes designed for the educated elite: *Mastermind, University Challenge, Brain of Britain, 15 to 1*. But nobody commissions shows like that any more. It's all about mass appeal: Big! Cash! Prizes! And Premium! Rate! Phonelines! In 1998, *Who Wants to be a Millionaire* (UK) changed the quiz world forever.

Once you had made it onto the show, you were pretty much guaranteed to walk away with thousands; if you also happened to be a general knowledge maven, there was a good chance you'd make it to a million. Naturally, Britain's quiz enthusiasts were even more taken with the programme than the rest of the nation. Olav has been applying for game shows since the innocent, pre-*WWTBM* mid-90s, but his love of trivia is now passionately coupled with financial ambition. He talks about his job at the *Times* –writing book reviews and setting their daily quiz – as if it were a stopgap packing shelves at Tescos. All energies are being directed towards the dream of a massive future windfall.

"I do... think... about *Millionaire*. Some of my friends have been on it, and won a lot of money."

Pat Gibson and Diane Hallagan, winners of £1 million and £250,000 respectively, are both part of the quizzing community; the ubiquitous Kevin Ashman won the top prize of a Jaguar Xtype in the stage version of the show. Not to mention Tecwen Whittock, the twice winner of the Welsh heat of *Brain of Britain*, who was convicted of "procuring the execution of a valuable security by deception" for coughing in aid of contestant and coconspirator Charles Ingram on an episode of *Millionaire* in 2001. Major Ingram, who won £1 million, was later stripped of his prize.

A remarkable coincidence: several quizzers from a select community getting on the show despite the "random" phone-in selector?

"It's just a willingness to get through," Olav shrugged.

That didn't make any sense, I pointed out. It sounded more like the old guard quizzing mafia were somehow muscling in on the new, high return shows.

"There are some shady circles… they flood the phone lines, it increases your chances of getting involved."

Flooding the phone lines isn't exactly cricket, although it's not against the rules. So in retaliation, most of the shows conceived since *WWTBM* have dumped the simplistic lottery selection process in favour of a labyrinthine series of auditions, in the interests of maintaining what Olav scornfully calls "programme equilibrium". He was turned down by *Eggheads,* a show that pits contestants against a panel of quiz experts (including, of course, Kevin Ashman), apparently on the basis that he was too good. However, he's currently made the third round of auditions for the *People's Quiz*, a new BBC show with a £200,000 prize. He's the last remaining QLL representative, after fellow Broken Heart Ian Bayley was rejected.

"Just try not to look too smart," Bayley warned him.

But money isn't everything, especially in the elite, rarefied world of the QLL. Broken Hearts suffered an unfortunate defeat that night in The Old Star, and Olav took up a forlorn position, leaning against the wall of the cove, sucking deeply on a Marlboro Red, watching through his eyelashes as the other players filed out. He really did look broken-hearted, although he remained laconic.

"I'm surprised you stayed for the whole of that," he said flatly.

I didn't mind: the alternative was going home to watch late-night TV, where *Quizmania*, the latest of a dubious new breed of phone-in game shows, would be offering viewers big prizes for solving apparently simple puzzles. In one recent example, the puzzle "What items might be found in a woman's handbag?" had answers including "balaclava" and "rawl plugs".

This kind of thing never happened on *Mastermind*.

Hard Drive Enema

Mil Millington

I'm sitting at my computer. My email client winks with yet another New Message. It's spam. Somehow, it's slipped past my filters, and sneaked into my life. The subject line reads "EXTREME COLON CLEANSING – SUMMER SALE".

Any irritation is eclipsed, however, by instant fascination. This taut mail header is perhaps the most brilliantly crafted phrase I have ever come across. It has the precision of both a Mozart symphony and of a sniper's bullet. Right from the off, it dismisses your lightweight, "weekend" colon cleansers and lets it be known that only those who are prepared to take their intestines to the limit are invited to *this* party. But it doesn't stop there. Because, to connect fully with this advertising copy, you have to be the kind of person who says, "Well, I've always *wanted* my colon cleansed in a way that redefines the boundaries of what's physically possible, but – pff – it's the cost."

That is: you have the alimentary canal and you have the will, but you're waiting for Matalan to get its act together. This perfectly constructed email arrives and every button in my head is pressed. EXTREME COLON CLEANSING – SUMMER SALE.

"Well, the price is right... and – now you mention it – it *will* be summer soon."

"What has this chilling glimpse into my Inbox got to do with our pretty lives?" I ask myself. I wonder what budding entrepreneur chose to market such a groundbreaking product, and how the trade was in the winter months.

What's interesting is that spam doesn't come overwhelmingly from America like it used to. Spam used to come overwhelmingly from America, and it used to be overwhelmingly for porn sites. Nowadays, spam comes from Asia, and – when it's not offering you the chance to have your bowels purified by the Khmer Rouge before you go caravanning for two weeks in the Lake District – it's offering pills that promise to help you lose weight, achieve an erection or "cum by the bucketful".

This email has probably come from China, in fact. China will soon be the world's major economy, and it's had the biggest population pretty much since the invention of reproduction. It will be the defining world power. Now, for the general public there, access to information about the outside world is... oh, what shall we say? "Imperfect." Their image of us is probably formed almost completely by inference pulled from "knowing" what our obsessions are – the things we'll pay hard cash for. And that list comprises:

1 Our physical shape shames and depresses us.
2 Our men cannot get erections. (Or, at least, not for long enough – basically, if she's wearing tights, the window of opportunity will be gone.)
3 We're worried about not being able to ejaculate with such concussing power and persistence that our penis could be turned on the crowd to suppress a civil rights demonstration. And presumably we want this because the prime desire of women here is to end lovemaking looking like they've just been thrown through a car wash.

That's the image that the Superpower Apparent and its tiger neighbours have of us.

"So what," I say to myself. 'It's not how we *actually* are. What others think is nothing: we define *ourselves*, daddio." But then I think back to the early days of spam, spam that advertised American porn; porn aimed at, and promoted by, sweaty 15 year old sad acts in Boise and Baltimore. What do these specific individuals crave?

Well, TEENS! – obviously. Of course they want TEENS! – their balls dropped only the previous afternoon: a 20 year old seems ancient and decrepit to them. Also (as their sole sexual experience of women up to this point has been secretly undressing their sister's *Barbie*) hairlessness. This originally represented the ideal of only one, *incredibly stupid*, group. But – as Goebbels liked to say – if you repeat a lie often enough, people simply accept that it's the truth.

Unsettled, I do what everyone does when queasy disquiet and uncertainty threatens: I Google. I browse the Web for porn, and I find women of 25 labelled 'old' – in the MILF niche or done for. What's even more illuminating is that I also discover that models with normal, natural, unshaven pubic hair have been pushed off into the "fetish" sections. Why this is especially interesting is because I know that many British women have also hit the razor and the wax, because now, for some people, it's seen as the norm. 15 years ago, it would have appeared deviant and vaguely creepy to have your pubes torn and scraped down to a tiny, ludicrous little strip of hair. Now, without a murmur – self-imposed – many women have adopted the look and the agenda set by pubescent American boys, to the point where a woman who *doesn't* go in for it might well find herself the butt of jokes. That's how culture works – it moves to the position occupied by reports of itself. I think we are, therefore I become.

So, the soon-to-be Rulers of the Earth, the Chinese, are mistaken. We are not insecure, self-loathing, clinically obese, borderline impotents who fritter away our days dreaming of crashing oceans of semen. But, in five years' time, we might very well be.

I still feel OK, though. Except, please, don't look at me: I'm so ashamed of my unwashed colon.

God I'm starving.

Cricket Makes No Sense, But Then Again Does Anything?

Patrick Neate

"You can learn everything you need to know about life from the game of cricket." This is a comment addressed by father (secondary character) to son (protagonist) in my latest novel. It's also a comment addressed by father (dad) to son (me) throughout my life. Many, many times.

I've always accepted the idea without question. I've accepted it since I was out first ball to a dodgy LBW aged 11 and my dad said, "It's character building. You can learn everything you need to know about life from the game of cricket."

The implication was and is, I guess, that cricket throws up the best metaphors. But what he was really saying was "life's unfair". Did I really need a metaphor to understand that? Probably not.

Cricket is undoubtedly a great source of metaphor but I'm beginning to suspect that dad's reliance on it arguably says more about him, me and the nature of our relationship than anything the metaphors say about the nature of this mortal coil. Do you follow?

I thought I'd write about cricket as a blueprint for understanding. It sounded neat. I might explain how life is sometimes like bowling: you can bowl full toss after long hop, dross upon dross, but one perfect delivery – pitching middle and leg, say, before cutting away to clip off stump – can be suddenly and shockingly redemptive. The lesson? Keep plugging away. I might explain how life is sometimes like batting: you can fall early or late but you'll always fall in the end.

The lesson? Stay humble.

I might even choose to suggest that cricket is still the best lens to understand the persistent national and racial stereotypes of the former British Empire. Look at the Aussies, physically tough and pragmatic and, in English eyes, determined to establish their nationhood through every defiant flash of bat. Look at Pakistan, clever and talented but, in English eyes, always to be regarded with suspicion. Look at the West Indies, all languid muscularity and, in English eyes, clandestine threat. And look at England: once imperially arrogant, then post-imperially diffident and now almost Australian (or perhaps, whisper it, American) in attitude. It's all pretty interesting stuff, right? And yet...

My dad played first-class cricket and later went on to captain a minor county. He was seriously good. We played together a few times. I'm not sure about this but I think the last was probably when I was 18 and he was pushing 50. I was out first ball and he hit a match-winning century. My sisters were never interested in cricket, and neither was my elder brother. Only me. I was a decent schoolboy cricketer, making up in application and ambition what I lacked in talent. Cricket, therefore, has always been a point of contact between dad and me. Even when our relationship was occasionally fractious, we could talk cricket.

Dad is a member of the MCC and every summer for the last decade or so we've headed to Lords for a one-day international and at least a day of the test match. These couple of days are when we do most of our talking. We start by discussing the cricket – the moisture in the pitch, the overhead conditions, the teams and the prospects – then, as the day progresses, we'll move to talking about ourselves, the family and, usually by teatime, more abstract subject matter from morality to politics to the morality of politics. The cricket is always there, of course, to lend a metaphor or two.

Over the last decade, I don't think it's my imagination that tells me that the make-up of those sitting around us has changed. Where once these were mostly old geezers in blazers who hummed and hawed and talked mostly ignorantly about the game over Chardonnay, now they are mostly younger, drunker and their ignorance is a lot louder. Recently there has been a lot written about the way in which football has been appropriated by the establishment. You can barely read about an MP, bishop or captain of industry without mention of their lifelong love (sincere or otherwise) of some or other football club. Cricket, it seems, has begun to go the other way; for good and bad. But it's not just the crowd that's changed. Over the same period, you see, the game has changed too. Where once batting in a Test match was about surviving one delivery so that you were still there for the next, now it's all about risk taking, quick scoring and mental domination. Where once a fast bowler looked forward to the out-swinging new ball, now many look forward to the old ball that "reverses" at the batsman. It doesn't matter whether you understand the technicalities of what I'm talking about, only that old truths have been turned on their head. What of the metaphors now?

My dad is a man of certainty and principle. I've always admired him for it and aspired to be similar. But just as he was a better cricketer than me, frankly he's a better person too. This is partly about, shall we say, "talent," but I suspect it is also partly because he developed his "game" in a time when the principles were easier to see, the certainties more certain and…

Ha! No, no, no… Even as I write that I can't let myself get away with it. Because the simple truth is that the good remain good whatever the uncertain circumstance and the uncertain, uncertain, however good the circumstance. As with changing life, so with changing cricket. You can, it seems, learn a lot about cricket from the game of life.

Go On Gourmand, Lick Your Plate!

Sarah Dohrmann

According to Jeremy Meyers, director of programmes for the James Beard Foundation – New York's most notorious gourmand club – a *foodie* is "an enthusiastic eater, someone who enjoys a wide variety of foods without the commensurate knowledge or understanding of the preparation involved in such food".

What he is saying is that James Beard members are *gourmands*; they know something about food, they have a pretty good idea about how it should be served, and this knowledge vaults them into a sparkly echelon in which foodies are not allowed.

Foodies and gourmands: status has traditionally separated these gluttonous tribes. While the gourmand enjoys a single estate wine paired with a slab of Argentinean beef, the foodie hunts through the bowels of Queens in search of the city's best taco stand. But foodies are catching up to gourmand status, because the American middle class is bulging. They're making more money (whether on credit or otherwise) and moving to New York where they eat US $200 dinners nightly. They compulsively watch the Food Network, along with 85 million other American households. Even their grandmothers back in Iowa now say they're 'braising' their rump roast instead of "letting 'er cook in the Crock Pot". And by god, they know who Bobby Flay is.

That's another thing foodies have going for them: every kid fresh out of culinary school wants to be a television celebrity chef like Bobby Flay. They'll work an 80 hour week, lose their girlfriend, take abuse, develop a drinking habit, get paid US $400 a week as long as it's at Babbo, Gramercy Tavern, Blue Hill at Stone Barns, Daniel, Jean-Georges, Per Se. And if they're still standing, they'll go on to open their own tiny restaurant on some godforsaken Brooklyn street where they'll cook the shit out of greenmarket fare (see Red Hook's 360 or The Good Fork); they're cultivating veritable bastions for foodie *branchés*. So foodies are eating the same daring and inventive concoctions as the gourmands, only paying less for it. And at the same time they're discovering new culinary talents that the gourmands have never heard of – in fact, who gourmands *won't* hear of until the press has finally written about them in *Gourmet* magazine or they've gotten enough backing to open their own mega-million dollar restaurant that comes with a US $350 *prix fixe* in a more desirable neighbourhood (see Masa).

The gourmands, though, still have one unconquered island. The James Beard Foundation. James Beard: post-WWII American chef who wrote more than 20 cookbooks, was hailed as "The Dean of American Cookery" by someone important and whose name is claimed to be "synonymous with American food".

The James Beard Foundation: New York non-profit "dedicated to celebrating, preserving, and nurturing America's culinary heritage and diversity in order to elevate the appreciation of [America's] culinary excellence." The James Beard House: said chef's former townhouse in the West Village where members pay up to US $500 annually to "enjoy information about the food world". They also get first-dibs on Beard House events – namely the fancy US $200+ private dinners prepared by America's most respected chefs.

One night recently I managed to find myself at the Beard House free of charge, throwing back wine amidst the *Chanel*-clad and pearl-collared social elite. I'd seen their kind before, but only as their waitress at some of the most high-end restaurants in town.

But it's my current gig as bartender and manager of Tía Pol ("the best traditional Spanish restaurant in town," according to *New York* magazine), where I've also become acquainted with New York's foodies: at Tía Pol guests wipe their faces with paper napkins. It's also where they'll wait for upwards of two hours aside the likes of Mario Batali, Dan Barber, Masa Takayama and copious other New York chef idols to experience Alexandra Raij's authentic *tapas*. It also happens to be where Nick Morgenstern goes for his weekly fix of *gambas a la plancha* with a side of spicy *aioli*. Nick Morgenstern: former pastry chef of Gramercy Tavern and current pastry chef at Gilt restaurant in the famed Villard Mansion at the New York Palace Hotel. And that's how I got the free seat. Nick and Gilt chef Christopher Lee had been invited to prepare a dinner at Beard House, and asked if I wanted to come along.

When I arrived, guests were packed into Beard's first floor drinking a "mystery sparkling wine" (one was to guess whether it was Old World or New, what its grapes were, and which *effervescent du monde* it was). Servers in black-and-whites entered the room, composed, with stocked canapé trays. After five seconds they'd leave the room limping. Still, they braved the pawing crowd to serve big-eye tuna rolls that looked like seedless watermelons; doll-sized teacups filled with black lentil soup and finished with some sort of foam; and Mediterranean octopus with blood orange pulp that was mounded atop dim-sum spoons. (Apparently there were also mini grilled lamb gyros with Greek yoghurt, but I wasn't quick enough to git to 'em.) Ladies wearing silk pantyhose and men wearing *Hermès* ties "ooh"ed and "ahh"ed with their friends, barking opinions about which *hors d'oeuvre* was best (it seems the lamb gyros were "just okay").

Huge oils of James Beard peered over the needy crowd. I thought he looked pleased, if not vexed. I heard one woman chastise her husband for eating a burger deluxe for lunch.

"But you *knew* we were coming here for dinner!" she whined.

He told her not to worry, he'd make room.

Soon, we were shooed to our assigned tables. Mr Meyers got

on the mic to say some nice things. On either side of my plate were four knives and four forks and two spoons of differing proportions. I felt glad I knew to work from the outside in. But even if I didn't, no one there would be able to tell. They were too busy ploughing through Japanese Kobe beef *carpaccio* with lemon pepper caviar and crispy shitake mushrooms; followed by diver sea scallops with fresh soy beans, passion fruit, lotus root and black truffle; followed by farmed-raised sturgeon with smoked potato *gnocchi*, golden beets, Meyer lemon, and caviar *crème fraiche*; followed by Pennsylvania venison with barley grains, macadamia nuts ("For some crunch!" the circling waiter crowed), kumquats and a *venison jus*; followed by Nick's *vacherin* of coconut cakes, *cassis* sorbet and coconut cream; followed by a chocolate tart of Tonka caramel and whole milk ice cream.

Each course was paired with two wines: one New World and one Old World of the same varietal. Everyone got wasted.

During dinner I chatted with my fellow diners. On my left was the chef's wife's best friend from childhood; on the other side of her was the chef's wife. They were making it a girls' night out, getting ripped and comparing childbirth stories; the friend had just had her first child 14 days before and even went so far as to show me her stretch marks as if they were wounds from the Front. The man sitting on the other side of them was quiet and well groomed; he was wearing a first-rate tie but also, I noticed, a *Swatch Watch* – a nice *Swatch Watch*, but still, it was plastic. The man immediately to my right was a natural gossip and a longtime Beardian. He delicately sipped wines as he told me about the man sitting directly opposite us. Apparently we were in the midst of a world-class interior designer – *he'd designed Jackie O's penthouse* – who had also been a member of The James Beard Foundation since its inception in 1986. I thought he looked like any other small man with an obvious toupee; his partner was even smaller, which made vague sense. During dinner everyone's austere gourmand façade stammered; they started to look an awful lot like foodies who might, in different company, lick their plates.

After dinner, after dessert(s), after New and Old World dessert wines, after coffee, the stars of the show lined up in front of us, our flies about to pop: Christopher and Nick stood in embroidered chef whites, their devoted staff trailing behind. Mr Meyers gave Christopher the mic, and boy did Christopher hog it. He talked about how he'd made it up the ladder to Gilt – his salad days in culinary school, his externship at Daniel, then running the kitchen at Striped Bass in Philadelphia, and now, coming back home (he'd been raised in New York) to Gilt – it was like a triumph, a dream come true. And he *never would have guessed* that someday he'd be cooking at *The James Beard House*.

Plastered glazed faces smiled back. It was a group hug. Then he introduced his staff, forgetting only two names.

Mr Meyers finally got the mic back.

"Questions for the chefs anyone?" I imagined us there all night, lighting candles and starting some ritual dance I'd have down by sun up.

It was sort of sad to see Christopher up there, dying to answer a question. And when it wasn't coming, you could see him slowly deflate: no one had curiosity. And no curiosity meant, gosh, lack of interest? But then, I reasoned, maybe gourmands already know all the answers. Mercifully, the world-class interior designer raised his hand. He said there was *something magical* about the Pennsylvania *venison jus*, but he for the life of him couldn't place it. What on earth made that *jus* so special? Lee tore it up. He talked fast, he used words like "reduction" and "low flame" and then he listed some foreign-sounding herbs until finally he landed on the ingredient the man had been racking his brain to place: chocolate.

"Oh chocolate!" the man squealed.

Christopher smiled. We all did. There were no more questions.

After Q&A the designer came around to chat with my gossipy neighbour and me.

"Fabulous meal, just fabulous, don't you think?" he said, "I'll be dreaming of that sturgeon into next week!" I thought, "*You would.*"

Nick came over to say hi. I introduced him to my new friends and everyone seemed quite impressed with me, that I was so close with one of the reasons for the season. There was talk of a drink down at a little beer and wine spot with artisanal cheese plates, but I was too tanked to keep on. Still, by that time I'd gotten greedy. You give a person a little bit of fine dining and suddenly they want the whole bag of chips.

"Hey do I get one of those goodie bags?"

I snapped on my way to coat check.

"Yes ma'am!" said some server in a penguin suit. Nick flashed me a "shame on you" glance and I felt bad. I got my coat, tipped five bucks, graciously accepted a goodie bag and then hailed a cab back to my hovel in Brooklyn. When I got home my cat mewed as I consumed everything in the bag: Nick's handmade chocolates, a mini-bottle of *Pouilly Fuissé*, and something else I ate too quickly to remember now. As I did, I looked over the evening's menu, reliving the gluttony, and eventually arriving at a description of the Pennsylvania Venison. I spat out laughter. There it was, plain as day: Barley Grains, Macadamia Nuts, Kumquats, and *Spiced Chocolate Venison Jus*.

The nerve of that guy.

The Invisible Journalist – Part One

Jack Roberts

Cologne, Germany. It's spring, 2007, and Günter Wallraff is halfway up the 15 ft rope tied to the bough of a tree in his garden. Demonstrating his fitness, he shimmies up to the top and back down in seconds. He's dressed in casual jogging gear; a black zip top with a red piped V collar and well-worn trainers. His hair is shaved short and his grey moustache is precise.

At 64, he's training himself for his latest undercover investigation; the topic is confidential, but he needs to pass for a 50 year old so that his prospective employers won't become suspicious. It's going well, and today he looks a good 15 years younger than his age.

Wallraff has been in the subterfuge game 38 years now, in which time he's become a master of reinvention. His successful ruses rate amongst the most astonishing feats in 20th century journalism. Posing as the secretary of a non-existent German fascist group in 1975, he negotiated a fake arms deal with General Antonio de Spinola, exposing his plans for a military coup in Portugal. As Levent "Ali" Sinirlioglu, a Turkish immigrant *"gastarbeiter"*– a project for which he spent two years in a wig and face make-up – he was exploited, discriminated against, and robbed of his wages by opportunist sub-contractors, all to uncover and publicise the maltreatment of immigrant communities.

Of all his roles though, his infiltration of the tabloid *Bild-Zeitung*, Germany's equivalent of *The Sun* newspaper, is perhaps the most high profile and controversial.

Wallraff spent four months working as a journalist at the

paper, and after publishing his book, *Der Aufmacher* (Lead Story), which documented their manipulation and deception of their readers, *Bild* attacked him with a litany of court actions, challenging the legality of his method. Although ultimately vindicated by Germany's highest court, Wallraff spent more than six years in trials, and it was only *Der Aufmacher*'s bestselling success that saved him from financial ruin. Despite the setbacks, he has always maintained his techniques are justified.

"Role-playing is the best way of acquiring new insights and knowledge, and getting close to people whom you otherwise don't understand," he tells me.

"If more people got involved in role-play this would be a much more open, humane society. We've forgotten how to play."

It's spring, 1977, and Günter Wallraff, 34, is researching a television documentary on *Bild*. Their circulation is topping five million, and their influence is enormous. They're easily Europe's bestselling newspaper, and as an institution are powerful and untouchable. *Bild* styles itself as "the peoples' paper", but the journalists who actually produce the tabloid describe it as an "excellent vehicle for employer's interests", and its readers as "thickoes".

In the past, Wallraff has written reports on how the newspaper consistently twists, sensationalises, and suppresses facts in its articles. In one investigation he discovers a woman who has left her abusive husband for a Turkish man, and whose reputation has been destroyed by *Bild*; the paper ran a "mother wanted" campaign on their front page, branding her a "heartless wife", and printed a letter she left for her husband declaring, "I have no further interest in my children." In reality, she was forced to write the letter at knifepoint by her husband, who threatened to kill their kids if she didn't. The woman was subsequently sacked from two jobs and fled to the Dutch border to escape tabloid reporters.

This time Wallraff is looking to produce a more in-depth work.

Alf Breull, 28, is a journalist at the newspaper and one of his key sources. Breull is "the poet", the rising star of *Bild*'s editorial team, but he has scruples, wants to leave the newspaper. The company that owns *Bild*, The Springer Group, is offering him more money and a new contract, but he is not enthusiastic.

"I wouldn't even work there for 10,000 DM a month. Working there, I have lost every shred of self-respect."

Breull has an idea for Wallraff.

"Why don't you get a job here yourself? That way you'll find out much more."

"But they know me already – they think I'm one of their enemies. I don't think I'll succeed."

"They're so full of themselves – they don't think anyone can touch them."

A plan is hatched: Breull gives notice to his employers, and puts his trusted friend "'Hans Esser" forward as a replacement. Now Wallraff must become "Hans Esser", 30, a former military man – officer in the department of "psychological warfare" – turned ad copywriter, turned tabloid newshound.

He shaves his straggly hair down to a close crop and wears coloured contact lenses. Looking in the mirror, Wallraff is unconvinced by his disguise though: he has wrinkles, and his nose is too distinctive. He contemplates plastic surgery.

A plastic surgeon friend at the University of Cologne advises against a facelift.

"This surgery is much too serious. Besides, you'll feel like a stranger to yourself for years afterwards."

Wallraff thinks it over: he can't afford 12,000 DM for the operation anyway. The surgeon advises him to change his body language if he wants to seem like a tabloid newsman.

"You need to be snappy, hard, smart, quick on the uptake. Not so reflective, defensive, and introverted. Show confidence. Where you feel insecurity, show yourself to be strong. Remember, you feel incredibly secure with the knowledge that you have this massive, powerful corporation behind you. You believe you are untouchable."

Meanwhile, Breull organises a meeting with Thomas Schwindmann, his editor at *Bild*, in the newspaper's Hanover bureau. On the morning of the meeting, Wallraff wears a large gold signet ring, borrowed from an aristocratic friend, and liberally coats himself with *Aqua Brava* perfume. He sprays it on his new 500 DM suit, and also under his armpits to hide the smell of sweat, of fear. Looking at his face in the mirror, he sees a different face looking back at him; it's the face of a successful manager, a face that has been trimmed for corporate convention – for a career. It's a face he has always hated when he has seen it on other people.

Driving up to *Bild*'s offices in Bemeroder Straße, Wallraff is given the impression of approaching a fortified military compound: the printing presses and editorial building are secured by a fence, and there is a guard patrolling the perimeter with an Alsatian.

Breull leads him up to the fifth floor, and walks him through the office doors, into the newsroom. Wallraff's pulse is racing. His throat feels tight.

Flash forward: Esser makes a great impression on Schwindmann, who approves his appointment. It is agreed Breull will oversee his transition to the workplace.

Schwindmann approaches Wallraff and Breull after work one day at 11 pm.

"Come back to my place so we can get to know each other a bit."

It is more of an order than an invitation; Wallraff and Breull are reluctant, but Schwindmann is the boss.

"Thank you very much Herr Schwindmann."

Leading the way in his BMW, Schwindmann races ahead of them to his penthouse apartment. Wallraff struggles to keep up in his worn out Peugeot *304*, but manages to stay in sight of the editor's distant taillights. The pursuit ends in one of Hanover's typical satellite suburbs, where they park.

Breull and Wallraff take the lift up to Schwindmann's living quarters. As they enter they are shocked to see that the apartment has been converted into a shooting gallery, starting in the lounge and stretching across a long corridor into the bathroom, where a large bullseye target has been erected. Schwindmann reaches into a draw and pulls out a gun, which he places in Wallraff's hand.

"Now show me what you've learned in the army."

Problem: Wallraff, the conscientious objector, has never handled a gun in his life.

"I'm kaput Herr Schwindmann. I no longer have a steady hand."

Schwindmann pays no notice.

"Doesn't it feel wonderful to have a gun in your hand? You feel like a different person…"

"I have a problem with my eyesight – an astigmatism. That was the reason I ended up in the psychological warfare department of the army. Next time I'll bring my own gun with me, one that has specially adjusted sights."

"The main thing is you shoot the target, and don't destroy my bathroom mirror." Schwindmann loads his weapon and takes aim at the bullseye.

The shooting match lasts until 3 am, although Schwindmann is a good marksman and easily defeats his opponents.

"You just have to imagine who your target is, then you're much more accurate."

A dark look of rumination crosses his face; any number of enemies could be ghosting around his imagination – Wallraff decides to leave him be.

Bored by the lack of competition, Schwindmann suggests they play "blitz chess". Blitz chess is a variant of chess in which players are given mere seconds to make a move; the trick is to react fast, to make something out of nothing. Schwindmann challenges Wallraff and sets the clock.

"You now have seven minutes."

Although Wallraff is a good chess player, Schwindmann wins

the first six games with ease.

"You have to learn how to do it! Blitz chess is like producing our newspaper. You can't shilly-shally around and think things over. Sometimes you have to hack out an article in a few minutes. You're under constant pressure to produce."

Schwindmann breaks to open his drinks cupboard for his guests.

"Cognac, gin, schnapps, or whisky? Your choice."

"Whisky," says Wallraff.

He hates whisky, but consciously chooses it over the other spirits. A manly drink might mitigate his repeated losses in his boss's eyes.

One drink follows another, and the games continue into the night. Wallraff starts to win blitz chess games, challenging Schwindmann's tally of victories, but the newspaper editor will not rest until the series is won outright. The competition continues in grim silence, until Schwindmann's eventual victory and the morning sunlight compels his guests to return to work.

Wallraff settles into the work at *Bild*. One day, he is sent out on assignment to report on a family in Celler. Their child is the victim of a fatal sex crime. Normally Schwindmann sends *Bild* photographer Heribert Klampf on such assignments: Klampf is a specialist at extracting family album photos from relatives of those who have recently died or been murdered. His methods are notorious, "If you don't give us access we'll use shots from the mortuary, and that wouldn't look too good." This time Schwindmann wants to test Esser.

"Get the photograph. We've set up space for it in the paper – and get a move on."

When Wallraff arrives at the house he sees the victim's brothers and sisters crying in the hallway. He's embarrassed to be there, but hasn't filed a story today and is under pressure to prove himself. Wallraff approaches the father, a butcher, offers his condolences, and asks for a picture of the child.

"You want to make money from our misery. You'll get at least 500 DM for the photograph from your newspaper," says the father.

It is the *Bild* reporter who responds, "There's nothing to it, it's a memory of your child, that's all."

The father makes it clear there will be no photo and Wallraff soon backs down, apologising profusely. Disgusted with himself, he is inconsolable for the rest of the evening – yet he is still under pressure to produce stories.

Soon afterwards, Wallraff's live-in girlfriend, a student, plans to give birth to a child at home, but it arrives unexpectedly early. There's a big drama; the midwife, Hanover's only home birth midwife, arrives late. Wallraff phones Schwindmann to explain he can't come to the office because he has been called in to provide first aid for a home childbirth.

"I can't work with you if you're not able to keep appointments," says Schwindmann, then, in a more measured tone, "... Home birth you say?"

At this time, home births are an extremely rare phenomenon in Germany.

"I think there might be a story for us in this. Interview the midwife and talk to the young mother – I'll send a photographer over."

Wallraff's girlfriend is completely opposed to the idea, but she's too weak to put up resistance and, in any case, Schwindmann has already put the phone down and dispatched a photographer. Later that day, when the midwife delivers the child, she holds him up for the obligatory slap on the backside. The baby is welcomed to the world by the *Bild* photographer's raging flash bulbs as his mother unleashes a curdling scream – her first of the day.

Wallraff leaves the room; the situation is too unpleasant to bear, and yet the sense of satisfaction he feels is undeniable.

"We got the photograph," he thinks to himself. "The story will stand up."

Back in the room, he reassures his girlfriend.

"Don't worry, you won't be recognisable, and newly born children all look the same anyway."

"Typical Esser," she says.

The story plays big in *Bild*, and the midwife later tells Wallraff that the piece led to a 100% increase in the number of Hanover home births – success.

Life at *Bild* grinds on though; Wallraff is again under pressure to deliver articles, having suffered three consecutive 'defeats'. His girlfriend decides to help him break the sequence of spiked articles with another taboo-busting personal interest story.

"I'LL SUCKLE MY BABY WHERE I WANT!"

Wallraff's *Bild* career is back on track, but he has recurrent nightmares in which he is found out, where the whole project dissolves in a cloud of smoke.

Back in the Hanover newsroom, journalists drink and puff cigarettes like world champions; most are incapable of filing copy without resorting to alcohol. Schwindmann is running illicit advertising "features" from casinos, nightclubs, and pubs in exchange for various "favours" One client is "Petra Breulla Herodus Meier", a sham-psychologist based at the Intercontinental Hotel. Meier claims that for 100 DM he can cure a smoker's addiction in mere seconds.

"The man is an idiot Esser, but do a nice positive story on him."

Wallraff meets Meier, notes his flashy props, and observes the snake oil act at close quarters. Returning to the office, he files a ludicrously positive story on Meier, and is offered a congratulatory cigarette by Schwindmann.

"No thanks. It really worked, I've stopped smoking."

In an attempt to look simpleminded and gain acceptance, Wallraff has decided to kick his habit. It works, and the exchange becomes a newsroom joke. Schwindmann will always offer Wallraff cigarettes after that.

"No thanks – I'm cured."

The other *Bild* journos have a good laugh at Esser's naivety – the man actually believes his own stories! Regardless, the newsroom powers mark him down as "one for the future".

Then, on July 22, 1977, Wallraff receives a phone call from a friend in Hamburg. A magazine has printed a story exposing him as Hans Esser – inconceivable – and the Springer Group are all over the revelation. Wallraff immediately ceases his work. The next day, the following story runs in *Bild*:

THE UNDERGROUND COMMUNIST WHO WORMED HIS WAY IN

Günter Wallraff, who has previously sneaked into Gerling and other institutions, has managed to worm his way into Bild *using a false name. Wallraff… who would drink a shot of Ballantines whisky in the morning… and swore when he lost at table tennis… said he used to work at an advertising agency in Düsseldorf, and wanted to see if he could work as a journalist. This story was as false as the name "Hans Esser"… the name on his* Bild *press pass, which he used when working as a reporter. He played a despicable game with his colleagues, who thought he was genuine. Exactly a month ago, he left work with "stomach pains", then disappeared into the shadows from which he came. Now he's writing about what he claims he has experienced at our editorial offices. We worked him so hard at* Bild *that he actually stopped smoking…*

30 years later, Günter Wallraff is seated at the large wood table that dominates his sparse office: a small building that sits at the back of his garden. The décor in the room is minimal; smooth aggregated stone towers – self-made artworks – rise up from the corners like flowers, and a grand piano sits unobtrusively in the background. Answering my questions, he makes animated hand gestures, sweeps his arms, drums the table with long, bony fingers, and speaks in passionate crescendos.

So what happened at *Bild*?

He grins wolfishly, "I was betrayed…"

The Invisible Journalist – Part Two

Jack Roberts

WALLRAFFEN/WALLRAFFA (German/Swedish): **verb**. To investigate and expose misconduct by adopting a false identity. *ORIGIN:* German undercover journalist Günter Wallraff, b. 1942, Cologne.

If I knew exactly where my perception of a story came from, I might not have the same motivation. I was damaged in my early childhood. When I was only four or five years old, I was put in an orphanage because my father was near death and my mother had to work. In the orphanage – I remember it like in a film – they took away everything I owned and I was completely depersonalised.

Between the ages of 16 and 18, I was a lyricist. I was interested in expressionism, in experimental American literature, and my role models were writers like E.E. Cummings and Ezra Pound. Although I was a conscientious objector, a pacifist inspired by Gandhi, I was conscripted into the Bundeswehr (the West German Army). I had never held a gun in my hand and was absolutely against the idea of killing my fellow man.

Back then, the army was full of old Nazis and the big heroes were the generals of the Hitler era. The SS symbols were up and they sang Nazi songs – you can't compare today to what it was like then.

For my passive resistance I was forced to carry a wooden stick when the others were marching around the place, so I tied flowers to the end of it and walked around with that instead. On one occasion I sneaked some flowers into the barrel of my companions' guns. Everyone laughed at that. The officers wanted to court martial me for it, but there wasn't enough evidence for them to go on.

Finally, they interned me in a closed psychiatric ward of a federal military hospital in Koblenz. The confinement ended after 10 months; they tried to break my will, but I kept a diary throughout and through my introverted world I began to experience a new reality. Afterwards they bestowed on me the honorary title of "Abnormal personality: unsuitable for war or peace". It was a great grounding for the work that I would later undertake.

Working as an apprentice at a bookshop, I learned to love books. I became consumed by my literary tastes and followed these interests to Scandinavia. It was a romantic journey through areas of misery. I would live in refuges for the homeless, and my heroes were Orwell, Jack London, Kerouac; I wrote about these experiences in my diaries but never published them. Years later, I discovered a diary entry in which I wrote, "I am my own secret 'Maskenbild' (masked image), I continually don new masks to search for myself and to conceal myself."

Looking back, this anticipated my entire role-play methodology, but in my wildest imagination I never thought then that it would develop in the way it did.

My first published journalistic work was in the youth magazine Twen, *which today has a cult status, and my reportage was used as a cover story twice. One of these stories was called "Me Against the Bundeswehr". That was the beginning; Heinrich Böll, the famous playwright, read my work and encouraged me to persist (I would later marry his niece, Birgit – sadly she died of cancer, but that's another story).*

My father had ruined his health by working on the production line at Ford Motors, so I decided I would spend several years working in factories. For two years I worked all over Germany: at Siemens, in a dockyard – the typical, alienating work of the proletariat.

In the beginning, the genuine workers gave me the nickname "the student", although I wasn't one and had never studied; the factory was my place of study, not the university. They thought to call me "student" because I gave the impression of being a bit detached from them, although much later I became more involved, part of the group. I also moved from being a purely passive observer to someone who became an active participant. In sociology, they talk of "participating observation"; I developed a method of appearing naïve to give the impression that I was stupid – playing the fool is the ideal way of getting at the real situation, to expose others.

My reportage was published in a newspaper run by IG Metall, an industrial trade union, and the pieces became very well known. They triggered a strike on one occasion, and mobilised the workforce. There were court proceedings against me and I became well known to the big business leaders, who circulated pamphlets to their factories, advising them not to employ me. After that, it became necessary to disguise myself.

The role-playing gave me a different identity. Originally I lacked conviction, but by finding situations in which there was social friction, I strengthened my sense of identity and my self-confidence grew. I became less afraid: out of a weakness, I managed to create something productive.

So there is my working methodology – a quite elementary form of camouflage. That is, I simply become someone else.

Since then, my work has become well known in Germany and elsewhere, and I have even had the honour of my name being added to the popular vocabulary with the word "wallraffen". Just as "Röntgen" (X-Ray) has become a verb "to see through something" in the medical sense, my name has become the verb "to see through something" in the societal sense. With "röntgen" you look right through to the skeleton – medically speaking you make it visible. With "wallraffen", it is society that is made visible.

Many people have questioned my methods, but for me there is one very clear guiding principle: my work stops where it begins to affect people's intimate private lives. In other words, where a tabloid newspaper like Bild Zeitung *begins my method stops. It justifies itself when the weak investigate the much more powerful and not vice versa.*

The ethics of such methods are important, and you have to be able to accept them being subjected to public scrutiny. Every opponent has the right to seek clarification through the courts to determine whether you acted within the law, or whether you went too far. In my case, I always had very powerful opponents who could exhaust all legal possibilities, and court proceedings against me lasted for years.

Bild *alone litigated against me for seven years trying to get my book,* Der Aufmacher, *banned. The lower courts supported Bild and said my methods should not have been used, but the highest court in Germany, the Federal Constitutional Court, overruled them and said they were legitimate.*

Their ruling was significant. My working methods had to be deemed legitimate, because with Bild *press engagement in German society had taken a wrong turning.*

To this day, I don't know who betrayed me while I was working undercover at Bild. *I would have stayed longer – I was seen as a big newsroom talent.*

Even before I had finished my book on Bild, *they started attacking me as their enemy. A troupe of reporters worked on my case for weeks, months.*

They went right into my childhood, to the place where I was born. They talked to school friends and neighbours and wrote a series of defamatory articles. Time and time again, I legally forced them to publish counter statements. I was never in the Communist Party, but they portrayed me as an "underground communist". "Underground communist" then had the same meaning as "terrorist" now...

In 1977, leading up to the first publication of *Der Aufmacher*, the picture *Bild* runs of Wallraff is unforgiving; his face is pallid, his skin is like paper, his cheeks sink into his jaw line. Under the photo, a caption:

Günter Wallraff: this is how everyone knows him, like something that's sprung from the pages of a psychiatry textbook.

This picture, several years old, depicts a man who has emerged from three months captivity and torture in an Athens prison. In 1974, Wallraff travelled to Greece to protest against Dimitrios Ioannides's military junta, and was arrested for chaining himself to a lamppost while handing out pamphlets. In the photo, Wallraff, badly underweight, ghoulishly recoils from the daylight.

Bild's repeated publication of the "madman" image in a series of negative articles is the prelude to a very comprehensive litigation. In a landmark case, Axel Springer's newspaper group demand that Wallraff's covert methods be declared illegal and his book banned.

The race is on: Wallraff now has to publish *Der Aufmacher* before the case goes to court or risk financially ruinous consequences. He talks into his recorder, types up the transcription, puts an editor to work on the text, and then rapidly re-edits. It's quick work, albeit unrefined, and in September 1977 the book is published in advance of the first trial.

Meanwhile, the *Bild*–Wallraff trial has become big news in West Germany. Surfing a crest of controversy, *Der Aufmacher* flies from bookshelves, rapidly rising to bestseller status. The book sells 300,000 copies by February 1978, and will go on to sell 2.5 million copies.

After the first court case, which Wallraff wins on appeal to the Federal Constitutional Court, *Bild* mounts another trial, and then another, lawsuit following lawsuit like a chain reaction of falling domino tiles.

The aim of the Springer Group is to break Wallraff financially, but every time they succeed in having a section of the text banned, Wallraff will go back, remove the offending passage, and replace it with newer, harder facts, then republish. He will publish 28 of these revised editions in total. Each edition stimulates sales, providing vital revenues to cover his mounting legal costs. Over the next seven years Wallraff will defend himself in over 30 cases.

Outside of the courtroom, the attention from *Bild* is unrelenting as the Springer Group intensifies its attempts to penetrate his private life; they bug Wallraff's home telephone, relaying the line through a complicated switching system so that "the boys" at *Bild*'s Cologne headquarters can listen in on his conversations.

Georg Bönisch, chief reporter at the *Kölnischer Rundschau* newspaper, informs Wallraff that the Springer Group has been employing agents from Germany's Federal Intelligence Service, the BND, to spy on him. When the courts discover this, they fine *Bild* for their behaviour, but the federal agents are never held to account.

Bild pursues Wallraff into the 1980s; increasingly stressed by the ceaseless attention, his mood darkens as continual court proceedings hamper his ability to work.

One day, a trusted friend – a photographer who accompanies him at public events – breaks down in front of him.

"I can't justify this anymore."

He confesses he has been working for Springer, spying on his friend. Wallraff forgives him on one condition: that he stays quiet and let him write the spy reports on his behalf. Wallraff drip-feeds the Springer Group misinformation for several months before they realise they've been burned. It is around this time that a female journalist knocks on his door. An attractive woman, she tells him she's from the BBC, that she's preparing a major documentary programme. He agrees to help her, offers hospitality, and almost becomes intimate with her before backing off (she's not his type).

When he learns from a friend that she's another agent working for Springer, he's distraught. Wallraff lapses into depression; he is powerless in the face of the "other", the malevolent agents who are nullifying his work, impeding his ability to do, to be. He decides to leave Cologne for a period, live abroad. The destination: Amsterdam, one of most beautiful cities in the world. Amsterdam, a place to breathe.

Cologne, 2007. Wallraff raps his fingers on the wooden table as he describes his motivation for transforming himself into a Turk in *Ganz Unten* (Lowest of the Low), his celebrated 1985 book that followed the *Bild* trials.

After years of wearying court proceedings, Wallraff decided to adopt a new identity, becoming "Ali Sinirlioglu", a dark-eyed immigrant. He remained in character for two years, applying make-up and contact lenses every morning, and was subjected to racism and callous exploitation working for an array of German factory employers.

"I'd heard of this district, where every second or third person was an immigrant, and I talked to some of the Turks living around there who said their working conditions were extreme and inhuman. I said to myself, "It's now or never. You're getting older, and it's going to be more and more difficult getting jobs like this.""

A couple of months after this conversation, Wallraff, now a far older man, will successfully pass as "Michael G", a 49 year-old casual worker at a call centre. In an article for the weekly magazine *Die Zeit*, Wallraff describes the call centre – of which there are approximately 5,500 in Germany – as "the coal mine of modern times".

He adjusts his clear plastic spectacles.

"Society today demands that these investigative methods are employed," he says, "Because in Germany – I don't know how it is in England – society is being increasingly divided between the new poor and the new incredibly rich, and this fissure is increasing dramatically. People no longer talk of the proletariat; instead, a new word has been invented by sociologists: '*precariat*'. Under that term, they include the unemployed, students, and academics – people who have got qualifications but can't find work. Salaried employees are now in the minority and there's an enormous increase in casual workers. Siemens, for example, will dismiss a thousand workers, and then re-employ them through another company a few months later, this time working for half the pay rate. That's normal these days."

Society may demand Wallraff's brand of journalism, but the challenges facing journalists, particularly young professionals, wishing to practise such covert methods of investigation are mounting; in a world of fragmented media sources, declining advertising revenues, and a digital culture that expects its content to be free, those without subsidy will struggle to support an investigative career.

"Things are becoming more difficult, and this is why I advise the young journalists I meet to learn another profession so that they can support themselves. By doing so, they can specialise over long periods of time, or even use a foreign language to work on specific topics across different regions of the world. Without doing so, it's virtually impossible to pursue a responsible form of journalism these days."

Those who would follow Wallraff might be missing the point though; the man is an ascetic repelled by the herd impulse, a natural loner, committed above all to a lifestyle of perpetual and often painful reinvention.

Despite the self-abnegation, Wallraff gives generously to others, and having finished his account of his experiences, takes the time to offer a tour around his living grounds – three terraced houses, merged into one property. In the garden, he maintains a small museum of ancient rock artefacts, to which he adds his own stone artworks, intricate objects he creates using a mineral slab and a metal drill. He leads the way to his kitchen, which, like the museum, is suffused with an unfussy sense of order – everything in its place – with granite work surfaces, antique furniture, and fine Ethiopian ground coffee: the sparse accoutrements of good taste and affluence.

Unlike many of his peers, Wallraff has managed to accumulate considerable wealth through a career in investigative journalism, and invests a large amount of that money in his foundation for immigrants. He has also accrued a reputation for unimpeachable integrity, although the assaults on his character continue.

In 2003, the release of declassified Stasi files, previously held by the CIA, detailed communications Wallraff had with the East German secret police in the 1960s. The Springer newspapers immediately pounced on the allegations and the opportunity to portray him as a communist agent. He claimed he was guilty only of naïvety in agreeing to even talk with Stasi agents, and in 2004 a Hamburg district court stated that these declassified documents gave no proof of his collaboration. The court also ruled that newspapers like *Bild* must desist from printing misleading descriptions of Wallraff, such as "Stasi collaborator" in their articles.

Once again Wallraff had seen off the wolves, although they will surely return. He has too many powerful enemies.

Watching him climb the tall rope in his garden, head shaved like a paratrooper, a sinewy outline propelling itself skywards by sheer dint of will, it's hard not to wonder what keeps this man going; Wallraff could easily coast through the rest of his life with money and public goodwill secured. He is entitled to do so: in the Germanic world and beyond his name is synonymous with benchmark, pioneering journalism and the crusade for social justice. Why not retire quietly while in credit?

Instead here he is, the professional orphan, still heaving himself up a rope, still seeking invisibility, still fighting and scratching and rolling like a child through his autumn years, chasing a shadow that grows longer by the day. And why?

To learn to see afresh: to get close to people and things, to divest my own selfhood by becoming someone else. To see the world with different eyes.

Musical Reincarnation in Manchester

Nicholas Royle

Friday night at the end of February 2005; Liverpool's Barfly is almost empty. Two rooms, a bar in the middle, a booth with a mixing desk. At one end a raised stage. It's getting on for 1 am. From backstage Performance's lead singer Joe Stretch appears, picking his way across looped cables like a crane while others set up equipment, tight black trousers emphasising his long thin legs. I introduce myself and remind him that we spoke on the phone; he apologises for the circumstances in which we meet.

"What circumstances?"

"Liverpool. It's so tawdry."

The band, like me, is from Manchester. They take the stage at 1.30 am. Stretch crackles with nervous electricity. He dances in a jerky, puppet-like way that reminds me of Ian Curtis. Half the time he looks about to burst into tears, while at other times he's struggling to suppress a grin.

Laura Marsden, fag hanging out of the corner of her mouth, never cracks a smile, but bats away relentlessly at lead guitar and occasional bass. Her sister Billie, on Korg keyboards, takes her style prompts from the decade in which she was born – the big hair, the cocktail dress, the tiny handbag hanging off the end of the synth. Joe Cross chainsmokes and presses buttons on a Roland sequencer, industrious, absorbed.

The crowd is small but enthusiastic. The band only play six numbers but they're electrifying.

I feel more alive than I have for months. I feel that coming back to live in Manchester was a good move, after all. I have a powerful sense of living in the moment and at the same time feel like I'm 17 again.

In 1980, I was 17. I listened to John Peel and Mark Radcliffe, whose show on Piccadilly Radio was named after Joy Division's first single. I went to see bands at the Manchester
Apollo – Skids, Tubeway Army, Siouxsie and the Banshees. Psychedelic Furs at Rotters. Or was it Rafters? Or Pips? I attended gigs by Corridor One, a band formed by boys from my school.

When I wasn't reading the *NME*, I had my nose in existentialist French novels. My 1980 diary is littered with quotations about death, existence and meaninglessness written in a strange italic hand I affected at the time.

When I went back to school after the summer, I found myself in the same class as Andy Wilson, guitarist for post-punk band Passage, who wore black drainpipes and nail varnish. His hair swung in front of one side of his face in a thick black wedge, while remaining short on the other side to expose his dangling diamond earring. The haircut appeared to owe more to the severe side parting of much-feared English teacher Peter Farquhar than to Phil Oakey of the Human League. Andy would quit school weeks before taking his A-levels to join Passage full-time. Their debut album, *Pindrop*, had just been released. I'd heard tracks on Peel – the distilled melancholy of "Watching You Dance", the panic attack of "Fear" – and knew this was a band that would affect me as deeply as Joy Division had.

On November 21, I went with my best mate, Nigel, to see another New Wave act called Fad Gadget at the Squat, a narrow shed of a venue located next to the Contact Theatre on Oxford Road. What impressed us the most though was the support band. Their music was accessible, each song had a hook and lyrics you could hear, even above the guitar's artful whine and keyboards that combined the jauntiness of Sparks circa 1974 with a slightly unsettling fairground vibe. The lyrics caught my imagination, chiming with favourite themes and obsessions, whether it was images of a Cold War-torn Europe ("Janek crossed his country's borders / Wouldn't obey his sergeant's orders") or references to the particular art movement with which I had become infatuated ("His face lit with exultation / Like a surrealist dream"). I was hooked.

Nige and I went backstage on a pretext of interviewing Fad Gadget and each acquired a copy of the support band's mini audio cassette, titled *That Obscure Object Of......*, featuring four tracks: "Baby Doll", "Next Train", "Night Masque" and "Janek".

I still have that cassette and still listen to it regularly 27 years later. If there were a fire in my house and I was allowed to grab only five things, that tape would be one of them.

The cassette is white plastic and bears a white label. The titles of the four tracks have been typed in capitals (the "I" has fallen more heavily on the paper than the other letters), the title of the mini-album in upper and lower case, the ellipsis comprising seven dots. In the top right-hand corner "4B" could mean almost anything. And in the bottom left-hand corner, in red caps, the red and black two-colour typewriter ribbon being the height of sophistication at the time, is the name of the band: "PERFORMANCE".

When I move back to Manchester, 23 years later, the gig listings in *City Life* feature a local band called Performance. For one giddy moment I wonder if it's the same band I saw at the Squat almost a quarter of a century ago, but a couple of minutes on the Internet reveals they have a website and songs that can be listened to online.

I like things that have the same name as other things, particularly if they're the same kind of thing, or, if we're talking about artists, if they're working in a similar field. I always had this predilection, even before I discovered there was another published writer called Nicholas Royle, author of *Telepathy & Literature and The Uncanny*.

Notwithstanding the name thing, I don't really expect to like the band's stuff. I'm not greatly exercised by the Kaiser Chiefs or Franz Ferdinand or any of the other new bands around. But when I listen, I do like it. It's a little bit like the Human League re-formed after listening to some Pet Shop Boys albums and a lot of early New Order and maybe some Ultravox (John Foxx era, of course). There's even, dare I say it, a hint of Performance – the other one.

Tastes change, fashions come around.

I get a number for Joe Stretch and shortly after the gig in Liverpool, I meet up with him and Laura Marsden.

Laura's mum has her hair done by a woman whose brother, Stefan, used to be in a band. I have with me my copy of the only single the original Performance ever released: "Sensation Extension (I Need)" b/w "Sandman"' The sleeve is signed: "Deepest Thanks, Stefan".

After a little research it transpires that they're the same Stefan. Stefan Korab, the band's guitarist, remains active in the industry, performing as Kid Voodoo and putting on club nights at the Tiger Lounge and other venues in Manchester. His sister is Laura's mum's hairdresser.

I make efforts to trace the other members of the original Performance. Bernard Cox is working at the department store John Lewis. Cox tells me he sold his drum kit to Andy Rourke of the Smiths and is happy to have left the music business behind. Martin Straffon, who played bass in Performance, went on to run a club at Manhattan Sound, close to Manchester's Canal Street, where Johnny Marr would DJ, but when the building was compulsorily purchased, Straffon got out and is now a director of a motorcycle hire company ("Europe's biggest – and sponsors of the Honda Racing team in British Superbikes"). According to Korab, Phil Walsh, the group's keyboard player, went on to work with Divine and then to record jingles and has since gone off the radar. No one I've spoken to knows what happened to lead vocalist

Pip Crompton.

It's not right to describe the 1980s band as "the original," of course. It suggests a link between the two bands that, hairdressing apart, does not exist. Just as it would be wrong to describe the author of *The Uncanny* as the "original" Nicholas Royle just because he was around first. But how else to distinguish between two bands with the same name? And what about that, anyway? Pure coincidence? I don't think so. Small world? Undoubtedly, but still. I like the fact that there's a link between the two bands, however tenuous, outside of my head. I make a copy of the Performance tape for Joe. Does he agree that there's a similarity? No, but I'll maintain there is.

On Wednesday 20 June 2007, I'm at the Roadhouse, a basement venue on Newton Street in Manchester's Northern Quarter. Performance take to the stage at 11.10 pm Their set is longer these days. For one thing, the debut album, once to have been released in a blaze of publicity by Polydor, is newly available from a table next to the bar. I buy two copies.

In the two years between encountering the band for the first time and seeing them tonight, I've been to a dozen or so gigs. I've got to know Joe Stretch and have been on a tour date with the band to the Underground in Stoke.

The Roadhouse gig kicks off with "Market Street", one of the best songs off the album. Joe Stretch is rubbing his face, massaging his gums, biting his fingers. He unfolds his body to its full height, upends a bottle of water over his head, lurches, manically gurning, over the front row. The Marshall amps behind him have had the letters "hall" removed, so they read "Mars". Stretch's wide-eyed gaze sweeps the room as he mouths indecipherably between songs, balancing precariously on top of the monitors before stepping backwards into midair and asking, in a clear and audible voice, "What's next?"

The Old Fool Who Fell for the Female Eunuch

Chris Jefferis

Herb Elliot's first impression of Australian athletics coach Percy Cerutty – the man who would coach Elliot to Olympic gold for the 1500m in 1960 – was one shared by many of his contemporaries: "sort of interesting, but a bit of an old fool."

At 60, the famous trainer lectured Elliot and the other students of Aquinas College dressed only in white shorts, high above the Canning River in Perth, Western Australia, where a thick sea breeze cooled the elevated playing fields. Elliot remembers he "talked to us about flying. I remember he was running around flapping his arms."

The thing is, Cerutty was a phenomenally successful old fool, using his eccentric techniques to coax world records and gold medals out of the athletes he trained. One of the driving forces behind the 1950s golden age in Australian athletics, by the 60s he began turning his theories on sport and modern life into books. A weird mix of new age philosophy and sports psychology, Cerutty's approach to fitness was all encompassing, coloured with grandiloquent historical examples and a quasi-religious zeal. In an essay "On Greatness," he wrote:

> *To become great, whether an artist, a musician, a writer, a philosopher or creator or scientist, even as one great in sport, the secret lies, assuming there is some native ability in the first place, in one factor above all others – emotion…*
>
> *So you are enjoined to develop your emotional life by all the means open to*

you. Feed it upon art, music, sculpture, architecture, even upon tragedy. Feed it upon the biographies of the Great Ones: how they suffered: how they won out: how they overcame: became supreme.

By the time I started sifting through the archive of his letters at the Victorian State Library, I already knew Cerutty was a man addicted to cultivating obsession. I just didn't expect to find him, at the age of 77, cultivating an obsession with Germaine Greer. But reading their brief correspondence, the relationship between the septuagenarian postal worker turned messianic sports coach and the most important feminist of the late 20th century began to make a strange sort of sense. Despite their differences, a shared fascination with the detrimental effects of modern life was enough to allow their lives to intersect for a few months.

In 1938, the year before Greer was born, Cerutty was 43 years-old, a Melbourne postal worker with a 60-a-day habit on the verge of a complete physical and mental breakdown.

After his collapse that year he was bedridden, and doctors gave him six months to live, but instead of wasting away, Cerutty set out on a lifelong quest for physical and mental perfection. He eschewed cooked foods, and began reading philosophy and history.

He exercised relentlessly, and by 1940 he was the Victorian marathon champion with a respectable personal best of 2 hours, 52 minutes. His unique personal philosophy was already under construction: at Flemington racecourse in Melbourne, he was known as "that Cerutty nut" for galloping around the track in imitation of the race horses. Claiming that the slouching caused by sedentary office life crushed the upper lobes of the lungs, Cerutty developed running drills designed to enhance breathing and fluidity by mimicking the motions of animals.

Through the 50s his reputation as a formidable athletics coach grew. He kick-started the career of John Landy, the record breaking runner who became the second man to run a sub-four minute mile; under Cerutty's guidance Herb Elliot established himself as the greatest mile runner of all time; and after Elliot's retirement in 1960, Cerutty helped bring sprinter Betty Cuthbert out of retirement to win the 400m at the 1964 Tokyo Olympics.

In Cerutty's mind, the perfect athlete was a kind of self-constituting Zarathustra, determined to escape the "life of business in a large city, where each person is, mostly, merely a cog in a gigantic machine".

The athlete dedicated to fitness must purchase a small block of land away from the city in the country or by the ocean and build a house (never buy one) to provide an escape, at every available opportunity, from the destructive and oppressive forces of life in the city.

At times, Cerutty's ideas verged on the messianic. His 1967 book *Be Fit or Be Damned* claimed that businessmen and those in government had become emasculated by their lack of physical fitness. Although financially strong, they were physically weak, prone to "desperations and panics" and nervous about the future. The result? The threat of nuclear annihilation:

"It is because of so many otherwise successful men, financially secure, what is termed in the vernacular 'well-oiled', that we see so many terrors: fears and desperations, if the nationalistic and ideological movements in the world appear to be jeopardising, much less sweeping away, the investments and sources of income."

Fortunately, Cerutty had designed his exercise regimes with a post-apocalyptic, primitive world in mind, so that a devotee would be "able to wrest a subsistence from his environment". He promised a guide for living which negated the need for any god apart from sport: "The fit man would never admit as a finality, the right of any man to absolution, nor will he bend his knee to any anthropological, or anthropomorphic, gods. It is far more intelligent to search out the laws of life, and living."

Looking through the archives at the library, it's evident he had some devoted followers. Peter Stanton, who had trained at

Cerutty's athletics retreat in Portsea, a small coastal town in southern Victoria, wrote in one letter:

I was not an apt pupil, but I found in your words and outlook something that struck a responsive chord in me, and it was of immeasurable benefit to my character to hear spoken truths that so few people dare to face… You have taught me the value of honestly held beliefs, however unorthodox, because I found one adult in all this world who could state in unadorned language things that I had always known were true but had not had the courage to stand up for. You have taught me to become a man.

Many of his protégés began mimicking his charisma and hyper-expressivity. One of Cerutty's correspondents adorned her letters with transcendent images of sunsets, beaches and semireligious new age iconography, addressing him as "Percy my daring, adorable, mad and eccentric high-voltage, super-speed, Friend".

A large part of the letter was written in capitals for emphasis.

In an interview in 2001 Herb Elliot described how he was less swayed: "There would be times where he would say something that was insightful for me, and it seemed to me to be genius. Then there'd be other times where he would say something, which I would think was ridiculous. But that never bothered me, I just ignored it."

It was while sorting through these letters that I found out about Germaine Greer. After Greer's debut book *The Female Eunuch* was released in 1970 – a ferocious feminist polemic that became an international best seller and made her an overnight celebrity – Cerutty fell headlong into what one journalist of the time termed "Germania".

His archives contained a variety of Greer-related newspaper clippings, accompanied by his scribbled notes, carefully attached with paper clips. In his journal he had copied out passages of *The Female Eunuch*, and mentioned attentively watching her TV appearances. He wrote notes to himself about his obsession, the feeling that "the picture of her: her face and expression, is with me most of my waking hours, heightened, no doubt, by re-reading her book most days".

He started writing to Greer in 1971. Cerutty set out to capture her interest by describing what he stood for and why he had a special emphatic connection with her ideas on women's liberation. In April 1971, he received her amiable reply:

Dear Mr Cerutty,

Thank you so much for a charming letter. You are perfectly right about cigarette smoking. I don't do it very seriously – it's usually a response to stress, of which Australia has been giving me plenty. I drink too much, too, and punish my body unmercifully, but it seems the only way to avoid punishing my mind. I'm sure you could teach me a great deal about avoiding stress and the old flight or fight reaction which drains my body of Vitamin C so that the slightest touch gives me a black bruise. My hands never shake, you know, but I have stomach pains and diarrhoea all the time.

Of course, I knew who you were, once I got to the signature, and I know that you are the one person who could heal me. But now it is too late. I'm off to torment myself further in Bangladesh tomorrow morning.

So let me just thank you for your letter, and all the kind and concerned things you found to say. And accept my love.

Germaine.

Greer's letters to Cerutty are peppered with comments about the frustrations of her personal celebrity. Describing an upcoming television appearance, she wrote to Cerutty about the difficulties of getting her ideas about gender and power across to the Australian public:

I shall be coming back to Australia very briefly to do four programmes in rather a hurry in Sydney. But they are all programmes in which we are trying to get other people to talk. I think I have been exposed sufficiently to the Australian public and they have made quite clear that they are not terribly interested in getting right what it is I tried to say to them. I really don't feel like inviting any more personal publicity in Australia. I would much rather try to demonstrate to Australians the sorts of things I wish them to understand about themselves and their country through their own words and actions.

Cerutty offered in his letters to minister to her particular stresses and loneliness, responding to Greer's admission of constant diarrhoea with a declaration of love, testifying to his vitality and strong character, and a page and a half of emphatic discussion about bowel function and migraine headaches:

I am not so sure as to all this about Vitamin C and bruises. I live on almost uncooked foods: there are no cooked foods in nature, just as the "natural", or those removed from all the idiot inhibitions, go to bed naked. What is apparent is you are a most unusual woman: that which applies to many, won't necessarily apply to you. So as to Diarrhoea: it is a symptom. (A mate has just called in a sherry or two – this does not mean the basic intelligence is affected, not at all: only, perhaps, the physical movements: mistakes in typing, etc. Indeed, alcohol can remove the inhibitions, take the cap off as it were: there was probably no great mind who was a vegetarian or teetotaller. But the means to greatness can also be the means for destruction: an early death, as history, many great minds, poets etc are the evidence. This doesn't mean that because I am 77, I am mindless, not at all. What it does mean is that I have learnt how to survive without any loss as to mind or brain. I like to think (and you could be the same!) the greatest male mind that has ever lived. I am certain you are the greatest female mind that ever lived. I expect this in nature and evolution.)

So back to diarrhoea: Before I understood these things I relied on the medical profession. Most hopeless: they cannot even keep themselves alive. So: when I suffered from what was a kind of paralysis of the bowel, all they did was prescribe drugs that in the end destroyed the natural functioning of the bowel. Now I never worry: never take any drugs: nothing. The medical profession are wrong as to bowel function. They say an evacuation of the bowel once in 24 hours is OK. IT IS NOT!

When I rise whether 8 am, 9 am, 10 am the first thing that happens is that I evacuate the bowel. 20 or 30 minutes after I go to the toilet again. Then another 20 to 30 minutes after – the evacuation of the bowel again. This means, that the content of the lower bowel is evacuated. Then something in the upper bowel drops down to be evacuated, a third lot. This means that my bowel is completely emptied. So all the disease causing contents gone, ejected. Nothing left to cause agedness, disease acidosis, anything. SO in my case I leave most men of any age for dead: heartwise, physically, the lot! Alcohol keeps the bowel open. You are the cause of these conditions. Your nature, dispositions: gifts, etc. The thing is to understand what we are: then no more real problems, physically or mentally.

I feel/realise: it could be I could help you. A letter is a poor medium: it is the person! When we meet someone we can believe in – that is half the cure. I feel we should get together. Too many men are jealous of women. Not me. I am devoted: adore them: because they are females. So, I respect: love and adore – YOU!

Could I be right? We are destined to meet? Between us we could straighten out this crazy world? I would like to think it is possible!

It's hard to understand how an aged athletics coach could become so obsessed with Germaine Greer, and also why a prominent young feminist, recently graduated from a PhD in Elizabethan drama from Cambridge, would be seeking cures for bowel dysfunction and celebrity ennui from a 77 year-old fitness guru. But I think there is a deeper connection between the two.

Those who have read *The Female Eunuch* will be familiar with the odd self-investigative style of the book. Greer looks at her body, and other women's bodies, and asks herself, why the shaved armpits, the coiffed hair, the arthritis-inducing stiletto heels and passive body language? Why the tamed and tortured body?

The forces supporting and threatening women's vitality, as Greer described them, had a lot in common with those Cerutty saw acting on anxious, tired, overweight businessmen: "Energy is the power that drives every human being, it is not lost by exertion but maintained by it, for it is a faculty of the psyche. It is driven to perverted manifestations by curbs and checks," wrote Greer.

"Nervous diseases, painful menstruation, unwanted pregnancies, accidents of all kinds, are all evidence of women's energy destroying them."

Although Greer's prescription for liberating body and mind went far beyond exercise, she shared ideas with Cerutty about how our debilitated bodies could come to twist the way we think and feel about life. Maybe these similarities go some way towards explaining Cerutty's obsession with Greer, although the young philosopher's beauty probably had something to do with it too. Eventually, Cerutty's correspondence became too much for Greer:

I will never be happy until I see you: meet you, face to face. You must accept it – no need for conceits – imagine one is the all, but it could be the most wonderful?

Greer's response was warm but unequivocal:

You must not say that you will never be happy until you meet me. That is foolishness. You will be happy everyday, all the time, except when you think about injustices and cruelty. These are the only things that can make you sad, certainly not my distance or strangeness.

Be happy – Germaine.

As far as I could tell from the records, that was the end of their four-month correspondence.

From postal worker to sports coach, to messianic theorist and unrequited lover of Australia's greatest feminist, Cerutty had traversed his own rigorously individual path through the changing and debilitating conditions of the 20th century. Just under four years after his final letter to Greer, he would die from motor neurone disease at the age of 80.

Arabian Vice: Sex, Lies and Videotape in Dubai City

Sachi Cunningham

Our last evening in Dubai and we're walking into "Cyclone", one of the largest night clubs in the city, known for its high quality mix of Eastern European, Asian and African sex workers.

The décor is decidedly cheap and neon, pulsing with clusters of coy women who bat their eyes at men circling the room. It's like any large club really, except the dance floor is eerily empty. I have taped a small video camera to my inner thigh, and have a *MiniDisc* recorder in my bag – that to the eye looks like a poor man's *iPod* – with stereo mics attached to it disguised as headphones. There is security and a metal detector at the entrance, but I don't get patted down.

In the bathroom I stare at a bloody pad drowning in the toilet as I move the camera to my purse. I join my reporting partner Mimi sitting at a table near the bar, the camera poking out of an open zipper on the side of my bag. Mimi takes a drag of her cigarette and looks around.

Kanye West's "Gold Digger" pumps through the speakers, as a herd of international businessmen and young women size each other up, bartering fantasies. Unlike regular clubs, where an interested look can start a conversation about your work, your interests or your astrological sign, the exchanges here are short and to the point.

"How much you want?" a man in a pressed blue shirt asks as he stops at our table.

"Too much for you," Mimi says.

Previously we had played along with these advances, but we are burnt from nearly two weeks in clubs like these, trying to learn more about Dubai's sex trade for our PBS documentary.

Like most boomtowns, Dubai has become a city full of paradoxes: a mixture of glamour, opportunity, desperation and human rights abuses. It's a city that shapes itself as a modern cosmopolitan paradise, a playground for international visitors, yet when 15 year old French schoolboy Alexandre Robert was raped by three local men in July this year, he was advised to flee Dubai because he could be prosecuted for homosexuality. It's a city with the tallest building in the world, the Burj Dubai (still under construction), yet that same building was the site of a 2,500 strong riot last year, when labourers on as little as US $4 a day smashed cars and offices in a dispute about pay and poor working conditions.

Most of these workers, and nearly 75% of Dubai's population, is foreign born: the city has become a Mecca for tax-free multinational business, luring a young, hungry, disproportionately male work force from India, China, Pakistan, Bangladesh and the Philippines. Dubai's utopian cluster of man made islands is literally rising from the sea to house the elite of this work force that totalled nearly 25,000 newcomers per month last year. Everyone from subcontracted kitchen workers to Halliburton's hired guns stop through for R&R from the war in Iraq. Here, the oldest profession in the world has found a ripe and thriving market.

"She ain't messin' with no broke..."

I mistakenly make eye contact with one of the guards patrolling the floor. Paranoid, I walk to the bar to see how visible my camera is to the passing eye. The camera can pass, but what sticks out prominently is Mimi and myself. The prostitutes are clearly divided into enclaves based on nationality. Mimi, a Bulgarian American, and myself, a Japanese American, appear to be the only women of different colours that are actually talking with each other. Depending on nationality these women are making anywhere from 200–2000 Dirhams for the night [approx. £26–£260]. The going rate for four hours is based on nationality, with the Arab women demanding the highest price and the Chinese the least.

"There's just so many of them," explained an American journalist that we had met at York, another popular club, earlier in our trip. He boasted that he could get several Chinese for the price of one, "and they clean your apartment in the morning too," he said with a pasty, pock-faced grin as a set of three longhaired beauties swarmed him.

I walk back to the table with two vodka tonics.

"Get down girl, go head get down."

Sasha, a Siberian prostitute that we interviewed earlier had sent home enough "gold" to buy her family a house. When she first came to Dubai she told us of being locked in a room where she would sleep with dozens of construction workers every night for less than a dollar per John. Now she could be selective. She had regular clients like the American from Texas who texted her a love note during our interview.

"He wants sex for free," she told us, but she wasn't interested in love. She was in Dubai for the same reason as every other foreign worker that we met: to get rich quick.

We'd come to Dubai as part of Mimi's photojournalistic investigation of the sex trade. She had focused on sex trafficking in Eastern Europe for the last three years. In Moldova she met a woman who had been trafficked to Dubai. The woman was supposed to return to Dubai this week to try to find the illegitimate child she had left behind, but in the end her paperwork didn't go through and the father, a policeman, discouraged her visit. We'd come to Dubai anyway, but it didn't take long to realise that women with illegal papers doing illegal work aren't so keen on talking in front of a video camera. So we got creative, combing the clubs and malls for documentary subjects.

After one more drink and a little more footage, we decide we've had enough and head back to our hotel to pack. I'm booked on a return flight to the US the next morning.

The first thing that I notice when we open the door to our room are our beds. The sheets are made despite hanging a "Do Not Disturb" sign on the door that morning. A few feet into the room and we see our clothes and belongings strewn all over the floor. My computer and hard drives are gone. Mimi's reporting notebooks have vanished from the night table. Mimi calls the front desk, but they refuse to contact the police.

"We've just been robbed, and you're telling me to wait until the morning?" Mimi asks with disbelief.

I open the safety deposit box to make sure that my passport, ticket and shot tapes are still safe. They are all accounted for. I walk down to the lobby and demand an explanation. Not wanting to make a scene, the worker finally places the call. Within five minutes a team of police are at the hotel. I take them to our room and explain the scene: that I have told the cleaning crew that morning not to come to our room, but that the beds were made when we returned that evening. We look through the remaining clothes to try and figure out what was stolen. I try to conceal the purses with holes ripped out for the camera on either side. The police assume it is an inside job. They tell us that all of the cleaning help, like most low paid labourers in Dubai, live together; finding the thief and stolen goods should be easy. Another crew of officers take fingerprints while a group of plain clothed officers are dispatched to search the cleaning crew's housing. Mimi photographs the crime scene. We're asked to come to the police station to file a report.

Problem is, we have to get our passports, tickets and tapes from the safe deposit box. Mimi has already disclosed that we're reporters.

"We were told that Dubai was one of the safest places in the world," she says as she takes another shot.

Something doesn't feel right though; I'm nervous about the police seeing the footage we've shot. We had recorded a side of

Dubai on those tapes that the local authorities would not be happy about.

Without any discussion Mimi, a good deal taller than me, grabs my purse and stands in front of door of the box in order to block the view as she fills the bag with tapes. Grabbing five at a time, one batch slips from her nervous clutch and crashes to the floor. My heart surges as I pick them up and Mimi hands me the filled bag.

The police station is empty apart from a drunk guy with a bloody head. We give our fingerprints and they copy our passports. When they see that Mimi is born in Bulgaria, their questions become more suspicious.

"Why are you here again?"

"When did you leave Bulgaria?"

We maintain that we are journalists and file written reports.

"Show me your camera," the police chief asks Mimi upon hearing that she had photographed the crime scene. A lump grows in my stomach beneath my purse filled with tapes.

"My camera is in the hotel room," Mimi says in her icy Eastern European accent, without skipping a beat.

I know she has her camera with her, and that the camera also contains photos of prostitutes.

An officer takes Mimi back to the room as I wait at the police chief's desk. A Somalian officer continues to take down my information. I remember a faulty memory card that Mimi had discovered at the start of the trip and wonder how she will ever be able to pull a switch off.

The morning call to prayer sounds as the glow of dawn comes through the windows. Mimi returns and hands her camera over to the police chief.

"What's wrong with it?" he asks, showing her the "error" sign that pops up when he turns the camera on.

"I don't know," she says, playing along. I find out later that, escorted by two officers, Mimi went back to the room, and pretended to find her camera in the far corner of the room where her broken memory card sat stashed in a side pocket of her camera bag. She put the card full of images in the tiny pocket of her jeans.

In front of the police chief she takes the camera card out and dusts it off. She does the same with the camera batteries. The error message still shows up.

"You can take it if you'd like," Mimi tells the chief.

He hands her the camera back and tells the officers to return us to the hotel.

I throw my clothes in a bag while we wait for our fixer to pick us up and take us to the airport. He arrives, and after running over the night's drama with him as he drives, he tells us that the hotel is owned by the Chief of Police, and that the robbery, conveniently staged on our last night in the hotel, was likely something more akin to a planned raid. We had probably been watched, he says. As he and Mimi try to piece together the evening's events, I pull all of the labels off of the tapes and disperse them throughout my bag. Mimi is scheduled to leave the next day, so I give her my video camera to take with her so as not to draw any attention when checking in.

At the airport I try to look nonchalant, but immediately after walking through the first security pass I am pulled aside, before even checking in.

Behind a curtained room, a veiled woman frisks my clothes and goes through my bags, collecting all of the tapes and putting them in a paper bag.

"Why are you taking those?" I ask, explaining that they contain video of the grand construction and sights of Dubai.

"Let's watch them now, together," I say. "There's nothing on them!"

Waiting on the other side of the security checkpoint, Mimi raises her voice.

"Why are you taking her things?" she asks. People in the airport start to turn their heads our way. I move out of the detention tent and start to call the numbers stored in our cell phone of the police officers that we met earlier that night.

The man who took my deposition tells me that airport security is a separate department and that he can't help us, but that he will send someone to see what the problem is. Almost immediately a plainclothes officer sitting against the airport wall stands up and walks towards the scene.

"Our hotel is broken into, and now I'm being detained?" I ask loud enough for onlookers to hear.

I continue making calls to everyone and anyone as Mimi does the same. The human rights worker we had interviewed earlier that week doesn't answer, but I carry out a pretend conversation anyway, and then continue calling in for help and with complaints to other locals.

With 10 minutes to go before my plane is scheduled to take off, my young UAE escort, outfitted in a traditional white cloak and headscarf, receives an order in his earpiece. He hands the bag of tapes to me.

"I'm sorry, but we made a mistake," he says without explanation. "We thought you were someone else." He walks with me to check in my bags and escorts me to the plane. Still in a state of shock, I unload the tapes into my purse as the plane takes off. Why did they let me go and how could we have been so naïve as to think that we could have filmed all that time without anyone noticing? But then, surely prostitution is so widely practised here, and so visible, that the authorities wouldn't really care if someone shot footage of it? Someone clearly did. Confused, but thankful that I'm flying home with taped evidence of the sex trade rather than a bunch of tall tales, I collapse into a deep sleep, clutching the purse strapped over my body.

I'd Rather Worship Jesus Than Go Christmas Shopping

Ron Butlin

There's a part of me that's always had a sneaky affection for Scrooge. When the horizon starts filling up with Santas, the streets are clogged with shoppers and the shops crammed with plastic holly, inflatable reindeer and the muzak of seasonal hard-sell, then it's time to bar the door, get out the gruel and light the single candle. Sometimes, turning my back on the lot of it can seem very tempting. And this year, 2006, Christmas will be the best yet. Thanks to the machinations of the global market, Britain has just about the lowest credit rates on record and its shops more to sell than ever before. Jingle bells, jingle tills.

I remember feeling just this way last year, until I heard the church bells ringing for Midnight Mass. Come on. They're calling us with their joyful clamour, with deep and thrilling bass boom-notes, and merry glistening *ding-dongs*. Great stuff. Come on, I say, it'll be fun. Off with the TV. Grab the coat, the scarf and gloves – it's icy out. Walk through the near-deserted streets, turn the corner – and we're there.

Entering the candlelit vault of stonework and darkness, we catch our breath at the intimate splendour of it all. Around us, there's the play of light and shadow on people's faces, the reflected gloss on the darkened wood, with flickering reds, yellows and blues coming from the stained glass windows. Ahead is a model of the Nativity. It's as if we've entered, not the past, but a moment that has endured for centuries. The interior is crowded.

Last minute arrivals, like ourselves, are finding their places. I pause at the end of a pew and just inside the door a woman moves along to give us room. She smiles. We sit down. Though non-believers, we do as everyone else. We stand and sing, we bow our heads and pray.

In the darkness above our heads, 12 chimes ring out for midnight. As the final stroke falls, its echo merges, it seems, with a long-ago echo coming from that small chapel of Santa Maria Maggiore Basilica. There, 440 years after the birth of Christ, and on the stroke of midnight – supposedly the moment of Christ's birth – midnight mass was celebrated for the very first time. The small chapel had been specially built by Pope Sixtus III. Every Christmas Eve from then on, this special mass was celebrated by an ever-larger congregation.

Gradually myths grew describing how, at the miraculous moment of midnight, the sand and the seashore, the rocks and the mountains, the oceans and valleys would open up, revealing all their hidden treasures. While the bells tolled midnight, farm animals would be given the power of speech, and anyone who listened to what they said risked being struck dumb or falling lifeless on the spot. In some countries it was believed that the dead rose from their graves, kneeling at the foot of the cemetery cross to say prayers under the guidance of dead priests. This eerie service would conclude with a blessing, after which they turned to gaze longingly at the villages and homes where they were born. Then, in silence, they would sink back into the ground.

Superstitions, I know, like religion itself. But to my surprise something happened as I sat in that candlelit Edinburgh church, one man in a congregation hundreds strong. I found myself suddenly moved. Deeply moved. I'm a complete unbeliever and I had to remind myself that those myths were touching, but quite absurd. But what of that? Their truth may be metaphorical rather than actual, but they still have real meaning. They're charged with the mystery lying at the very heart of our lives. More profound, surely, than the emptiness of frantic Christmas shoppers and stressed-out assistants: all the choreography of our grab-and-go consumer culture, set to the relentless muzak-din of disco-carols.

Listening to the church bells' echoes fading into the past, I was all at once overwhelmed by the certainty that each one of us had his or her place there. Quite unexpectedly, I sensed a deep and unqualified peace. This peace didn't come from God – whether Christian, Muslim, Hindu or whatever – but from something very human: a sense of genuine belonging.

How different to the rhetoric we hear outside those doors, from the politics that have set our world lurching from crisis to crisis. Uncertainty has come to us as never before: we are as much at the mercy of our own democratically elected leaders as at the hands of any terrorist. With profiteering and fanaticism tearing everything apart, we are being made to live in a state of permanent threat. Our fears are stilled with platitudes of reassurance, our hopes are exploited, our expectations are diminished to a petty selfishness that can be placated by loyalty cards, electronic gadgets and special offers. These are toys to keep us amused. Like children we are supposed to be grateful, and trusting.

Of course, there were toys there, too – a cardboard stable, a wooden crib, the papier mâché figures of Mary and Joseph, the animals of straw and cloth. But these we could see clearly and we knew them for what they were.

We were invited to rise and sing a carol about Christ being born. And, though I didn't believe one word of it, I sang out loud. The vault of the church resonated with the communal voices of men, women and children – some of whom might very well have been jostling with me for the last of the Christmas goodies. But so what? By staying at home, Scrooge might very well have avoided the frenzy and clamour of commercial Christmas – but he would've missed out on that moment of utter peace, which endured long after I left the church.

Those Mao Badges and the Red Stars and All That Crap Have to Go

Rose George

The Trans-Siberian takes a long time to get from Moscow to Irkutsk. One day into fourth class carriage life, and we – 70 or so do-gooding volunteers on Operation Raleigh – were bored. The view was always trees. The food was dull. Valentina, the samovar-controlling carriage attendant, was a dragon.

Then we met the conscripts. Two carriages down, still in fourth class – though it may have been third and a half – were two carriages full of young Russian boys-to-men, heading for Chita, three days beyond Irkutsk, to do a couple of years of military service that would make the train look unbearably exciting.

We made friends with them and their vodka. We learned that Valentina, when she wasn't feeling dragon-like, sold vodka from her samovar cubbyhole for 1000 roubles – or nearly nothing. We got drunk, we played cards, we tried each other's languages. And then they got their kit off.

"We can sell you," they said.

It was only a couple of years after the Soviet Union had crumbled. Their caps and belts and shirts and trousers were, for them, the symbol of two years of impending hell. To us, they were hip. The red stars and green caps, the badges and the Cyrillic: it was all so *Smiley's People*. So unknown. So chic.

Communist chic kitsch had only really been available to gawping Westerners for two years, and here was an entire department store of the stuff, for a pittance.

The commerce lasted a day or so. Then one conscript – Yuri? Sergei? The names are all vodka – arrived during a transaction. He was angry.

"You should be ashamed," he told his fellow conscripts, "you are selling off your uniforms for money?"

He looked at us.

"You should be ashamed too."

The selling stopped.

Yuri/Sergei was a proud man. He was angry at the rapid dismantling of his country, and he thought that selling its remnants to these noisy Westerners showed a lack of pride. He's probably an oligarch by now.

I kept my Red Army belt and cap, but they never emerged from the drawer. I'd not forgotten being chastised. Nevertheless, eight years later, I did it again. In Saddam's Iraq, in 2001, images of the man were everywhere. You couldn't move for seeing the jowly face and the black moustache. They were on the hotel receptionist's desk; on posters in every shop; on watches and pens and books. I succumbed. I bought six Saddam watches, a few Saddam posters, and a collection of Saddam's books, including his masterpiece, *One Trench or Two*.

When I returned, friends were desperate for the watches. They thought they were fashionable. They thought they were kitsch enough to be hip. They thought – and I didn't disagree – that a homicidal dictator, whose son reportedly had people mauled to death with attack dogs, who kept eight million people on an emotional spectrum that began with dread and ended with terror, was comical. His bushy black moustache. His hilarious speeches. His face on a watch! It was all so cute.

But this year something odd happened. Maybe I grew up. Maybe it was penance for having turned the iconic symbols of monstrous regimes into arm-candy. Maybe it was China.

This summer I went to China for the first time. For a while, I did what first-time visitors all probably do. I marvelled at how good the food was there, and how crap it was here. I noted down the hilarious Chinglish. I goggled at the smog and the thoughtless, relentless construction. But I never, ever, bought any commie kitsch.

It was everywhere. In tourist "villages" from Chongqing to Beijing, there were Mao posters, badges, pens. There were kiosks selling nothing but *The Little Red Book*. There were figurines of teachers and intellectuals being tortured and humiliated, forced to crawl on their knees with placards round their necks as they had done during the Cultural Revolution. Toy teachers with toy tormentors. In the tourist crafts market in Beijing, the *lo wei* – foreigners – were rapt. They bought everything. And I felt different. I bought nothing.

In East Germany, nostalgia for communist days is pervasive enough to have a name: "*ostalgie*", or nostalgia for the East. There are "*ostalgie*" discos. There was a globally famous film – *Goodbye Lenin* – which saw nothing wrong in laughing at the past. But it's such a recent past. In the Stasi museum in the former East Berlin, the perfectly preserved 1960s furniture, Honecker's bathroom and phone, are all interesting enough. But upstairs, in the Stasi library, people still go to find their personal files and map out exactly how their lives were derailed by the East German secret police.

In China, it's not even about the past being recent. The past isn't the past yet. Mao is dead, of course. Though his portrait still hangs in Tiananmen, he can be publicly criticised for the failed "Great Leap Forward," which caused 30 million Chinese to die of hunger, even if his wife and her fellow three in the "Gang of Four" took the rap for the "Cultural Revolution" The less observant visitor, and the stubborn expat, can even claim that China now has a free market economy, that the police never interfere with citizens unless they break the law, that – a common expat refrain – "I feel freer in China than I ever did in Berlin/London/Chingford." But on my hotel television the BBC magically went black whenever anything "negative" about China came on – a segment about blogging? ZAP.

"And now we go to the protests over the new China–Tibet rail – ZAP."

There is no Wikipedia. During the month I was there, two reputable journalists were imprisoned for spuriousness. A blind lawyer who defends people against forced abortion was arrested for turning up at court. *The Little Red Book* is still everywhere, even if it's now got a Gucci cover. And I won't buy it. On reflection, I won't buy Saddam or Stalin either. I've got over it. The icons of homicidal dictators and their murderous regimes have lost their charm.

I'd say they should be banned, but that's a bit communist.

The Architecture of Illness

David Foster

The patient's journey: in this case it starts with my mother's persistent sickness, a visit to the local GP. The doctor makes some preliminary checks, takes blood, and then refers her to hospital for tests.

Then I am accompanying my mother to her bronchoscopy. This is the first journey we make through the hospital corridors. We park in the nearby terraced streets, and then walk into the hospital on a subterranean level. The corridor takes us past urology on the right: banks of alarm systems on the wall. Round a sharp corner, and we get to choose between the stairs or joining the silent, nervous strangers waiting together for the lift.

A bronchoscopy is a probe of the respiratory system using fibre optics, which are inserted through the trachea into the lungs. Like so much of the medical technology now common in diagnostic procedures, it allows the medical gaze to descend deep into the anatomy of the human body.

I see none of this. I remember the waiting room: toothpaste green with a floral frieze. Posters giving health advice. Assorted seats with leather effect finishing. The obligatory stack of backdated magazines. Next to us three generations of Pakistani women carry on a bi-lingual conversation. Despite the language barrier it's clear that the oldest, dressed in a sari, nervously awaits similar tests.

From the waiting room we are taken into a tiny anteroom for an initial consultation, before I leave my mother in the larger medical preparation room. As specialist instruments follow the passageways of her respiratory system, I wander the hospital corridors to waste away the waiting time, and hang around in the Belle Vue Restaurant.

My mother's blood oxygen levels are so low that she is immediately hospitalised. A few days later she is diagnosed with lung cancer, which she will battle with for a year.

My sister arrives home and we go to the hospital.

Crossing the road we spot our mother, a minute figure gazing out of the fourth floor window in the late-80s extension block. She is watching for our arrival.

Later in a letter she writes, "I am much too healthy to be here, I'm running around at night helping the old ladies pushing their buzzers and move their blankets" Looking at her handwriting is what impresses her absence on me most.

She is placed in private rooms in another unit to prevent the risk of infections, which her diminished immune system cannot withstand. The entrance to this block is always surrounded by the excited chatter of women and men visiting the neo-natal units. This section of the hospital was built in the 1970s, and was an award winning design at the time. I climb a stairwell next to a floor to ceiling window, which reveals the patchwork of roofs and passageways that have swallowed the ground below: refuge for expelled groups of smokers.

Upstairs my mother is sitting in bed, weekend supplements strewn around her. Sunlight reflects off the opposing hospital block's glass façade and into the room.

"I'm going out of my wits here. I've read all the papers. I can't see anyone, although there's a nice West Indian nurse who comes to see me."

In the century that this hospital has stood, its wards have changed from Florence Nightingale's long communal corridors to designs that place precedence on patient privacy.

At the same time as this, my grandmother has suffered an acute stroke and is in a hospital over in Peterborough. She appears to be in a deeply comatose state which resembles uneasy sleep. At her bedside the notice board reads "NIL BY MOUTH", then, "WEEKLY OBJECTIVE: sit Evelyn in the space chair to stimulate movement."

Who knows how conscious she is of our presence? Stunted monologues on family news are spoken to her with overemphasised intonation, as if delivered down a bad international phone line. We are always watching for any sign of response. But there's only so long I can keep it up before looking for other distractions: staring at crumpled blue sheets, a burst of ward chatter, a Catherine Cookson novel on the window shelf, a view of unkempt back gardens. These are the things I see when I look away. As prospects diminish for recuperation, Evelyn is moved from the specialist ward to a high care ward: back down broad corridors that reach toward her vanishing point.

I remember the quality of the light, the echoes, and the distance that the corridor stretched. The memory of the corridors of different hospitals becomes mixed together.

Why is it that now I can only remember the journeys made back and forth from the wards rather than the visits themselves? From these, I have the vaguest recollection of small talk that barely scratched the surface of what we probably wanted to say.

At my mother's bedside, conversation has run its course; sometimes it's hard to keep it going in such a sterile environment. It's time to go.

"Do you need me to bring in anything? I have an old personal stereo. I'll bring you some tapes."

Then comes tiredness and frustration at her own state:

"David, I'm sorry I'm not doing much."

"Mum!"

"You know the towels, the washing towels, in the bathroom.

They might be dirty."

The hospital corridors are calm now. Visiting time is over, evening meals have been served. She walks to the lifts with us and as we retrace our steps back through the building, we know she'll be at the window again, watching us leave.

I Killed Britney Spears

Jean Hannah Edelstein

It's Britney, bitch

I was unhappy when I heard that she had broken up with Justin Timberlake. I was saddened when she married her hick friend from Louisiana on a drunken night in Las Vegas. I felt troubled when she wed the horrible Kevin Federline.

I winced when, barefoot and pregnant, she wept on national television before an audience fixated on the spectre of her decline. I frowned when she was photographed stumbling about Hollywood with Paris Hilton and without her knickers; I worried when she shaved her head. And when I saw Britney Spears stumbling fitfully across the stage of the 2007 Video Music Awards, grabbing the crotches of her male back-up dancers without feeling, mouthing the words to a song that was clearly not coming from her heart, something died inside me.

She's so lucky, she's a star / but she cries, cries, cries in her lonely heart

I fell in love with Britney Spears on a cold winter's day in the December of my 18th year. I was shopping for accessories in a tatty store for teenagers; she was dancing through the halls of a high school in a sexy uniform on a large flat-screen television suspended above a rack of Christmas earrings with flashing red-and-green lights.

Baby, I'm so into you / You've got that something, what can I do?

While I had heard Britney's first earth-shattering single, "… Baby One More Time", on the radio occasionally before that particular moment of epiphany, the depth of her growling voice had led me to believe that she was a middle-aged African-American woman. Thus, I was quite taken aback by the juxtaposition of the basso profundo and the pink bowed mouth of a blonde pigtailed nymphet.

Oops, I did it again / I played with your heart / got lost in the game

It is not, I will mention here, as a small caveat, that my affection for Britney Spears was ever romantic – or at least not very much. Rather, my worship of her was heroic. Britney Spears, I decided, embodied all of the possibility of my young female life. In my case these possibilities had been trampled over by the ambitions of my parents in a not dissimilar way from that in which Britney's infamous mother Lynn had guided her daughter's career with an iron fist.

The path my parents selected didn't involve nearly as exciting a wardrobe though: without consulting me too much, they carefully moulded my life with the ultimate aim being the receipt of a respectable undergraduate degree, instead of a Video Music Award. Adolescent, I necessarily resented it.

Say hello to the girl that I am / You're gonna have to see through my perspective / I need to make mistakes just to learn who I am / And I don't wanna be so damn protected

Britney was an apt figure upon which to fixate my girlish dreams because she was (as discussed in the various celebrity magazines which I consumed in shameful secret) the same kind of girl as me: born in 1981, in a small, boring, American town, the middle of three children. At 17, still a virgin, although (as evidenced by the way in which she writhed through the frames of her videos) replete with all the pent-up sexual frustration of a nice American girl who had been strictly forbidden to have sexual relations with her boyfriend... and was probably struggling to understand the meaning of sexual relations thanks to the exploits of her very own President. Except that while these things filled me with secret shame, she made it into a brand: Miss Britney Jean Spears, the whorish virgin, the untouched slut.

I'm not a girl / Not yet a woman / All I need is time

Time has marched on for both of us: for me, the transition into womanhood has been comprised of a mundane string of typical middle-class benchmarks, struggles, minor triumphs: tertiary education, unsuitable boyfriends, a string of chilly rented flats, career starts and stops and missteps. Through it all I've kept an eye on what Britney has been going through.

At first, it seemed, in contrast to me, that she was going from strength to strength. But then, at some point, the trajectory of her life seemed to go in completely the opposite direction from mine. Where my interest in her was once based on envy and aspiration, it now became all about Schadenfreude: any time that things felt a little tough, I could always check to see how Britney was getting along and feel relieved that at least I still had all of my hair. It was as if our roles had reversed: I couldn't help but think that maybe if Britney had known about me she would have wished to have my life as I had once longed for hers.

With a taste of poison paradise / I'm addicted to you / Don't you know that you're toxic?

Although my fandom was quite half-hearted and cynical, I nonetheless was one of millions who fed the Britney machine. I gave her family and managers a reason to continue bleeding her dry as it became increasingly apparent that she was no longer able to fit in the box that made us all love her, be fascinated by her, want to be her or sleep with her.

Flicking through the gossip blogs, I wince when I see the pictures: her bloated, spotty face, her ratty hair extensions, the enormous soft drink perpetually clutched in her chewed fingers, her two unhappy looking children who are the unassailable proof that she, too, has fallen victim to base carnal desire. It's like the Britney who I once loved is dead. And I can't help but feel that every time I lurk in a newsstand, flicking through a copy of *OK!* to glean the latest developments in her tragic decline, I am at least partially responsible.

When I see that dead look in her sad, bewildered eyes, I feel like maybe, in a little way, I killed her.

Contributors

Laura Barton is a feature writer for *The Guardian*. Originally from Wigan, she now lives in London, and is working on her first novel.

Billy Briggs is a former staff writer with *The Herald* in Scotland, and has won awards for his journalism from Amnesty International and the European Union. As a freelancer he has written for *The Guardian*, *The Sunday Times*, and *The Scotsman*, amongst other publications.

Sarah M. Broom is a writer living in her hometown, New Orleans, Louisiana, where she works for the mayor's office. Her work has appeared in *The New York Times Magazine*, *The Oxford American*, *O: The Oprah Magazine*, and elsewhere.

Ron Butlin is a writer and poet, whose novels include *Belonging*, *Night Visits*, and *The Sound of My Voice*. The latter novel won the French 'Prix Mille Pages' in 2004 and 'Prix Lucioles' in 2005, both for Best Foreign Novel. He lives in Edinburgh.

Sachi Cunningham is a filmmaker and staff video journalist for the *Los Angeles Times*. Previously, she produced and shot video for the American PBS television series *Frontline* and *Frontline / World*.

Sarah Dohrmann is a Brooklyn-based writer, currently living in Morocco on a creative writing fellowship from the US Fulbright Commission. There she is continuing work on her first novel, as well as researching contemporary Moroccan women's writing.

Jean Hannah Edelstein is a New York-born, London-based journalist. She is a regular contributor to a number of British national newspapers and magazines and is an editor of *PPR*, the journal of the Institute for Public Policy Research.

Chris Flynn is the editor of fiction quarterly *Torpedo* (falconvs-monkey.com) and writes for magazines such as *The Believer*, *Swindle* and *Nuke*. Born in Belfast, he now lives in Melbourne.

David Foster is a Welsh photographer and writer. He teaches English in London and works for the Trevillion Images photo agency.

David Gaffney is a Manchester based writer, and the author of two short story collections, *Sawn Off Tales* and *Aromabingo*. His first novel, *Never Never*, is published in 2008.

Lauren Gard is a former staff writer for San Francisco's *East Bay Express*, and a former associate editor at US *Marie Claire*. She's currently working as a private investigator in California.

Rose George was formerly senior editor of *COLOURS* magazine, and now works as a freelance journalist in London for various national newspapers and magazines. Her second book, *The Big Necessity*, is published in 2008.

Nikhil Gomes is a Peterborough based writer. Having recently completed an MA in Creative Writing at the University of East Anglia, he is working on his first novel.

Niven Govinden's first book *We Are the Romantics* was published in 2004, and his latest novel *Graffiti My Soul* came out in 2007. He lives in London.

Chris Jefferis is an Australian writer and academic. He graduated from the University of Sydney in 2006 with a Masters in History, and is working on a PhD in Political Economy and Finance.

Alyssa McDonald is the editorial coordinator for *The New Statesman* and is contributing editor of BAD IDEA. She also plays bass guitar for Scritti Politti and The Brian Jacket Letdown.

Leesha McKenny is a staff writer for *The Sydney Morning Herald* in Australia. Previously, she has worked for *The Newcastle Herald* and *The Phnom Penh Post* in Cambodia.

Martyn McLaughlin is a senior reporter for *The Scotsman* newspaper, Scotland's national title, and formerly worked for *The Herald* as a reporter and magazine writer. He lives in Glasgow.

Mil Millington is the author of three books, *A Certain Chemistry*, *Love and Other Near Death Experiences*, and *Things My Girlfriend and I Have Argued About*. He regularly writes for *The Guardian*, and maintains a popular blog from his home in Wolverhampton.

Patrick Neate is the author of six books including *The London Pigeon Wars* and *City of Tiny Lights*, and runs 'Bookslam', the monthly London literary event. In 2001 he won the Whitbread Award for 'Best Novel' with *Twelve Bar Blues*.

Jack Roberts is a founding editor of BAD IDEA magazine. A Londoner, he has contributed to national newspapers including *The Daily Telegraph*, *The Sunday Telegraph*, and *The Guardian*.

Nicholas Royle is a Manchester based author of five novels – *Counterparts*, *Saxophone Dreams*, *The Matter of the Heart*, *The Director's Cut*, and *Antwerp*. His last book, a collection of short stories called *Mortality*, was published in 2006.

Nikesh Shukla is a London-based author and musician. As 'Yam Boy' he has performed in the UK, the US, and India, and at music festivals such as Glastonbury and 'Rise' in London.

Daniel Stacey is a founding editor of BAD IDEA magazine. Originally from Perth, Western Australia, he is a literary correspondent for *The Australian* newspaper.

Tat Usher recently completed an MA in Creative Writing at the University of East Anglia, and is working on her novel, Goatman.

Max Wheeler is a Brighton based writer, musician, and youth worker. He works with various youth organisations across the UK, and was previously a member of the hip hop group Dirty Diggers.

Acknowledgements

We would like to thank all the writers, artists, and photographers who contributed to BAD IDEA in 2006-2008. Without their talent and generosity of spirit there would be no magazine: they are the ones who keep us moving forwards.

Being young and with relatively limited resources, few people offered us much hope or encouragement at the outset of our project, when we were just another pair of gibbering would-be magazine creators, scuttling around the filthy streets of London. Belief can be a fragile commodity, and – in England particularly – concentrating and speculating upon failure can sometimes seem like the national blood sport. When we started out two people especially gave us heart and inspiration for which we will always be grateful. Thank you Lou McLeod. Thank you Clay Felker.

We also owe a debt of gratitude to our families, who – against their better judgment – seem to have found a method for coping with the borderline psychopathology and messianic tendencies that come with the independent publishing game; Gwynne, Sadie, Tom, Michael, Jenny, Pat, Claire, Richard, Sarah and Co. Thank you all for your love, help, and patience.

Much love and appreciation is also due to the extended BAD IDEA family: Steve Sawyer, Alyssa McDonald, Sebastian Meyer, Jean Hannah Edelstein, Sarah M. Broom, Lauren Gard, Simone Radclyffe and David Foster. Heroes all.

To Patrick Neate, Mil Millington, Rebecca Gray of Serpent's Tail, Francesca Sears, Simon Wheatley and Jonas Bendiksen of Magnum Photos, and the Le Gun artists collective, all who went out of their way to contribute at early stages, many thanks for your noblesse oblige.

Finally, we would like to thank everyone at Portico and Anova Books for giving us this opportunity, especially Tom Bromley, Polly Powell, Malcolm Croft, and Helen Ponting – not forgetting Charlie Campbell, who was quick to judge when called upon.

The BAD IDEA/Portico Writing Competition

In November 2007, BAD IDEA magazine and Portico Books launched a writing competition, requesting submissions on the topic 'Is the pen mightier than the keyboard?'

The competition finalists were announced in February 2008. They were:

Emma Hooper
Susan Jackman
Caroline Moran
Tom Williams
Benjamin Wood

The overall competition winner, in a very close contest, was Emma Hooper, a 27 year old Doctoral Candidate in Creative Writing at the University of East Anglia.

Congratulations to Emma and all of the successful finalists.

Warm commendations are also due to the many competition entrants not mentioned here, whose efforts ensured the general standard of submissions was remarkably high.